The Complete Idiot's Reference Card

Interview Questions

1. *Tell me about yourself.*

   First, prepare in advance, using this formula:

   1. "My name is … ";
   2. "I've worked for X years as a [job title]";
   3. "Currently, I'm a [job title] at [company]";
   4. "Before that, I was a [job title] at [company]";
   5. "I love the challenge of my work, especially the major strengths it allows me to offer, including [A, B, and C]". Second, help the interviewer by focusing the question with a question of your own: "What about me would be most relevant to you and what this company needs?" Then answer this more specific question.

2. *Why did you leave (do you want to leave) your most recent (current) job?*

   Never answer with negative reasons, even if they are true. Frame your answer positively by answering why you want to move to the target company instead of why you left or want to leave your most recent (current) job. For example, instead of answering, "I don't get enough challenges at Acme Industries," respond, "I am eager to take on more challenges, and I believe I will find them at XYZ Company."

3. *Tell me what you know about us.*

   Using the techniques you'll find in Chapter 2 and the resources listed in Appendix B, research the target company before the interview. Basic research is the only way to prepare for this question. Do your homework, and you'll score big on this question.

4. *What experience do you have?*

   Pre-interview research will help here, too. Try to cite experience relevant to the company's concerns. Also, try answering this question with a question: "Are you looking for overall experience or experience in some specific area of special interest to you?" Let the interviewer's response guide your answer.

5. *What don't you like about your current job?*

   Refuse to answer negatively. Respond that you "like everything about my current position and have acquired and developed a great many skills, but I'm now ready for a new set of challenges and greater responsibilities."

6. *How much are you making now? How much do you want?*

   It's always best to put off discussing salary until you are sure that the interviewer is "sold" on you. However, you can't avoid answering the first question, whenever it comes. Frame the reply this way: "I'm earning $32,000, but I'm not certain that helps you evaluate my 'worth,' since the two jobs differ significantly in their responsibilities." In answering the second question, avoid stating a specific figure. Instead, quickly list the skills, talents, abilities, and responsibilities the target position entails ("If I understand the full scope of the position, my responsibilities would include … "), then answer the question with a question: "Given all of this, what figure did you have in mind for someone with my qualifications in a position as important as this?"

7. *What's the most difficult situation you ever faced on the job?*

   Remember, you're talking to a prospective employer, not your best friend. Don't dredge up a catastrophe that resulted in a personal or corporate failure. Be ready for this question by thinking of a story that has a happy ending—happy for you and your company. Never digress into personal or family difficulties, and don't talk about problems you've had with supervisors or peers. You might discuss a difficult situation with a subordinate, provided that the issues were resolved inventively and to every-,one's satisfaction.

8. *What are you looking for in this job?*

   Flip this one over. Despite the question, the employer isn't really interested in what you are looking for. He's interested in what he is looking for. Address his interests, rather than yours. Use words like "contribute," "enhance," and "improve" in your response: "In my current position, I've discovered just how much one person could contribute to a company. As production supervisor, I increased efficiency an average of 10 percent, which meant a quarterly bottom-line increase of $20,000 in net revenue for our department. I'm looking to do even more for XYZ Industries. That's what will give me satisfaction in this job."

9. *Why should I hire you?*

   This may sound suspicious, negative, or just plain harsh. Actually, it's a call for help. The employer wants you to help her hire you. Keep your response brief. Recap any job requirements the interviewer may have mentioned earlier in the interview, then, point by point, match your skills, abilities, and qualifications to those items.

alpha
books

P9-CEI-871

Quick Fixes for Common Interview Disasters

On the way to the interview, bus tires churn into a mud puddle and splatter you head to foot. Duck into the nearest public restroom and tidy up as best you can. Walk into the interview and announce "A funny thing happened on my way to the office … " Quickly tell the tale, then conclude: "I apologize for my appearance, but this meeting is too important to me to postpone, and I didn't want to put you to the inconvenience of rescheduling. Take my word for it: This *was* a very impressive suit."

You feel ill during the interview. Excuse yourself and go to the restroom. If you cannot compose yourself, return to the interviewer and explain that you have been fighting the flu (or some other common ailment), which you thought would go away, but that you feel too ill to continue the interview: "I don't want to expose you to the risk of catching my flu. I hope we could reschedule in a day or two, so that I can perform at my best." This is no time for heroics, no employer wants to spend time near someone who is sneezing and hacking.

The interviewer is interrupted, in mid-interview, by some office crisis. Don't take the interruption and the interviewer's distraction personally. Give the interviewer the time and space she needs: "Please, go ahead and attend to your call. I've blocked out ample time for this meeting." Do *not* suggest rescheduling, but if the interviewer suggests it, do your utmost to cooperate.

The interviewer is interrupted by frequent phone calls and other distractions. Use this to your advantage by saying: "You really *are* busy around here! It looks like you can use all the help I can give you."

You've been fired, and you are afraid of what your former boss will say if he is contacted by current employment prospects. This may be hard for you, but you should contact the former boss: "I'm in the process of looking for a new job, and I'd like to find out how I stand with you. If you are asked as part of a reference check, how would you describe the circumstances of my leaving the company? Would you be willing to say that I was laid off rather than fired? The problem is that every time I tell a prospective employer about my termination, I blow another shot at a paycheck."

You trip, stumble, and fall as you enter the interview room. Don't ignore what just happened, but don't beat yourself up about it, either ("I'm such a clumsy oaf!"). Get up, dust yourself off, and say: "I've always prided myself on a talent for making a memorable entrance." Then offer your hand for the greeting handshake: "Hello, I'm John Smith."

At a dinnertime interview, you accidentally spill a soft drink on one of the interviewers. Apologize immediately, then *ask* what you can do to help. Do *not* start wiping down your fellow diner. Suggest club soda to remove the stain: "Let me call the waiter over and get some club soda for that." Do not offer to pay for dry cleaning, but do offer help: "I have a really great dry cleaner. Can I send you to him—or, perhaps, take the suit there myself?" After the excitement dies down, offer one more apology: "I am very embarrassed—and very sorry."

You are asked a question to which you have absolutely no answer. Don't fake it, but don't give up, either. Instead, comment on the quality of the question, tell the interviewer that you don't have an immediate answer, then explain how you would or could go about getting the answer: "That is an extraordinarily good question, to which I don't have a ready answer. To answer the question fully, I would need to study how your customer service staff usually addresses such complaints, then assess the effectiveness of this response over time. Only with that data could I give an informed, meaningful response. Anything else would just be guessing or manufacturing an opinion."

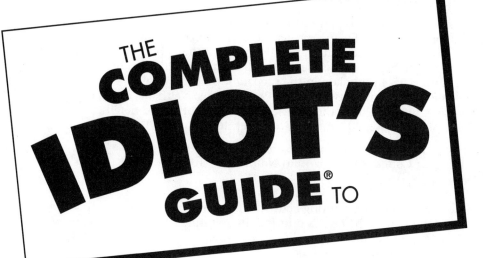

THE COMPLETE IDIOT'S GUIDE® TO

the Perfect Interview

Second Edition

by Marc Dorio

alpha
books

Macmillan USA, Inc.
201 West 103rd Street
Indianapolis, IN 46290

A Pearson Education Company

International Standard Book Number: 0-02-863890-5
Library of Congress Catalog Card Number: 00-100787

02   01   00   8   7   6   5   4   3   2   1

Interpretation of the printing code: the rightmost number of the first series of numbers is the year of the book's printing; the rightmost number of the second series of numbers is the number of the book's printing. For example, a printing code of 00-1 shows that the first printing occurred in 2000.

Printed in the United States of America

Note: This publication contains the opinions and ideas of its author. It is intended to provide helpful and informative material on the subject matter covered. It is sold with the understanding that the author and publisher are not engaged in rendering professional services in the book. If the reader requires personal assistance or advice, a competent professional should be consulted.

Publisher
Marie Butler-Knight

Product Manager
Phil Kitchel

Managing Editor
Cari Luna

Acquisitions Editor
Amy Zavatto

Development Editor
Joan D. Paterson

Production Editor
Billy Fields

Copy Editor
Abby Lyon Herriman

Illustrator
Jody P. Schaeffer

Cover Designers
Mike Freeland
Kevin Spear

Book Designers
Scott Cook and Amy Adams of DesignLab

Indexers
Angie Bess
Amy Lawrence

Layout/Proofreading
Lana Dominguez
Mary Hunt
Eric S. Miller

Contents at a Glance

Contents

Part 4: Special Settings and Challenging Circumstances

16 Creating an Interview

17 Getting Through the Gatekeeper Interview

Foreword

How many times during a job search have well-intentioned friends or family members offered you advice on how to conduct yourself in an interview? I am willing to bet that these words of wisdom have for the most part been varied, confusing, and even contradictory.

One person tells you to "be yourself, and don't hold back," while another suggests you "play the game" and don't get "boxed in" by the crafty interviewer. Really, with all this "sage" advice it's no wonder that most job candidates approach the interview with the same enthusiasm as they would an IRS audit! There must be a better way.

Over the years, both as a corporate Human Resources professional and now as an executive search consultant, I have personally interviewed hundreds of candidates for positions ranging from nonprofessional to top-level executives. These individuals have come from diverse countries and cultures. This interviewing experience has taught me two valuable lessons. The first is that preparation is key for interviewing success. What you do to get the interview in the first place, as well as preparing for it, is critical. Second, there is no pat way to interview. Each situation is unique. Flexibility and being able to correctly "read" each interviewer's style is, therefore, essential for a job seeker to hit the mark. *The Complete Idiot's Guide to the Perfect Interview, Second Edition* will teach you both lessons and more.

Most books I have read on interviewing address only one issue; namely, how to conduct yourself during the interview itself. *The Complete Idiot's Guide to the Perfect Interview, Second Edition* certainly does that, and much, much more. This book offers practical and proven methods and techniques for getting an interview. The techniques contained in this book will enable you to research the marketplace and discover the potential employers' needs. It will provide you with the skills to conduct a thorough job search, prepare for the interview, interview effectively, and negotiate the final offer. You will be able to do it all better than you have in the past.

Professional interviewers like myself can quickly assess a job candidate's level of preparation and confidence. This book is an invaluable tool in your job search and career management tool box. You'll enjoy reading it and refer to it often.

William Myers
Vice President, Tarnow International Executive Search Consultants (formerly Corporate Vice President of Human Resources, International Flavors and Fragrances, Inc.)

Introduction

Question: How do you measure the effectiveness of a resumé?

Obvious answer: Whether it gets you a job or not.

Try again. Because the obvious answer is wrong.

The objective of an effective resumé (or cover letter, query letter, cold call, and all the other early steps in the job hunt) is not to get you a job. It is to get you an *interview*. The job interview is your ultimate opportunity to "sell" yourself to an employer, even as you gauge whether that employer is right for you. It is a doorway to a job and a portal to a career.

At least, that's the way it is supposed to be.

Even as we joust and jockey in quest for that interview, many of us look forward to the event as to a grim interrogation. We think of it as an obstacle rather than a path to employment. Many of us are intimidated by a process that makes us feel small, in-adequate, inept—like a complete idiot.

Why a "complete idiot"?

Well, we don't know what questions will be asked. Don't know if we'll be able to an-swer the questions when they're asked. Maybe, too, we don't know how to dress for the interview. Don't know how to negotiate salary. Don't know enough about the job. Aren't good at remembering names. Can't think on our feet. Are easily rattled and afraid of drooling.

There's plenty of *bad* to feel about interviewing—a process that *should* be filled with bright hopes and great expectations. A lot of us are afraid we'll just plain blow it. More than any other aspect of the job search, the interview is a mystery to most peo-ple. Even job hunters who are confident of their resumé-writing ability and their ex-pertise with a cover letter often feel unsure of themselves when it comes to interviewing.

If you're leery of the interview, well, at least you're in good company. But why stay there?

How to Use this Book

The Complete Idiot's Guide to the Perfect Interview, Second Edition, cannot, of course, guar-antee success. But reading the book will help you get excited—in a productive way—about interviewing. It will help you see the interview as an opportunity rather than an obstacle, a positive event instead of a reason for terror. The *Complete Idiot's Guide to the Perfect Interview, Second Edition* is designed to take the mystery out of the interview by showing you how to "read" the employer's needs and how to present yourself as the solution to the employer's problems.

Here's what you'll find in the pages that follow:

Part 1, "Getting There," faces the fact that before you can ace an interview, you have to *get* an interview. You'll find advice on how to transform your resume and cold calls into interviews, and how to prepare for those interviews so that you'll come across as a winner. In this section of the book, you'll also find pointers on "looking the part"—how (and how not) to dress.

Part 2, "Being There," begins with valuable things you can do in the reception room: last-minute preparation and assessment, as well as exercises to keep you psyched up while you're trying to calm down. You won't find cut-and-dried interview "scripts" here, but far more useful tools to help you listen more effectively, to answer the most common questions, to answer the really tough questions, and to take charge of the interview and steer it in the direction *you* want to take it. All this leads up to a chapter on the bottom line: salary negotiation.

Part 3, "Do You Have Any Questions?" (You'd Better!), is devoted to the questions *you* should ask. These are designed not only to gather the information you need to evaluate an employer and an offer, but to help you "close the sale" and get that offer.

Part 4, "Special Settings and Challenging Circumstances," explores many of the less typical, but still important, interview scenarios, including the informational interview that *you* arrange, the preliminary or screening interview, and the telephone interview. You'll also find tips for handling such situations as the mealtime interview, the panel interview, the sequential interview, and the computer-assisted interview.

Part 5, "On the Spot," is a special section on mastering performance and stress interviews—certainly the most intimidating and challenging of interview scenarios—and turning employers' objections into persuasive selling points.

Part 6, "To Follow Through, Follow Up," covers the all-important post-meeting phase of the interview process, beginning with the follow-up interview and what to do, say, and write after all the interviewing is finally over.

Three appendixes bring up the rear, including a glossary of interview buzz words, sources of information to help you prepare for an interview, and exercises to help you conduct an inventory of your skills.

Extras

Throughout the book, you'll find loads of helpful sidebars that give you extra bits of important information. Here's the description of the different kinds of boxes:

CPR

Common interview mishaps—from faux pas to catastrophe—happen more than you'd like. The tips you'll find in these boxes will teach you how to overcome mishaps gracefully.

Talk the Talk

The path to a terrific interview is strewn with jargon, catch phrases, euphemisms, and hot-button words. These boxes will tip you off to the most important ones.

The Skinny

For nuggets of knowledge that will help you perform at your personal best, look for these boxes.

Clincher

These are tips and "extra-mile" advise on how to make your interviews more effective.

Don't Call Us ...

Put your foot in your mouth, and a prospective employer will send you hopping out the door. Look in these boxes for advice on avoiding pitfalls, verbal and otherwise.

Special Thanks from the Publisher to the Technical Editor

The Complete Idiot's Guide to the Perfect Interview, Second Edition was reviewed by an expert who not only checked the technical accuracy of what you'll learn in this book, but also provided invaluable insight and suggestions. Our special thanks are extended to Ron Smith.

Ron Smith is a project manager at IBM Global Services. He has published three books on application development and ten computer-related articles. Ron is also a past president of the Greensport Area Toastmasters in Houston, Texas, and enjoys racquetball.

Trademarks

All terms mentioned in this book that are known to be or are suspected of being trademarks or service marks have been appropriately capitalized. Alpha Books and Macmillan USA, Inc. cannot attest to the accuracy of this information. Use of a term in this book should not be regarded as affecting the validity of any trademark or service mark.

Part 1
Getting There

If this isn't the first interview book you've read, you already know that a big problem with most of the books on this subject is that they just plop you down in the interview and then start issuing whatever advice they have to give.

But how do you get that interview in the first place? And how do you go about preparing—not only for a particular interview, but for interviewing in general?

Here are five chapters on developing productive interview attitudes, acquiring the "inside" knowledge you'll need, securing the interview, preparing for your very next interview, and dressing for the occasion.

Chapter 1

Myths and Reality

In This Chapter

➤ Correcting misconceptions about interviews

➤ How to help the interviewer interview you

➤ Why most interviewers aren't sadists

➤ Putting the focus on the interviewer

➤ What employers look for

When my friends and I played baseball as kids, we used to rattle the opposing batter, poised for the pitch, by shouting some "friendly" advice: "Don't choke! Don't choke!" I guess the encouraging words in the title of this chapter are about as helpful to you, facing an interview.

But isn't it exactly what you're thinking?

If it's not what you're thinking, great! Positive thinking promotes positive results. But, in my experience, too few job seekers approach an employment interview positively. If you can think of the interview not only as a job opportunity for yourself, but as a hiring opportunity for the employer—a chance for the employer to meet you, the perfect person for her needs and the solution to her problems—you are already well on your way to an offer. But many face the interview as if they were Oliver Twist asking for just one more dollop of cold gruel. Some even see the interview as a brick wall rather than a doorway. The result? If you see the interview like this, you aren't driven by upbeat, hopeful energy, but by fear and loathing. On this important day, you feel bad. And that ain't good.

If you feel this way about interviews, I hope this chapter will help you begin to change. And if you're lucky enough to feel good about the interview process, I hope this chapter will help you feel even better.

Interview Myths

Even veterans of employment interviews tend to think of them the wrong way. They go into each interview assuming that the interviewer holds all the cards, a deck that he has craftily stacked against them—in order to probe them, wear them down, and expose their every flaw. That is one of several interview myths. There are more.

Myth 1: Employers Know What They Want

So, most of you are scared—*really* scared—when you interview. Because you're scared, you go into a defensive mode, an inherently negative stance that prevents you from showing the world your best.

Okay, sure, but even if you could manage to show your "best," how do you know it would be good enough? How do you know that *your* "best" is *the* "best" that this particular employer is looking for?

So you're in the dark, and fear of the dark is a pretty common—pretty *primal*—fear. Right?

You have some choices to make. You can stumble around in the dark and feel more and more afraid as you bruise yourself on all the end tables you can't see. Or you can try to find some light. Although you can't know for certain whether your "best" will be seen as good enough or not, you *can* go into an interview knowing quite a bit about how this employer defines "best." In the back of this book you'll find Appendix B, "Information Sources for Job Searches and Interview Preparation," which supplies strategies and resources for learning about the needs, wants, desires, and problems of prospective interviewers *before* you walk in the door.

Clincher

Don't think of the interview as something that is done *to* you, but as an assignment you share with the interviewer or interviewers. Cooperate with them to successfully complete the "assignment." Transform a scenario of "you versus me" into a "we" situation.

But this brings us to the crux of our first interview myth. You can research and prepare thoroughly, then brilliantly analyze the problems of an industry and the needs of a particular firm. And believe me, doing so will shift the odds very much in your favor. Unfortunately, doing so is no guarantee that the interviewer knows what the problems of his industry are or even what his company needs.

The interviewer does *not* always know what he wants. In fact, interviewers who have a clear and clearly formulated idea of what they want are probably in the minority.

To be sure, most employers have vague, general notions of what they're looking for. I've summed that up in "What Every Employer Wants," a bit later in the chapter. They may also have a job description that lays out the "duties and responsibilities" of a particular position: "The widget analyst is responsible for A, B, C, and D." But distressingly few interviewers take the time to *think through* the specific qualities, qualifications, personality traits, and broader background that would make up the perfect widget analyst for their particular situation.

If you accept this proposition, your first impulse might be to bury your head in your hands: "Not only am I not sure what this guy wants, now you're telling me *he* doesn't even know!"

But take a breath, and don't despair. Many interviewers are precisely in the position of, say, a technically unsophisticated customer in the market for his first personal computer. He has a vague idea of what he wants and how much he wants to spend, but the salesperson—as any good salesperson does—must educate and guide him. The salesperson doesn't go so far as to tell him what to buy, but does walk him through the process, in order to determine what product and combination of features will most satisfy his particular needs.

Your job as the interviewee is to prepare sufficiently for the interview so that you can meet the interviewer at whatever level of preparedness you may find him. Then you have to be ready to educate and guide him. This, of course, puts you in a tremendously powerful position. You, the job candidate, will help the employer decide what he needs. In the fullest sense, you *sell* yourself.

Myth 2: Employers Are Experts at Interviewing

Granted, the interviewer may not have fully explored every dimension of his firm's needs in regard to the job in question, but, certainly, a manager with the power to hire *must* know people. And this means that he *must* have substantial experience and skill as an interviewer.

In a pig's eye.

Most interviewers are full-time something else: engineers, managers, financiers, accountants, whatever. Anything but professional interviewers. They have not been trained as interviewers; in fact, they've had relatively little experience interviewing people. More often than not, interviewers feel awkward and uncomfortable in the role. They might actually consider the interview a necessary evil, at best, and, at worst, an unwelcome interruption of their "real" work. To top it all off, the interviewers don't typically spend hours reviewing your resume and other documentation. More than likely, your paperwork is given a quick once-over a few minutes before the meeting—probably while you're waiting in the reception room.

Now you have another choice. You can bemoan and bewail the interviewer's lack of skill and his absence of preparation, or you can see these "deficiencies" as opportunities.

You'd really be sweating if you walked into the interview unwilling and/or unprepared. Well, it's likely that the interviewer *is* unwilling and unprepared. He could really use some help, and would be grateful for it. Go ahead, help him out.

This means walking into the interview prepared to take it over and give it direction. (You'll find out more about how and when to do this in Chapter 8, "Listen Carefully.") The beauty of taking over the interview is that it does much more than transform a doomed meeting into a productive one. It instantly casts you in the role of problem solver. You see, before you walked through that door, you were just part of today's problem: "A million things to do, a million deadlines to meet, a million clients breathing down my neck, and *this* of all days is the day I've got to interview Joe Blow!" But sit down with the interviewer, assess the situation, take over, and turn it into a piece of cake for the interviewer, and you've miraculously become part of the *solution*—one of the few really good things that happened today.

The Skinny

In "normal" times, unemployment in the U.S. ranges between 4 and 6 percent. The good news is that during such times, two million jobs open up *monthly*.

Myth 3: Employers Like to See You Squirm

You could conceivably come up against a genuine sadist, but the prospect isn't very likely. Few interviewers are warped enough to enjoy watching the discomfiture of the candidate, let alone set out deliberately to humiliate or embarrass the interviewee. Indeed, if anyone squirms, it's more likely to be the interviewer, who feels that the candidate is judging *him* and judging the company through him.

That said, some interviewers will use so-called *stress interview* techniques, which you'll read about in Chapter 23, "You're On Fire! The Stress Interview." These techniques are meant to put you on the spot, to see how you react and operate under pressure. Relatively few jobs call for a stress interview, although you may be subjected to one if you are up for a particularly high-pressure sales position involving lots of difficult customer and client contact. But even in these cases, it's rare to find an interviewer skilled enough to sustain his side of a stress interview.

No, you're far more likely to find a reasonably polite interviewer, fairly eager to make the meeting a pleasant one. Why? The reasons are pretty intuitive:

Talk the Talk

A **stress interview** employs harsh, high-pressure techniques—long silences, deliberately offensive questions, impossibly difficult questions, a very brusque questioning style—to test your mettle. Relatively uncommon, the stress interview is most often used to evaluate candidates for high-pressure jobs in which difficult or hostile customer contact is anticipated.

➤ Few people enjoy being party to an uncomfortable, unpleasant conversation. They do whatever they can to avoid starting such a conversation.

➤ Few people actually enjoy being mean.

➤ Most people want to be liked and to create a favorable impression.

➤ Most businesspeople understand that the world of business—in a particular community or in a particular industry—is a *small* world and that what goes around comes around. Even if this particular employer doesn't hire you, he understands that he may end up doing business with you someday. No sense in abusing you.

➤ Even if the two of you never see one another again, no businessperson wants bad word of mouth. If this interviewer treats you poorly, what will you tell the world about her company?

➤ And what if she *does* hire you? Why create a situation that will produce bad feelings from day one?

Clincher

Don't picture yourself as asking for a job. See yourself as offering the employer the opportunity to acquire your expertise, judgment, initiative, creativity, and commitment.

Interview Reality: They Don't Really Care About You

I've tried to dispel some prevalent and pervasive interview myths. Now, for a dose of reality. I'll give it to you straight: *The employer doesn't really care about you.*

Before you sputter in righteous outrage, ask yourself this: Do *you* really care about the employer?

Be honest, now.

No, of course you don't. If you did, you'd work for free. The fact is, it's not the employer you care about, it's yourself: providing a good living for yourself (or for yourself and your family) right now, while carving out a productive and lucrative career for the long haul.

Just as you don't really care about the employer, then, the employer doesn't really care about you. She cares about herself and about her business. Insofar as you can help her and contribute positively to her business, you *do* count. Beyond that, however, you are a stranger.

This revelation isn't meant to cast a cloud over your day, but, rather, to change your focus. Naturally, gearing up for an interview, you're thinking about yourself:

➤ Will I make a good impression?

➤ Will I screw up?

➤ Will I look good?

➤ Will I answer the questions correctly?

➤ Will I remember everything I want to say?

➤ Will they like me?

➤ Will the salary be high enough?

➤ Will I negotiate shrewdly?

➤ Do I have enough experience?

➤ Will I get the job?

It's only natural, but that doesn't make it all good. You need to shift your focus—*unnaturally*—to the employer, what she needs, what she wants, what problems she faces, what concerns her.

Look at it this way: One of the questions an interviewer might ask, point-blank, is "Why do you want this job?" It's possible that the answer uppermost in your thoughts is "Because I need the money." Giving voice to that answer, however, while admirably honest, will almost certainly result in a hasty end to the interview and absolutely no job offer. Obviously, that's not what the interviewer wants to hear.

What *does* she want to hear? Answers to all her problems. She wants to hear how you're going to contribute to her bottom line. She wants to hear how you're going to make her look good. She wants to hear about how *you* will make a positive difference for *her*.

Clincher

Ask not what the interviewer can do for you, but what you can do for the interviewer.

Not only will forcing yourself to focus on what the employer cares about—namely herself—greatly improve your chances of bagging the job, the effort will also yield an added dividend: You'll be less nervous and less afraid. Veteran actors learn that stage fright comes from focusing on yourself—on how *you'll* perform, on how *you'll* feel, on how *you'll* look—rather than on your audience. Think more about the audience and less about yourself, and stage fright becomes largely a thing of the past.

What Every Employer Wants

You need to prepare for an interview knowing three important things about the employer's needs, wants, and desires:

1. You can discover a lot about what an employer needs, wants, and desires by taking the time to do your homework: Research the industry in general and the company in particular before you walk through the interviewer's door. If at all possible, also research the interviewer himself; this may not be so difficult, if he has any degree of prominence in the industry or company. See Appendix B for research sources and methods.

2. What you discover may very well be *more* than the interviewer knows. Be prepared to educate him about his needs, wants, and desires.

3. Each employer needs different things, but there are some major things that *all* employers want from their employees.

Let's explore point #3 in detail.

A Solution, Not a Problem

The employer wants to hire a solution, not a problem. Present yourself accordingly. This means coming into the interview prepared (see points #1 and #2 above), having fully scoped out the issues that concern the industry and the company. It also means working with the interviewer to make the interview itself pleasant and productive. Know when to listen and when to take the lead (see Chapter 11, "Take Control and Start Selling Yourself," for more on taking control).

Clincher

Being prepared for an interview and being willing to take the lead not only benefits you directly—by ensuring that you deliver the information you need to deliver—but also benefits you indirectly by helping the interviewer. To the degree that you make his job easier, you will be perceived as a problem solver, which is something *every* organization wants and needs.

Do *not* come into the interview bristling with demands, objections, and complaints. Some candidates who have a healthy regard for their own qualifications and value misuse their sense of self-worth by playing "hard to get" and "driving a hard bargain," as if they were temperamental movie stars. This attitude makes you look like a problem, not a valuable asset. By all means, think highly of yourself, but don't let self-esteem transform you into a prima donna. Instead, emphasize cooperation and a willingness to strike a bargain. You can always negotiate or, if necessary, turn down an offer. But you have to *get* the offer first.

You will also probably be perceived as a problem rather than a solution if you complain about your present job or present employer, or if you complain about *anything:* the weather, the traffic, the subway—whatever. Adopt a cheerful, positive, upbeat tone.

Finally, one sure way to come off sounding like a problem is to enter into the interview as unprepared as the interviewer probably is. Few situations are more awkward, painful, and problematic as a meeting in which neither participant has anything to say. Nor will the interviewer, sitting in silence, be thinking: *Oh, what a terrible person I am. I should have been more prepared!* No, unfortunately, it will be more like: *How much longer do I have to sit here with this lox of a human being?*

Someone Who Can Do the Job

While many—perhaps most—interviewers have only a vague idea of their own requirements, most do understand that they need someone who can do the job. The interviewer may not think about this beyond the dimensions of raw ability and experience as defined in some official job description, or as defined more crudely by the interviewer's generalized concept of the job: *The job is* selling. *This guy's gotta be able to* sell.

Address this "can do" aspect of the interview by ensuring that your qualifications are clearly and convincingly spelled out in your resumé and other pre-interview paperwork. Be prepared to back up your claims with specific examples, anecdotes, and, wherever possible, facts and figures. Prepare and make use of the "Interview Kit," which is discussed in Chapter 4, "Get Set."

Accent the positive, even when you're not entirely sure of your qualifications. Don't shoot yourself in the foot by expressing self-doubts or other reservations that may intrude into your consciousness during the interview:

Interviewer: You'll also have to analyze widget sales on a quarterly basis.

You: Gee, I have to admit I've never done that before ... I'm not absolutely sure ...

Such a response, while honest, will probably get you a one-way ticket out the door. Don't deceive the interviewer with false claims of unmerited expertise, but, at this point, it's best to cloak any doubts and self-doubts with a mantle of positive attitude:

Interviewer: You'll also have to analyze widget sales on a quarterly basis.

You: I look forward to that opportunity.

If the interviewer asks you point-blank if you have widget sales analysis experience, answer honestly, but positively, citing related experience, as well as a willingness and capacity to learn:

Interviewer: Do you have experience in widget sales analysis?

You: I have experience in sales, and I've certainly made extensive use of analytical reports. I look forward to developing expertise in widget sales analysis.

Someone Who Will Stick Around

Searching for, interviewing, relocating, training, and breaking in a new employee are expensive propositions. Each day that a new employee is on the job represents an investment for the firm—an investment in education and development—and no employer wants to see his investment evaporate after only a few months. Be certain to convey to the interviewer an image of stability and commitment.

What happens if your resumé reveals a history of using multiple jobs as stepping stones? Put this in the best light possible: "One of the things that most excites me about this position, Mr. Burns, is that it is truly worth my long-term commitment. I have been searching for a job in which I can grow while developing a great program for the organization."

Someone Who Will Fit In

Learn everything you can about the environment and "culture" of the prospective employer. This includes making an effort to find out how people dress (suits? casual wear?) and groom themselves (beards okay? long hair okay on men?), as discussed in Chapter 5, "Clothes Call." It also involves demonstrating social ease, which is most loudly proclaimed nonverbally, through body language. Check out Chapter 7, "Shall We Dance?" for a discussion of this.

Make an effort to discern something about the politics of the potential employer. Is the orientation conservative? Liberal?

If it becomes apparent to you, as the interview conversation develops, that you do *not* fit in— that you just don't like these people—try not to let your doubts show. It's always better to secure an offer, which you can evaluate in calm and tranquillity before rejecting. For now, do everything you can to keep your options open.

Don't Call Us ...

Beware of volunteering too much about your political and social beliefs at an interview. You don't know whose toes you might step on. Also note that it is inappropriate (and illegal) for the employer to ask you questions relating to your religious beliefs, ethnic background, sexual orientation, age, disabilities, marital status, or plans for raising a family. See Chapter 10 for more on handling difficult interview questions.

Someone Who's Likable

Related to the question of whether the prospective employee will fit in is whether she is likable. In certain positions, such as sales and customer service, "likability" is a job prerequisite, but even in positions that require little or no customer contact, it's important to be pleasant and enjoyable to be around—likable. No one wants to work with an obnoxious or disagreeable person.

Sure, you're nervous, but do your best to project a forthcoming, friendly, open image. Avoid single-sentence or one-word responses to questions. Don't chit-chat aimlessly, but do open up. Be approachable. Smile and make eye contact. Speak with enthusiasm.

Someone Who Will Return the Investment

Whatever else an employer may or may not say he wants, you can be certain that he is looking for an employee who will work hard, is motivated, and who takes interest in the work. In short, every employer wants good value for his investment. Be prepared to speak with enthusiasm about the mission of the company, department, or division and how you intend to dedicate yourself to it. Be prepared to discuss how you will go "the extra mile" to ensure that the mission is always accomplished.

Introduce Yourself as a Solution

What all of this adds up to is not a vague and nerve-wracking game of guessing precisely what formula or combination of qualities an employer is looking for. It is, instead, a matter of presenting yourself as an answer rather than a question, an asset rather than a liability, a solution rather than a problem. If you make the transmission of *this* message the goal of each of your interviews, they will become less murky, less confusing, and far less intimidating. Instead, your interviews will come to seem what they were always meant to be: an experience in positive communication and a fair exchange of value between a prospective employer and employee.

The Least You Need to Know

➤ Think of the interviewer as your customer—someone who has some idea of what he wants, but who will greatly benefit from your guidance.

➤ Shift your focus from yourself, from what you feel and from what you need, to what the interviewer feels and needs. Address these issues during the interview.

➤ Needs and wants vary from employer to employer, but rest assured that *all* employers look for employees who will solve, not create, problems.

On Your Mark

Let's start with a jolt: *Don't bother to prepare for* an *interview.*

Let me explain.

What's the *critical* difference between a good salesperson and a great salesperson? A good salesperson makes a sale, while a great salesperson creates a customer. The difference is one sale versus infinite sales.

Take a lesson from the great salesperson. Don't prepare for this interview or that. Don't hang all your career hopes on a one-time shot in the dark. Instead, invest your precious time in preparing yourself for the upcoming interview *and* for any number of interviews to come. Prepare to present yourself as what *every* employer, *everywhere* and *always*, desperately wants and needs: a remarkable person with skills not only specifically suited to the job at hand, but also with the manifest capability and character to manage anything thrown his or her way.

This chapter is not about last-minute cramming for tomorrow's interview, but about taking the longer view. After all, you're likely to live beyond tomorrow—and even beyond your next job.

Transferable Skills

In taking the longer view, then, don't focus on skills specific to a certain job; rather, put the focus where it should be: on you. The skills you carry with you matter more—to you as well as to any of your employers—than the skills that a certain job happens

The Skinny

Odds are that you'll change employers seven times during your working life. You'll change careers three times.

Talk the Talk

Transferable skills are specific to you rather than to a particular job. They describe a function—that is, how *you* work with people, data, or things. For example, knowing how to write computer programs in the C++ programming language is a job-specific skill, whereas the ability to analyze and synthesize information is a skill you can transfer from job to job.

to require. Because such skills are yours, rather than peculiar to some job, they are transferable.

Now, you probably already think you know what you're good at and what your skills are. For example, you might say of yourself, "I am persuasive," but that is a description of a trait, not a transferable skill. On the other hand, declaring, "I am a salesperson" is just a job description, but it likewise says nothing about transferable skills. Take a step toward redefining the trait and the job description as a *transferable skill* by transforming the adjective describing the trait into a verb: "I am persuasive" becomes "I persuade."

Next, expand the narrow job description. This is rather easy once you learn that transferable skills fall into three categories: skills in relation to *people*, to *data*, and to *things*. Decide whether "salesperson" chiefly involves working with people, data, or things. The answer is *people,* and your description of a transferable skill becomes "I persuade people."

Climbing the Ladder

Notice that "I persuade people" describes a function—that is, *doing something* with *people, data,* or *things.* And notice, too, that, expressed as a function, it is a very powerful skill that is of tremendous value in a great many jobs.

You can, however, make the statement even more powerful and the skill yet more compelling to an employer. Transferable skills are rungs on a ladder that ascends to levels of increasing complexity. *Persuading* is on a middle rung. It is a more complex "people" skill than merely *communicating*, which, in turn, is more complex than a bottom-rung skill such as *following directions*. But *persuading* is less complex—on a lower rung—than *negotiating*, while *mentoring* is even higher than *negotiating* on the people-skills ladder. If you can convince an interviewer that you persuade people, you may well get a job in sales. If you can convince her that you negotiate with people, you may score a position as an account executive. Demonstrate to the interviewer that you excel at mentoring, and maybe she'll see in you the makings of a Director of Sales.

The Higher the Better

In short, you want to identify your highest-level transferable skills

➤ The higher your transferable skill level, the more unique you
for employment and the less competition you will face.

➤ Jobs that require higher levels of transferable
skills usually pay more and are more interesting than jobs calling for lower levels of
these skills.

➤ Jobs requiring higher levels of transferable
skills tend to be careers (that is, jobs with a
future).

➤ The higher your transferable skills, the more
control you are likely to have on the job.
Positions requiring only the lower levels of
transferable skills are usually cut and dried,
whereas higher-level positions invite and require creativity.

Clincher

Be prepared to present to
interviewers the most complex
(highest-level) transferable skills
to which you can legitimately lay
claim.

Free-Form Exercise

So, let's get started. Find three blank sheets of paper, and write "PEOPLE" at the top
of one sheet, "DATA" at the top of another, and "THINGS" at the top of the third.
Below these headings, on each sheet, write "I am good at ..." Next, complete that
sentence in as many ways as you can for each transferable skill category: people, data,
and things. For example:

PEOPLE

I am good at ...

persuading

selling

helping people make purchase decisions

explaining how machinery works

being patient

listening

... and so on.

If you find working with a blank sheet of paper intimidating, flip to Appendix C, "Skills Inventories," and use the checklists I've provided.

Your Marketable Skills

Use either the free-form method, the checklists in Appendix C, or a combination of the two to put together a list of six to eight of your strongest and highest-level transferable skills. Then, put each of these in a complete sentence, beginning with "I am good at …" If, for example, you've decided that *negotiating* is one of your top skills, you would write, "I am good at negotiating."

But don't stop now. You're on a roll. Include an object in your sentence: "I am good at negotiating *prices*." Try going another step by tacking on an adjective or adverb or a clause that includes these parts of speech: "I am good at negotiating prices *that are satisfying to both buyer and seller.*"

Step-by-step, you should be able to identify your top transferable skills and then define them in a way that not only describes you accurately and vividly, but sets you apart from the teeming masses yearning for the very job *you* want.

Even You Can Do Research

Now that you know something about yourself, you'd better find out something about the rest of the world. Research can serve three interrelated purposes:

1. It can help you identify a job/career/field suited to what you know about your transferable skills.
2. It can help you locate specific job opportunities.
3. It can provide information about an industry, field, or even a particular company that will make you sound highly impressive and well informed in an interview.

Make New Friends

Start with whatever is closest to you. If you are currently employed, open your file drawer and look over past projects. Identify firms and individuals who interest you as potential sources of information and potential employers. Do your best to get around and meet people in your field and in other fields that may interest you. Collect business cards, and keep a file. Also keep these contacts alive with an occasional friendly phone call or, if appropriate, a breakfast or lunch. Pretty soon, you'll find that you've got something a lot more meaningful than a file of names. You've got a *network*.

Joining a professional group or organization in your field is another great way to network. Not only are you likely to meet potential employers, you will usually get access to newsletters and magazines that publish industry-specific want ads. If you can't find an appropriate organization in your field, consider Toastmasters International (714-858-8255), a most supportive organization for the would-be networker who not only wants to make contacts, but also wants work on self-expression and self-esteem.

Your growing network serves two purposes:

1. It generates information. Each of your contacts is a potential source of news about a job, an industry, or a field.

2. Each of your contacts is a potential employer or referral to an employer.

You don't need to be currently employed to build a network. Potentially, everyone you know—friends, neighbors, old school chums—can be useful nodes on your network. Talk to the people around you. Ask them what they do. Ask them how they like doing what they do. Ask them how they got started doing what they do. (If you want to know more about networking, look into Douglas B. Richardson's *Networking*.)

Get a Library Card

While you are looking around your office (if you have one) for the names of folks to induct into your network, check out those stacks of trade journals and newsletters that you've been meaning to read "when you have the time." They contain valuable industry talk that not only will expand your knowledge of the issues and trends current in your field, but may also alert you to job opportunities and the needs and desires of specific firms.

Talk the Talk

A **network** is an informal set of business and personal contacts the job hunter deliberately develops in order to acquire information and employment leads.

Clincher

Former coworkers don't just vanish from the planet. They can become live-wire nodes in your employment-opportunity network. Never forget the personal and professional friends you've made in a company you left. Give 'em a call. The time is now.

Don't Call Us ...

Review your list of contacts carefully before calling on any one for a referral. Make certain that the person you tap for good words will, in fact, have nothing but good words to offer. Beware of hidden agendas, and be aware that your contact may be a potential competitor for your target position.

Clincher

Appendix B, "Information Sources for Job Searches and Interview Preparation," gathers some of the most useful printed and electronic sources of employment-related information. Check it out.

If you don't have an office, or your desk isn't cluttered with periodicals and newsletters, or you want to look beyond your current job, career, or field, go to the nearest public library and get yourself a library card. Then, consult the following:

➤ *National Trade and Professional Associations of the United States* (Washington, D.C.: Columbia Books). This reference lists not only the associations that are relevant to your industry, but any publications those associations may produce.

➤ *Reader's Guide to Periodical Literature* (available in most library reference departments). Use this reference to look up a subject and find magazine and journal articles relevant to it.

Don't scan trade and business periodicals just to find want ads. Also look for:

➤ Articles that tip you off to hot firms and solid opportunities

➤ Articles that inform you about industry trends and developments, and that identify growth and opportunity areas

➤ Names of article authors (if they are industry professionals) and the names mentioned in the articles; these are potential job contacts and sources of *inside* information

➤ News about promotions, executive moves, retirements, and, yes, even deaths; such information will help you identify possible openings at specific companies

➤ Product and service ads; these may tip you off to companies that are producing hot new merchandise and trend-setting services

Use a Computer

Access to the Internet and the World Wide Web can make your job search easier, faster, and more comprehensive. Peter Kent's *The Complete Idiot's Guide to the Internet, Sixth Edition* (Macmillan Computer Publishing, 1999) suggests some places to start poking around for electronic want ads and job postings, as well as information about entire industries and specific companies. Alfred and Emily Glossbrenner's *Finding a Job on the Internet* also contains a wealth of suggestions for logging on to specifically job-related sites.

Using the vast Internet has been made easier in recent years by a variety of "net browsers" and "search engines." You can begin research on almost any subject, including careers, industries, and specific companies, just by typing a few well-chosen keywords. You should be able to locate the home pages of larger companies or organizations that interest you.

In addition to general Web search engines, pay a visit to the following gophers (series of menus from which you can access just about any type of textual information):

➤ The RiceInfo Gopher, which presents Internet resources by subject area. You can get to the RiceInfo Gopher through the Web (**www.riceinfo.rice.edu**) or Gopher to **riceinfo.rice.edu**. Type in a specific industry or field of interest, and you will find a wealth of specific information, including material directly related to employment.

➤ The Gopher Jewels (cute, huh?) takes the menus from the Internet's major Gopher sites and classifies them by subject. The result is the closest thing you're likely to find to a subject index of the Internet. Get to the Gopher Jewels using the Web (**http://galaxy.einet.net/GJ/index.html**) or Gopher to **cwis.usc.edu**.

Don't Call Us ...

Avoid relying on outdated reference material. When you use reference works in the library, make sure you consult the latest edition of the work available. The reference librarian can help.

Talk the Talk

A **home page** is an Internet site created by an individual or organization; it contains "hypertext links" to data relevant to the individual or organization. It is roughly equivalent to an electronic table of contents.

While seemingly inexhaustible, the Internet can be quite exhausting—or, at least, overwhelming. If you're willing to pay, such subscription online services as Dialog, Nexis, Dow Jones News/Retrieval, and Newsnet provide targeted business information. The most popular mainstream commercial online providers, such as America Online, CompuServe, and Prodigy, provide some company profiles, and America Online features "Employer Contacts Databases," a collection of brief profiles of some

,000 companies, and an "Occupational Profiles Database," which contains job and ~~eer~~ descriptions.

If you're willing to pay even more, consider hiring an information broker, a professional researcher who will find and deliver information in whatever area you specify. Really good information brokers will conduct a "reference interview" with you in order to help you determine just what data you should be going after. For a directory of reputable information brokers, check out *The Burwell Directory of Information Brokers*, which may be available in your local library or by calling 713-537-8344.

Leverage What You Learn

You get a phone call. XYZ, Inc. wants to interview you. Great!

What's even greater is that you've done the research and you can now walk into the interview with an insider's knowledge of the needs, goals, and problems *specific to XYZ, Inc.* All you have to do is filter the information you've already obtained. Get a hold of XYZ's annual report, brochures, and other published material, and cross-reference it with whatever industry research you've turned up; then, you can specifically identify:

> ➤ **Company issues.** Do your sources emphasize certain themes or issues as critical to the firm?

> ➤ **Industry issues.** Do your sources emphasize certain themes or issues as critical to the industry as a whole?

> ➤ **Relevant current events.** What's going on in the world, nation, community, or neighborhood that affects the company or the industry?

You want to walk into the interview armed with plenty to say about:

> ➤ **The business of the company.** What does it do or make?

> ➤ **The scope of the company.** How large is it? Where does it do business?

> ➤ **The competition.** Who are they, and what is the target company's standing among them?

Clincher

Chapter 4, "Get Set," begins with a discussion of how to handle the "Big Phone Call." If possible, use that call to obtain more information about the job—especially a formal job description (if you haven't gotten one yet).

What, Me Worry?

Here's my final word—for this chapter, anyway. You'll need days, weeks, or months to find a job. You can spend that time just looking, or you can invest it—leverage it—in order to acquire knowledge that will make you look like an insider when the interview finally comes. It's your time. It's your call.

The Least You Need to Know

➤ Prepare for *interviewing* rather than cramming for a particular interview.

➤ Become intimately familiar with your "transferable skills" by taking a thorough inventory of them.

➤ Invest in research time—it will make you a knowledgeable (and therefore compelling) interview candidate.

➤ Build a network, starting with friends and colleagues, and making use of the appropriate professional organizations in your field.

Chapter 3

Target: Interview

In This Chapter

➤ Being proactive—*making* (not hoping) interviews happen

➤ A more effective approach to the resumé

➤ Turning want ads into interviews

➤ Getting interviews through unsolicited "cold calls" and "cold letters"

➤ Uses and limitations of employment agencies

I know there are other how-to-interview books out there. And my publisher is eager for me to assure you that this particular one is the best of them all. Fortunately (because I don't like to lie), that happens to be true. You see, most interview how-to's just plop you down at the interview, as if the interview were a given, something that just magically materialized. The fact is that if you *wait* for interviews to *materialize*, you'll probably be unemployed for a very long time. Take some advice from the first line of a classic recipe for rabbit stew: "First, catch your rabbit." First, make the interview happen.

Making an Interview Happen

Capitalism! The free job market! Ain't it grand? Hey, it works like this: You need a job. You've got certain skills, education, and experience. An employer out there—somewhere—needs an employee with your skills, education, and experience. You find one another. She interviews you. You're hired!

In your dreams.

It's true that most employers aren't stupid enough to actually *hide* the jobs they have. But that's about all the reassurance I can give you concerning the American employment system. *System?* It's hardly that organized. You'd think that because companies desperately need talent, they would employ full-time talent scouts. Well, very few do; most, however, do not. It's up to you not only to make your presence and availability known, but to appear before an employer as the perfect fit, the key to his lock, the answer to his prayers.

Those Old Resumé Blues

It's important, first, to know who you are, what you have to offer, and who may be looking for it. That's the business of Chapter 2, "On Your Walk." Once you've done your homework, tradition dictates that you present yourself in the form of a resumé. Now, everyone knows what a resumé is: a document that summarizes your experience. But here's something else everyone *should* know: For every 1,470 unsolicited resumés sent hopefully to the nation's employers, 1,469 end up in the wastebasket (as cited in *What Color Is Your Parachute?* by Richard Bolles).

I'm not saying you should abandon the resumé. After all, employers do need summary information about you. But this book is about interviewing, not resumé writing. (For help on resumé writing, check out *The Complete Idiot's Guide to the Perfect Resumé, Second Edition* or *The Complete Idiot's Guide to Getting the Job You Want.*) That said, it's important to make a critical point here: The problem is not that employers are uninterested in resumés; rather, it's that they are far less interested in your *experience* than in your *qualifications*. Here's the difference: *Experience* is what you've done in the past, whereas *qualifications* are experience *plus* the qualities, skills, and abilities that make you (in the words of the third edition of *The American Heritage Dictionary of the English Language)* "suitable for a particular position or task."

Clincher

Job hunting can be discouraging. You *will* suffer rejection. But it is a mistake to be discouraged by rejection. Use each rejection as an opportunity to learn about yourself and about your approach to the employment process. Rejection is a valuable opportunity to learn. Exploit it.

Obviously, the qualifications you want to present in your resumé are the qualifications for the job at hand. But this is precisely where most resumés fail—which is why 1,469 out of 1,470 resumés never produce an interview. Most resumés concentrate on the needs of the applicant rather than on the requirements of the job—that is, the *needs of the employer*. Avoid the resumé blues by focusing on what the employer—not you—wants:

➤ Describe abilities instead of job duties.

➤ Include indications of performance that tell just how well you do your job.

➤ List accomplishments instead of responsibilities.

➤ Begin by asserting your "objective"—a statement about how you will address the needs of the employer.

Let's talk about the last point for just a moment. Many resumés don't even begin with a statement of objective, and those that do usually do so with an *ineffective* statement of objective—one that fails to make clear how the applicant's objective will benefit the employer. Here's an example of a typical narrowly stated objective:

OBJECTIVE: Quality Assurance Engineer

This tells an employer nothing beyond the fact that the applicant wants a position, and unless the employer has a position with this precise title available, it's not likely that he or she will pursue the applicant's candidacy.

Here's a broader statement:

OBJECTIVE: Seeking an opportunity to utilize my skills, education, and energy in a working environment that offers a good, solid career path.

Great—for the applicant. But why should the employer care? What's in it for him or her?

Here are three progressively more effective statements of objective:

OBJECTIVE: To obtain a position where my 15 years of material, production, and inventory control experience will be a company asset.

This one says something about what the applicant brings to the employer's table. But try transforming *experience* into *qualifications*:

OBJECTIVE: To obtain a position where my 15 years of creating innovative and cost-effective systems for material, production, and inventory control will be a company asset.

The Skinny

According to one prominent authority, 78 percent of resumés "fail to do justice to the people they describe." Reason: They describe *experience* rather than what employers are really interested in—*qualifications*.

The phrase "creating innovative and cost-effective systems" transforms passive experience into active qualifications. Notice the use of the verb form *creating*. Well-chosen verbs—*creating, developing, inventing, marketing, selling*—always energize a description of qualifications. They are your best shot at prompting the target employer to take his or her feet off the desk and call you for an interview. But let's not stop here:

OBJECTIVE: To be a member of a team that needs my 15 years of experience creating innovative and cost-effective systems for material, production, and inventory control.

In this objective, the applicant goes beyond merely stating his or her qualifications. Instead of concentrating on the simple fact that he or she has skills to offer, the applicant focuses on how this set of qualifications fits with the employer's particular needs and wants. Suddenly, the employer is no longer considering a job application, but an answer to what his or her *team needs*.

The Awful Truth About Want Ads

Even a strong, employer-focused resumé is a long shot if it's unsolicited. For this reason, most job hunters scour want ads in newspapers and trade journals rather than just roll the dice. But a Department of Labor survey from the early 1990s reported that only five out of every one-hundred American job holders got their positions through newspaper want ads, and other surveys have placed this figure even lower, at two out of every one hundred. Worse still,
if these surveys had been restricted to upper-level employees, the numbers would have practically evaporated. The overwhelming majority of want ads are for entry-level or lower intermediate-level positions.

Don't get too depressed. After all, responding to want ads does increase your chances of getting the job you want by 2 to 5 percent (over sending unsolicited resumés). Better yet, in responding to want ads placed in special-interest, professional, and trade publications, your "hit rate" should be higher—and the jobs more attractive. Just don't base your job search entirely on the classifieds section.

Do, however, maximize your chances of transforming a response into a call for an interview. You'll sharpen your edge once you understand the dual purpose of a want ad: It is both a *net* cast to snare likely candidates, and a *screen* used to sift out and discard 95 (or more) resumés out of every 100 received.

To get by the screen, take the following steps:

➤ Respond quickly. Employers expect to receive most resumés within 96 hours of the ad hitting the streets. Day three is the peak, and by day four or day five, the employer starts going through the pile in earnest.

Don't Call Us ...

It can be tough to confine your response to the parameters of the ad. Resist your natural tendency to give the employer a little "something extra." That something extra could end up convincing the employer that you don't quite fit in.

➤ Respond briefly. Your cover letter should be short and to the point.

➤ Mention the source and date of the ad in the first sentence of the cover letter and state that you are interested in the position because it is such a great fit with your qualifications: "Your advertisement for a widget analyst in the May 18th *Widget World* intrigues me because my qualifications so closely match what you are looking for."

➤ In the next part of your cover letter, paraphrase the qualifications asked for in the ad, then address only those.

➤ Present your qualifications in a bulleted list rather than in sentences within paragraphs. Your cover letter must "sell" you *at a glance*. Don't make the reader work to find out who you are.

➤ Don't ignore criteria you don't meet. Invent some way to address them. For example, if an ad asks for "experience with database programs"—experience that you lack—respond that you are "interested in database programs."

➤ If you're not asked to state your salary requirements, don't. Pick the wrong target figure, and you may get screened out.

➤ Even if you are asked to state salary requirements, don't. Difficult as it may be, just ignore this request.

➤ Set your letter apart from the crowd by timing it to arrive on Tuesday, Wednesday, or Thursday rather than on Monday or Friday. (Employers tend to feel overwhelmed at the start of the week, and pinched by deadlines at the end of the week.) Or invest in a reply via overnight mail or courier service.

Clincher

If you absolutely must respond to a query about salary needs, compromise. Don't pinpoint a figure; just allude to the subject of salary: "As I have moved upward from position to position, my salary has increased commensurably." Or respond with a range. If you're looking for $30,000, but would settle for $25,000, set your range at $25,000–$35,000, adding the phrase "depending on the scope of my responsibilities."

What About Want Ads on the Internet?

The Internet is a rich source of employment information, but most job seekers who rely exclusively on want ads posted on the World Wide Web end up disappointed. Why? The truth is that Internet want ads are neither more nor less effective than want ads posted in newspapers, professional or industry journals, or elsewhere.

This said, turn to Chapter 19, "The Internet Interview," for some suggestions on using the Internet as an aid to job hunting as well as employment-related communications.

Turning a Cold Call into a Warm Reception

You needn't rely exclusively on sending unsolicited resumés or responding to want ads. After researching the job market and the suitable firms in your field, try some cold calls. A *cold call* is an unsolicited employment query/application over the phone. The target employer doesn't know you and hasn't asked you to call. You could make cold calls based on a Yellow Pages search, but you'll more likely make a meaningful connection if you do some research on your target em-ployer and industry first (see Chapter 2 for more help).

If the prospect of calling a stranger to ask for a job seems daunting, don't be too intimidated. The object of a cold call is nothing so momentous or terrifying as actually *getting a job*. The goal of a cold call is to keep you from getting screened out. It should generate sufficient interest to get you an interview—or, second best, a receptive reader of the resumé you will send.

Don't Call Us ...

Some authorities advise sending a want ad reply in an envelope marked "Personal and Confidential." This may well ensure that the intended target opens the letter, but it could also irritate the employer, who will feel deceived.

End the Run-Around in Human Resources

So who do you talk to? When you contact larger companies, the Personnel, or Human Resources (HR), department is the obvious target. Obvious, but not the best. In many—perhaps most—organizations, the function of HR, so far as recruitment is concerned, is to eliminate unsuitable candidates from the pool of applicants. Why talk to a screen? The more effective strategy is to speak directly to a person with the authority and power to hire you.

Follow the Clout

Your research may tell you who that person is, or you could call HR now and tell them that you are researching careers in X field and that you would like to talk to a senior staff member in the X department: "Could you give me the name of that person?" Emphasize that you are not applying for a job, but only seeking information. Once you have the name of the contact person, you might indeed start with a request for an informational interview, as discussed in Chapter 16, "Creating an Interview." Just tell the cloutmeister that "your Human Resources department recommended I speak with you." If you decide to bypass the informational interview and proceed directly to the cold inquiry, warm it up a bit by mentioning that "your Human Resources people suggested I contact you."

Phone Tips

Chapter 18 is all about the telephone interview, but you can use some quick advice about the cold call now.

Make your call with one primary and three fallback objectives firmly in mind:

➤ **Primary objective:** To arrange a meeting.

➤ **Fallback #1:** To arrange a time to talk further on the phone.

➤ **Fallback #2:** To secure a receptive reader for your resumé. This may be combined with Fallback #1, to discuss your resumé.

➤ **Fallback #3:** To secure a lead on a job possibility elsewhere or to seek information on future prospects for employment at the target company.

Keeping these objectives in mind will prevent you from suddenly going blank when the voice answers on the other end of the line.

Snuff Out Spontaneity

No law dictates that a telephone conversation has to be spontaneous. You wouldn't "wing" *any* major presentation, would you? So why not script the cold call? Here are the parts:

1. Greet the recipient and identify yourself. If you're calling on someone's recommendation, make this the third thing you say: "Good morning, Mr. Smith. My name is Joseph Billing. Your client Pat Mitchell strongly recommended that I give you a call."

Clincher

Beware the "voice of fear"—the thin, tight, quavering, high, breathless, and utterly unpersuasive voice that comes out when you're scared. Combat the voice of fear by breathing deeply and always pushing your voice into a deeper register. Male or female, you command more respect if you speak in a relatively deep voice. And slow down! Take your time. Give value to each word.

2. Reel out your "hook," a statement designed to appeal to the recipient's self-interest. For example: "As you know, the new government regulations have created a climate of crisis. But, Mr. Smith, I see them as a challenge and an opportunity."

3. Now that you've got him hooked, develop the recipient's interest: "I'm assistant to the Director of Regulation Compliance at Acme Widget, Inc., and I've been part of a team that's been achieving cost-effective compliance."

4. Then, transform interest into desire: "I'd welcome an opportunity to sit down with you and share some of the cost-saving strategies I've been a part of. I'd like to explore how my work might benefit your firm."

5. Prompt the recipient to take action—or take action for him: "I'll call you next week to determine a time when we can get together."

The Hardest Sales Letter You'll Ever Write

While the cold call is generally more effective than an unsolicited letter—a "cold letter"—you may feel more comfortable sending one of these. As you would with the cold call, research your target employer before writing a cold letter; don't just take a shot in the dark. The letter can be structured identically to the cold call; start with a *hook* (in this context, an appeal to the employer's self-interest), then write a few sentences to create *interest*, and continue the discussion to generate *desire*. The letter should end with a call to action.

Clincher

Use the cold letter as a cover letter to accompany your resumé. Just as you tailor your letter to the individual employer, so you should modify your resumé. The resumé is not carved in stone, and its content should detail the highlights you give in your letter.

The cold letter is a sales letter, and the merchandise is you. The savvy consumer buys value. To be sure, your ultimate goal is to sell yourself as high-value "merchandise," but remember that your more immediate objective is to secure an interview. Therefore, offer value in return for the chance to interview: "I would welcome the opportunity to talk to you about how my approach to widget analysis can increase your sales." This tells the target employer that you will give him something. It is far more effective to *give* than to ask for an interview so that *you* may *be given* a job.

The Letter-Call Formula

Why think in terms of a cold call *versus* a cold letter? Combine the two, beginning with a cold letter and following up with a cold call designed to underscore the points made in the letter.

If the cold call yields an interview and there will be more than a two-week lag between the call and the meeting, follow the call with a letter thanking the recipient for agreeing to the interview, underscoring how much you are looking forward to it, and briefly recapitulating the benefits—to the employer—you outlined in your phone conversation.

Working with an Agency

Employment agencies generally get a bad rap in job-hunting books. This isn't entirely fair and is the result of expecting too much from an agency. The fact is that the overwhelming majority of hopefuls who sign up with an employment agency fail to get jobs through it. It's not that the agencies are incompetent; rather, while you may believe the agencies are working on your behalf, they are well aware that they're really working for the people who pay their bills: the employers. Think of the employment agency as a combination talent scout and screening service. First and foremost, the agency's mission is to find suitable employees for its clients—not a job for you. So, in working for the employer, the agency may or may not also be working for you—it all depends on the agent's judgment.

The Skinny

Only five of every one-hundred job hunters who walk into an agency actually get a job through the agency.

Presenting Yourself

In many ways, presenting yourself at an employment agency interview is no different from presenting yourself at an employment interview, but there are a few key differences:

➤ **Be clear about what you want.** Don't define yourself and your needs so broadly that you waste everyone's time getting called for jobs you'd never even think of taking, but do define yourself and your needs broadly enough so that you are not eliminated from consideration for jobs that might actually be a good fit.

➤ **Don't use the agent as an employment counselor.** That's not his job. Remember, he works for the employers, not for you.

Don't Relax Yet

The employment agent works for the employers, not for you. Don't put your professional life in the hands of an employment agency. It's fine to sign up with several agencies, but pursue the job hunt on your own as well. Regard the agency as nothing more than an adjunct to your primary employment campaign.

Is This the Best Place for You?

Courtesy pays. Treat the people at the employment agency with respect and pleasantness. But don't take your manners to an extreme. If you ever begin to feel that you are being unfairly pigeonholed, bullied, or just plain ignored, don't stick around out of courtesy. Walk away and go on to the next agency. There are plenty of them.

Clincher

At the very least, your encounter with the employment agency is valuable as an opportunity to practice your interview skills.

And because there *are* plenty of them, you don't have to confine yourself to a single agency. Sign up with several. Your chances of getting "placed" by any one agency are about one in twenty, so registering with a few of them betters these long odds at least to some degree. Don't feel guilty, don't misplace your loyalty, and don't worry about receiving duplicate job offers. Few employers use more than one agency for any single position.

The Least You Need to Know

➤ Interviews rarely "just happen"; you need to proceed vigorously and proactively in order to *produce* them.

➤ Take a long, hard look at your resumé. Is it focused on the needs of the *employer*?

➤ All of the traditional approaches to job hunting have limitations, so don't rely solely on any one approach. For example, respond to want ads while making cold calls and using an employment agency.

➤ Never lean too heavily on an employment agency; the agency works for the employer, not for you.

Get Set

In This Chapter

➤ How to respond to a request for an interview

➤ What to tell your boss (protecting your present job)

➤ Scheduling the best time for the interview

➤ Developing and deploying your "interview kit"

➤ Rehearsing for the "performance"

➤ Logistics: Getting there—on time

➤ The night before ...

You've landed an interview. You should feel just great—rarin' to go. Right?

Well ... maybe.

Or maybe you're feeling more like Elmer Blurque, the reluctant door-to-door salesman on an old-time radio comedy show, who'd tap ever-so-lightly on his prospect's door, pause, and announce to the audience in the goofy voice of a consummate rube: "Maybe nobody's home—uh-hope, uh-hope, uh-hope."

Jubilant excitement, high anticipation, second thoughts, out-and-out doubt, and naked fear—all are part of the pre-interview stew. Well, don't just simmer. Your time—now—is a precious asset. Here's how to use it.

Go!

The big news may come to you in a letter, but more than likely you'll hear by phone. Either way, answer promptly. Before you rush headlong into a response, check and double-check your calendar to make certain that you have no conflicts. Once you set a date and time, it's important that you don't make any changes. The last thing you want is to annoy the interviewer right off the bat by making her rearrange her schedule for you.

What to Do with the Big Call

These days, a request for an interview will usually come by phone. Respond to the call with pleasant enthusiasm, but don't go wild. Be certain to:

The Skinny

Forty-eight of every one hundred job interviews result in a job offer.

➤ Speak loudly enough to be heard.

➤ Use correct grammar.

➤ Speak in complete sentences whenever possible.

➤ Avoid long pauses.

➤ Focus your voice, pitching it somewhat lower than normal.

➤ Smile when you speak; that's right—even though the caller cannot see you, smiling will often naturally inject warmth into your voice.

➤ Respond in a businesslike manner; this is not the time to get chummy or shoot the breeze.

Clincher

It's possible that your first telephone contact will itself be a preliminary screening interview rather than a request for a face-to-face interview. See Chapter 18 for a discussion of the telephone interview.

What to Ask Now

Your first assignment is to listen. In your excitement, it's all too easy to hear without really listening, so be certain to jot down the information you are given. Don't hang up until you have obtained the following:

➤ The caller's name and title

➤ The name of the company

➤ The address of the company—or wherever the interview will take place

➤ The date and time of the interview

➤ The names and titles of the person(s) with whom you'll be meeting

➤ The telephone number of the caller and of the key person with whom you'll be meeting

If the interview location is familiar to you, great! But if you need directions, ask for them: "I'm not familiar with that part of town. Can you tell me the best way to get there from such-and-such street?" It's better to ask now than to get lost later.

Close the conversation by repeating essential information back to the caller: "I'll be at 1234 West Street, Suite 3456 on June 3 at 9:30, and I'll ask for Ms. Carlson." If you are speaking directly to the person who will interview you, end with an expression of pleasant anticipation that also serves to confirm vital information: "All right, then, Ms. Carlson. I look forward to seeing you at your office at 1234 West Street, Suite 3456 on June 3 at 9:30. Thanks so much for calling."

You *should* have your calendar and date book by the telephone, but if you don't and you're not certain whether the proposed date and time are free, it's better to ask to call back. Be sure to promise to call back at a specific time: "I need to check my schedule. It's 10:30 now. Can I call you back in a half-hour, at eleven?" Then be certain to call back at exactly that time.

If you *know* that you have an irreconcilable conflict (such as another job interview, you lucky dog), reply that you can't make it at the time proposed. Don't explain why, and don't invite discussion of the issue. But do offer an alternative: "Any time Wednesday or Friday would work well for me."

Clincher

You've sent out X number of query letters and, therefore, have some right to expect a call or two for an interview. Why not tack up a note by the phone with a checklist of the information you need to obtain from a would-be interviewer?

What to Say (and Not Say) to Your Present Employer

If you are currently employed, you need to decide what to tell—and not tell—your employer. Perhaps he or she knows that you are looking for another job and is even supportive of your efforts. Wonderful. More likely, though, you're conducting your job search without your boss's knowledge. If this is the case, you need to practice discretion at your place of work.

Being discreet begins with how you handle the phone call summoning you to an interview. Take the call, and greet the caller. Then ask for a moment to shut the door. Just say, "Can you give me just a moment? I need to shut my door." You don't have to say why. The caller *knows* why, and he understands.

Clincher

If you know you can't take job-hunt-related calls at work, plan a way to handle them elsewhere, but make sure you return calls *before* the end of the day. If you live close enough to the office to go home for lunch or have a friend who lives nearby, ask to call prospective employers back around midday. If you have a cellular phone, make sensitive calls from a private area, such as your (parked) automobile.

Don't Call Us ...

Do *not* express fear to the prospective employer: "My boss would can me in a heartbeat if he found out I was interviewing." Nor should you imply that you are skulking around behind your boss's back; after all, you'll be interviewing with your potential *new* boss. Just ask that the interview be kept confidential. That is all that needs to be said.

If you don't have a door to shut, try to get the essential information without betraying the nature of the call. Should your caller begin to transform the call into a telephone interview, you will have to stop him: "Mr. Smith, I'm in a high-profile, high-visibility position here, and I can't discuss this matter with you now. May I call you back this evening at six?" Or just say, "I'm sorry, Mr. Smith, but I'm not in a position to discuss this matter with you now. Can I call you back this evening at six?"

As a ploy to get a raise or a promotion, you may be tempted to do away with discretion and actually start dropping hints around the office that so-and-so wants to interview you. This is almost certainly a bad move. Instead of getting what you really want with your present employer, you'll more likely persuade him that you are disloyal or, at the very least, a grumbler and malcontent. Maybe you feel confident that you'll get the job you're about to interview for. That's a very healthy way to feel, but the hard fact is that you might *not* get the job or that the offer might not be all that you expected. In the end, you might want (or need) your current position for quite a while.

The best policy, then, is to avoid talking about your job search with anyone at your present workplace. You'll find, to your chagrin, that swearing even your most trusted confidantes to secrecy is effectively akin to posting an announcement on the coffee room bulletin board. Always be discreet—at *and* away from work.

It's a Small, Small, Small World

You've just hung up the phone. An interview! Great!

Then, a persistent little thought wraps its icy claws around your medulla oblongata: What if this *prospective* employer blabs (inadvertently or otherwise) to your *current* employer?

You try to dismiss the notion as mere paranoia.

In truth, you're not paranoid. It could happen. In most cases, it's a fairly remote possibility, but the smaller and more tightly knit a particular industry is, the greater the likelihood of a "security breach." It would be wise, then, to stress to the prospective employer that you would prefer to keep the upcoming interview in strict confidence.

A Little Bouquet of Graceful Lies

You will need time for the interview. And that means taking time away from your current job. If you have a flexible lunch hour, plan to take an early or late "lunch" so that your interviewer can keep her regular lunch hour—you don't want her going hungry just to interview you.

Of course, squeezing an interview into a lunch hour can be uncomfortably confining. What if someone is late? What if the interview runs overtime? The last thing you want is to have to watch a clock or—heaven forbid—cut your own interview short.

The better strategy is to tell your current boss a graceful lie that will allow you maximum flexibility.

➤ As part of your general job-hunting strategy, hoard a cache of vacation days. Deploy these as necessary to leave an entire day free for an interview.

➤ If you are entitled to personal days, use them. You have a "dentist's appointment," a "doctor's appointment," "a parent-teacher conference," "automobile trouble," a "visit from the plumber." Any of these should free up, at minimum, a morning or afternoon.

➤ Keep your lie simple. The best lies are the most basic. Elaborate stories are usually too flimsy to stand up for long.

Don't Call Us ...

Don't let your clothes betray you. If you usually wear a casual shirt and khakis to work, nothing will broadcast, "I've got an interview!" more loudly than your suddenly showing up in a spanking-new suit and tie. Make up an excuse: "Boy, I *hate* wearing a tie. But I've got to talk to Johnny's teacher this afternoon, and I don't want to look like a bum."

Best Time for an Interview

If you have any choice in the matter, schedule your interview at the optimum time—neither on Monday nor Friday. The middle of the week is best, because it's apt to be less hectic than the start or end of the week.

➤ Ten o'clock in the morning is a great time for *any* meeting, including an interview. The interviewer(s) will have settled in for the morning, alertness and attentiveness are usually at their peak, and lunchtime (with growling stomachs and accompanying impatience) is still in the comfortably distant future.

➤ Avoid late-afternoon meetings. Your energy level, as well as that of the interviewer, tends to be at its lowest.

➤ Avoid hectic times (such as the day or two before a big sales conference) and hectic seasons (for example, Christmastime in the retail industry).

Resolving Scheduling Conflicts

The best way to resolve conflicts is to prevent them altogether: Don't forget to consult your calendar in your eagerness to schedule an interview. You do maintain an engagement calendar, don't you? You should keep it accessible, next to your telephone.

If a conflict does develop, first try to resolve it without involving the potential employer. Always move your schedule to accommodate his. If that proves impossible, call the employer immediately. Put the conflict—and the consequent need to reschedule the interview—in the best light by explaining that an "urgent professional commitment" or "urgent professional emergency" has suddenly come up. Then continue, "I am really sorry to cause you inconvenience, Mr. Smith, but I just can't let the rest of my team down." Putting the matter this way at least testifies to your ethical character and high degree of professional commitment.

Life, of course, is uncertainty. Illness, accident, and family emergencies do arise and force you to change your plans. Inform the prospective employer immediately. Describe *briefly* the nature of the emergency, apologize, and—if possible—reschedule immediately. If you can't, give the best estimate that you can. Never fabricate personal crises or family emergencies as an excuse for rescheduling an appointment.

Trust, But Verify

When you make an appointment, you must trust the potential employer to keep it. However, if more than a few days will elapse between the phone call and the appointment, telephone the employer the day before the interview to confirm: "I was just calling to confirm our ten o'clock meeting tomorrow at your office."

Build an "Interview Kit"

Odds are that you didn't buy this book because you happen to love interviews. Well, there's often someone else who doesn't love interviews. That person is the employer. Some employers see interviews as a necessary evil, and they consider them interruptions in a busy day. More importantly, some employers are uncomfortable in the role of interviewer. They often put off preparing for them, and sometimes don't even prepare at all. The result: a lot of talk about the weather punctuated by awkward silences.

Your prime objective in approaching a prospective employer is to appear to her as *the* answer to her needs. Come to the interview as part of the solution rather than just another part of the problem. And the interviewer's problem at the moment is how to get through the interview comfortably and productively.

So, how can you be part of the solution?

Come prepared with great questions; Part 3 will show you how to do that. And come prepared, too, with one very handy prop: the interview kit.

What Goes into the Interview Kit?

The interview kit is a kind of scrapbook, which may contain such items as additional copies of your resumé (three should be enough; avoid carrying around a sheaf, which makes you look desperate) and, perhaps, a half-dozen copies of an executive briefing, which hits the high points of your resumé in a single narrative paragraph. Your interview kit should also include letters of commendation, awards, copies of business presentations you have made, photos of equipment you have worked with, and so on.

If the work you do—or want to do—involves creating ads, artwork, and so on, don't try to stuff samples of everything into an interview kit. Instead, prepare a full-scale portfolio of your work. Your portfolio may be a big, bulky thing, or you may be able to put it on a computer floppy or CD-ROM and present it on a color laptop/notebook computer you bring to the interview.

Don't Call Us ...

Be careful *not* to include in your interview kit anything that may be construed as trade secrets or confidential and/or proprietary material that belongs to your current employer!

How to Use Your Interview Kit

The purpose of the interview kit is not only to exhibit some of your wares and highlight your qualifications and accomplishments, but, quite literally, to serve as a conversation piece: something to look at, something to spark comment, something to prevent awkward silences.

It is best, however, not to let the interview kit become the object of rapt attention; use its contents as springboards to further comment and discussion:

> **You (as you and the interviewer look through the interview kit):** I received this letter after I completed a project that saved my client $40,000.
>
> **Interviewer:** Oh. Tell me something more about that.
>
> **You:** Well, this was the client's situation as I saw it ...

Each item you select for inclusion in the interview kit should have a strong, positive, compelling story to go along with it.

Stay in Control

It is important to remember that *you* control the interview kit. You may give the interviewer one of the copies of your resumé—especially if he has failed to bring in the copy you sent by mail—but the interview kit itself always stays in your hands. Don't give it over to the interviewer, but merely let him or her look. Your objective is to convey that the work it contains is yours, is of great value, and is not up for grabs.

Rehearse It and Nurse It

The renowned trial attorney Louis Nizer once wrote a book called *Thinking on Your Feet*. I've often thought about that title, and about how intimidating the notion of thinking on your feet is. Few things are scarier than relying on spontaneity, especially if your career, your very livelihood, depends on it. No wonder most of us dread job interviews! Even when we're sitting down, we're thinking on our feet.

Or so we believe.

The fact is that a job interview does not have to be conducted under the tyranny of spontaneity—*if* you stop thinking of the interview as an event over which you have little or no control. Instead, conceive of it as a *performance*—more like a speech or presentation than an interrogation.

Once you start thinking this way, your next step becomes obvious: Rehearse.

The Skinny

According to *The People's Almanac Presents the Book of Lists*, the 10 worst human fears in the U.S. are (from bad to worst): dogs, loneliness, flying, death, sickness, deep water, financial problems, insects, heights, and—in the number-one position—speaking before a group.

Gather Ye War Stories

After you have thoroughly researched the employer and industry you're aiming to join (see Chapter 2), you should review your own "war stories"—the achievements, accomplishments, problems encountered, and problems solved that relate to what you have determined to be the needs and requirements of the prospective employer.

➤ Select three or four concise, solid war stories that show you off at your best and relate to what you believe the employer needs.

➤ Structure your war stories. They need a beginning, middle, and end. This structure effectively corresponds to problem, analysis of problem, and solution to problem.

➤ If possible, coordinate your war stories with the contents of your interview kit. It should include letters and other documents that illustrate your narratives.

➤ Write out the war stories you select. Use this document as an actor would use a script. Rehearse it. Commit it to memory.

The Rest of the Script

You've done all the research, organized your interview kit, and memorized your war stories; you're ready, right? Wrong. Now you need to review and rehearse the rest of your "lines":

➤ Conduct an intensive review of your research about the target employer. Bone up on three or four major industry issues, problems, and trends that you will want to discuss at the interview.

➤ Review your personal information as well. Know your skills, qualifications, achievements, and interests. These constitute your basic, general sales pitch. Know them cold.

➤ Adapt your general sales pitch to meet the needs of the target employer. It's like a game of connect-the-dots: Certain dots represent your skills and qualifications, while others represent the employer's needs; you should be able to link all the dots to form a complete picture.

When you rehearse alone, consider videotaping yourself. This is a great method for zapping nervous tics, bad posture, fidgeting, wild gesticulations, or jittery hands. If the person you see on your TV screen is not smiling, you'd better make a conscious effort to do just that. (You'll find a concise body-language primer in Chapter 7.)

Don't Call Us ...

If you're reviewing and memorizing your strengths, shouldn't you do the same for your weaknesses? Yes, you certainly should. A favorite interview question is "In what areas do you feel you could use improvement?" Just remember *not* to initiate discussion of these issues yourself. If the interviewer asks, respond. If not, pitch your strengths only. See Chapter 9, "How to Answer Questions Everybody Asks," for tips on turning negatives into positives.

You might also ask a friend or family member to role-play with you by acting the part of the interviewer. You can prime your co-star's pump by furnishing a list of some questions, but also invite her to invent questions of her own.

Questions, Questions, Questions

Now is a good time to read Chapters 9 and 10. Take time to anticipate the most likely questions and prepare answers. You should write these out.

Once you have the answers to the tough questions you're anticipating, go ahead and read the chapters in Part 3 about questions *you* should ask. Prepare a short list of questions to ask. These should raise issues that put your skills, qualifications, interests, and accomplishments on display.

Clincher

When *should* you arrive? If your appointment is early in the day, be careful that a premature arrival doesn't intrude on your host's morning routine. Four or five minutes before the scheduled time is acceptable. If you arrive even earlier, tell the receptionist that you're early and would rather not disturb Ms. Whomever yet. Could she announce you in 5 minutes?

Interview Logistics

Don't become so immersed in the Theater of Interview that you neglect logistics—you've got to get to the interview site, and you've got to get there on time. Plan your route in advance. If possible, make a trial run over the route at the same time of day that the interview will be taking place, so that you can better estimate travel time. And be sure to give yourself plenty of extra time, especially if the office is in a city where traffic can be a problem.

It's better to allow a little too much time and end up arriving early than late. Use the spare minutes to clear your head and collect your thoughts. Take a look at Chapter 6, "Reception Room Savvy," for ideas about how you can make effective use of the time you spend in a reception area.

If you arrive early at an unfamiliar destination, use your extra minutes to familiarize yourself with the building. Determine just where you have to go. If you're *really* early, get in the elevator, ride it up to the correct floor, make certain that you've come to the right place, then go back down, walk around the block, and return on time.

Travel: Who Arranges and Who Pays?

If you are interviewing out of town, you should clearly establish who will be arranging your travel. Typically, it's your responsibility to book a flight, but the employer will often make the hotel arrangements. That said, don't assume anything. Always ask. If you're expected to reserve a hotel room yourself, ask for advice on the most conveniently located hotel—not the "nicest" or "best," but the "most conveniently located."

In most industries, the employer will usually pay for your travel and accommodations, including meals. However, you may have to front the money, then put in for reimbursement. Accordingly, make sure you:

➤ Save all receipts.

➤ Secure the name and address of the person to whom you should mail your expense report and receipts.

➤ Ask if the company has a preferred travel agent, hotel, or air carrier that you should deal with.

Even if the employer prepays all or most of your travel expenses, collect and save any receipts, including those for your airline tickets and for your hotel. The employer may want these for bookkeeping purposes.

What if *you* are asked to foot the bill? Then you're faced with a tough decision. Should you stake travel costs on the interview? What does this say about the prospective employer? How serious is she about considering you for a job?

And don't just ask these questions of yourself. Talk to the employer: "I am not accustomed to paying my way to an interview. Is this usual with your company?" Or: "I have to tell you, Mr. Johnson, that I don't ordinarily pay my own way to an employment interview. Before I commit to this investment, can you tell me how many others you are interviewing for the position? Where do I stand?"

Wake Up! You're Jet-Lagged!

If you're traveling great distances, especially overseas, reserve your arrival day as a day of rest. Don't try to hit the airport in the morning and rush to an interview. You'll run out of steam. Jet lag is a harsh reality and can hit you with the sandbagging impact of the flu. Allow time to sleep. Definitely arrange for a wake-up call, and back this up with your own alarm clock. Jet lag wreaks havoc on your body's internal clock.

The Night Before

Here's this chapter's hardest piece of advice: Relax. Devote the night before your interview to relaxation. Free your mind to prepare for the day ahead. Don't allow family problems, financial worries, or other events and crises in your personal life to intrude on this time. If they're eating at you right now, take out a pad and pencil, make a list of your worries, then promise yourself that you will deal with them—*after* the interview. You might try *positive visualization,* in which you imagine yourself at the interview, impressing the interviewer or interviewers.

Talk the Talk

Positive visualization is a mental exercise in which one imagines what success in a given context will look and feel like. A runner might prepare for a race by *seeing* herself leaping the hurdles. A job candidate might visualize himself successfully answering the most difficult questions or accepting a congratulatory handshake at the end of a great interview.

43

See a Show, Walk the Dog

Distract yourself with something mindlessly pleasant. Go to a movie. Have a nice dinner. Don't stay out late, and, if you can avoid it, don't drink.

The Last Supper

Eat well, but this is not the time to experiment with exotic or unfamiliar cuisine. Choose a meal you know will agree with you. Again, avoid overindulgence in wine or liquor. Your best bet is not to drink alcoholic beverages the night before an interview.

Into the Land of Nod

Do what you can to get a good night's sleep. It's a bad idea to force yourself to go to bed early, since you'll probably wake up in the wee hours and may not be able to fall back to sleep. Retire at your usual time. Avoid unpleasant discussions. Remember to set your alarm. Congratulate yourself on having landed the interview. Now, have a good night.

The Least You Need to Know

➤ Don't fly to pieces when you are called for an interview. Obtain all the information you need, and consult your calendar before committing to a time.

➤ Be discreet about the interview; it is important to protect your current job. Avoid using the interview as a ploy to improve your situation with your current employer. You could end up losing your job.

➤ Make good use of the days before the scheduled interview: Review your skills and qualifications (as well as your weaknesses); anticipate the interviewer's questions and prepare answers; prepare questions of your own; rehearse; and assemble your interview kit.

Clothes Call

Doubtless, your mother or father or somebody who was supposed to know better told you something to the effect of "It's what's inside a person that counts, not what's outside." Or, maybe you got the "don't judge a book by its cover" version.

Right.

The truth is, whether we like it or not, appearances are *very* important. Although dressing a certain way will not magically produce a job for you, poor, indifferent, or inappropriate grooming may very well get you screened out of a job before a single word is exchanged. This chapter gives you some dressing strategies to show you at your best.

Evaluating Your Employment Wardrobe

Now—*before* you are called in to an interview—is the time to take stock of your "employment wardrobe." You need to ask yourself two questions:

1. Do you have clothing appropriate to the position, industry, company, and department in which you are seeking a job?

2. Is this clothing in excellent condition: clean, neat, in impeccable repair, and not obviously "dated"?

The second question is self-explanatory, I believe, but the first could benefit from some discussion. "Appropriate" dress: What is it? I mean, this is a free country, right? I'm not applying for a military career. I don't have to wear a uniform.

CPR

A rainy day. You've gotten off the bus and are walking to the interview. A car speeds around the corner, tires churn into a mud puddle, and you are splattered head to foot. What do you do?

Let's face it. There's no way that this is a desirable event. However, you can turn this disaster to your advantage.

If possible, duck into a restaurant or other place that has a public restroom, and tidy up as best you can, particularly your face and hands, if they were splashed. If you can't find a place to do this, try to find a public washroom at the interview venue. You might explain to the receptionist what happened to you and secure from her a key to a washroom.

Looking as clean as you can under the circumstances, walk into the interview and announce: "A funny thing happened to me on my way down here ..." Narrate the incident, then conclude: "I apologize for my appearance, but this meeting is important to me, and I didn't want to postpone it or cause you the inconvenience of rescheduling. I hope you'll bear with me. This *was* a good-looking suit, up until a few minutes ago!"

Handled this way, the incident won't make you look foolish. The interviewers will be treated to your healthy sense of humor, your unflappable nature, your ability to put matters into their proper proportion, and your professionalism: Nothing, but *nothing* could stop you from getting to this interview.

You're not joining the army. But don't be so sure that this gets you out of wearing a uniform. You're probably already well aware that many career fields and professions have unspoken dress codes. If you walk into an interview dressed right—that is, wearing the appropriate "uniform"—you broadcast that you understand at least something about the job, without even uttering a word. If hiring were 100-percent fair and logical, you'd get job offers based strictly on your abilities. In the real world, however, an employer's decision to hire is to a significant degree influenced by *feelings*—and one of those feelings is that you will "fit in." So, go ahead: Walk in the door already suited up as a member of the team.

But how do you know what to wear? There are a good many dress-for-success books on the market, including N.J. Golden's *Dress Right for Business*, Anne Fenner and Sandi Bruns's *Dress Smart,* and Pamela R. Satron's *Dressing Smart*, as well as the original, *Dress for Success*, by John Molloy, first published back in the 1970s. The problem with consulting these is that fashions change, and none of the available books explores the dress codes of specific industries, let alone how those dress codes may be influenced by regional preferences and individual corporate cultures.

So where do you get the lowdown on the right "uniform"? Well, the best place to get any information is straight from the horse's mouth: As a company's "dress code" is on public display every day, just pay a visit to the target company in advance of the interview and take a look around. If you can't do that, or if the nature of the company's business is such that it does not allow for a casual visit, check out any newsletters or other literature the company publishes; look for photos showing staff members. How do they dress? Plan your interview wardrobe accordingly.

> **Don't Call Us ...**
>
> Be careful about visiting the firm on a Friday. In many offices, Friday is "casual day" and does not reflect the prevailing dress code. Don't be misled if the prevailing look is casual on that day.

Dress Codes

There is more to the "dress code" than just trying to look like everybody else. Effective interview dress is a combination of what makes you comfortable, what expresses how you feel about yourself, *and* what is appropriate to the field or industry in which you are seeking employment.

You all know what "comfortable" means, but just be aware that what is comfortable at home—say jeans and a T-shirt—will make you very *un*comfortable at an interview for an investment banking position. Remember that comfort has physical, emotional, and cultural dimensions—consider all three in choosing your interview wardrobe.

And what about "expressing how you feel about yourself"? This is fine, dandy, and wholly positive—as long as what you feel about yourself is appropriate to the position you're seeking. Dressing with a generous serving of panache may send the right signals if you're angling for a job as art director of an illustrated magazine, but, no matter how you *really* feel about yourself, donning something more conservative will almost certainly give you a better shot at that accountant slot with Dewey, Cheatham & Howe.

I Gotta Be Me (You Gotta Be Kidding!)

Here's a short and sweet prescription for interview dress and general grooming: Male or female, the best interview look is the *safest* look—conservative and traditional or, if you prefer, *classic*.

Accept this as the base on which you can build a more individual look, if you wish.

Clincher

Sales professionals make it a practice to dress just a little better than their customers. Apply this thinking to your interview attire by dressing up from the interviewer just a bit.

The "safe" look extends to personal grooming as well as wardrobe:

➤ **Avoid dousing yourself in perfume, cologne, or after-shave.** The sense of smell is highly charged emotionally. If you flood the office with too strong a scent, you may be perceived as annoying and intrusive—or, at best, inconsiderate. You should also be aware that some people suffer allergic reactions to perfume and could become ill from it. The last thing you want is to make an interviewer sick!

➤ **Do feel free to use your favorite scent sparingly.** A hint of perfume or cologne can create a pleasant, inviting, clean, and polished aura. Just remember, the scent should be *barely* perceptible.

➤ **Reevaluate your hair.** Hair length—especially for men—was a downright inflammatory issue during the 1960s and 1970s. These days, the social controversy has died down, but it hasn't disappeared. Very long hair on men is still widely perceived as a token of rebellion or, at least, a hang-loose kind of sloppiness. On the other hand, some people associate excessively *short* hair (the "buzz cut") with hyperconservatism or "skinhead" attitudes.

Women don't have to be as concerned about hair length. Just be aware that some interviewers may find a severe "mannish" cut intimidating or offensive.

➤ **If you have a mustache or beard, ensure that it's neatly trimmed.** In some corporate cultures, however, beards—and even mustaches—are frowned upon. If you have any misgivings, scope out the situation through a pre-interview office visit.

CPR

Employment in the United States is regulated by some excellent laws barring hiring practices that discriminate on the basis of age, gender, or race. However, no law can regulate the emotions, including those associated with humanity's uglier sentiments.

Although a growing number of employers not only accept but positively encourage ethnic and cultural diversity in the workplace, you may want to reconsider "ethnic" hairstyles that represent significant departures from what is generally perceived as the cultural mainstream.

Just as it is illegal to discriminate on the basis of race or ethnicity, so it is unlawful to do so on the basis of age. Nevertheless, employers continue to place a premium on youth or, at least, the appearance of youthful vigor. You will have to decide for yourself whether gray hair is an advantage—conveying an aura of experience and wisdom—or a disadvantage, suggesting that you are older than your years.

From Executive Assistant to VP

Warning: Don't get carried away with all of my conservative advice. *Dress appropriately for the position you are seeking, not for the position you currently have.* For example, if you are an office assistant accustomed to wearing a sport jacket, shirt, tie, and jeans, you should invest in the best conservative suit you can afford before you interview for the position of assistant account executive. If you're an assistant account executive now, don't look like one when you interview with the "creatives" for an advertising copywriter position.

Clincher

Remember that fashion is a powerful form of communication. Just as you shouldn't open your mouth to speak without something to say, so you shouldn't put on your interview clothes without knowing what you want them to "say."

The First Commandment: Be Thou Sharp and Clean

It matters little how carefully you select your wardrobe and how much you pay for it if what you wear fails to be sharp and clean. This, above all, is what an interviewer will notice. Suits—for men and women alike—should be dry-cleaned immediately prior to the interview. Shirts and blouses should be freshly laundered; medium starch is best. The clothes you wear need not be brand new, but they must be in impeccable repair.

And whatever you do, don't stink. Interviews can rattle your nerves. Rattled nerves can make you sweat. Sweating can make you—well—stink. Shower or bathe as close to interview time as practical, and, of course, use deodorant.

Traveling Clothes

Travel is hard on clothes. Fold and pack everything neatly and carefully. These days, airlines usually don't hang your garment bag in a closet, so, you'll have to fold it in half. Your suits, shirts, and blouses will survive this torture with fewer wrinkles if you keep them in the plastic bags the dry cleaner delivers them in. Professionally laundered shirts are best transported in the boxes most cleaners provide for folded shirts.

The Skinny

More than one in six airline passengers who participated in a recent *Consumer Reports* poll reported problems with checked baggage. While few suffered misdirected bags, many had to endure long waits at baggage claim. Not good, if your schedule is tight.

If you fold suit jackets in a suitcase, try folding them in half, lengthwise, *away from* the lining—that is, so that the lining shows. This tends to fight wrinkles.

Needless to say, you should transport important documents—resumé, interview kit, and so on—in your carry-on luggage only. Along with your key documents, you should also carry at least one change of clothes and your toiletries with you. This way, even if your checked bags go astray, you'll still have something to wear.

If you've got the time, consider availing yourself of the hotel's pressing service. This is less time-consuming than dry cleaning (which you should have done before you left, anyway). Alternatively, carry a travel iron or a portable clothes steamer. In a pinch, steam out wrinkles by hanging clothes in the bathroom while the shower is running on hot. Of course, be careful not to scald yourself or end up soaking your clothes.

For Men Only

In general, dress to communicate an impression of reliability and attention to detail. Don't allow any single article of your outfit to become the subject of attention or discussion. (*You*, not your clothes, should be the focus of the interview.)

➤ Be aware that dark colors suggest authority, and that dark blue conveys the greatest degree of authority. (Why else is a police officer's uniform dark blue?)

Black certainly qualifies as dark, but wearing a black suit may strike the interviewer as funereal. Avoid it.

➤ Don't bother with synthetic fabrics. They generally have a sheen and texture that make them look cheap—even if they aren't. Also, they don't "drape" as attractively as natural fibers do, and they tend to retain body odors stubbornly. For your interview, wear natural fabrics only.

Suit Yourself, Sir

Dark colors convey authority, and dark blue does it best. Solids and subtle patterns are fine. Be aware that "banker stripes"—muted, narrow pin stripes—are associated with conservative finance and power politics. If that's the message you want to deliver, fine; some interviewers will be impressed, while others might find it mildly pretentious.

You're on safe ground limiting your choice of fabric to 100-percent wool. Even if you are interviewing in the summer, you'll be better off in a summer-weight wool suit than a light-colored linen or linen-blend suit. Linen wrinkles quickly and badly.

A decade or more ago, three-piece suits were *the* business uniform, but, more recently, two-piece suits have predominated, and vested suits have started looking stodgy. It pays to monitor prevailing fashion and to go, conservatively, with the prevailing trend, always staying slightly behind the cutting edge.

If you have a slender build, the smart European cuts can look great, especially if you are interviewing in a "young" industry (such as television or advertising), but you are generally safest wearing a more generous—and conservative— American cut.

Don't Call Us ...

Avoid loud checked patterns that conjure images of disreputable hucksters or a Technicolor Robert Preston in *The Music Man.*

That designer-logo tie you paid a bundle for—chuck it (or at least, don't wear it to your interview). Many interviewers feel that designer ties broadcast insecurity, as if you needed a designer's imprimatur to certify your good taste.

Keep Your Shirt On

Wear only long-sleeved shirts. Period. Wear a white or very pale blue shirt. Avoid patterns and stripes.

Be careful about monograms. Many interviewers interpret the presence of a monogram as a mark of individualism, prosperity, and pride in appearance, but others will see in it ostentation, even vulgarity. While the safest course is to avoid mono-grammed shirts altogether, if you do get them monogrammed, put the initials on your left sleeve, at the top of the cuff, rather than over the breast pocket.

As with the suit, natural fabrics are best for the shirt. Since cotton wrinkles more readily than polyester blends, it is absolutely essential that you get your shirts *professionally* laundered with medium starch.

Fit to Be Tied

It's up for debate whether the first thing the interviewer will notice is your tie or your shoes. Regardless, the tie is important. The wrong one can make an expensive suit look cheap, and the right one can lift even modest attire a notch or two.

There is only one acceptable choice of fabric for ties—100-percent silk. Linen wrinkles instantly, wool is too casual, and synthetics don't knot well and always look cheesy.

If you do as you're told and wear a white or very pale blue shirt, you won't have any trouble finding a coordinating tie. As for the suit, the tie should complement it rather than match it. If your suit is patterned, don't wear a tie with a pattern that competes with it. Tie widths expand and contract with the tides of fashion, but the width should always be in proportion to the suit lapels: A reasonable rule of thumb is that the width of the tie should be approximately equal to the width of the lapel.

Don't Call Us ...

How about a bow tie? Nope. Not at an interview. And don't even *think* of clip-on *anything*.

Go with the traditional patterns: foulards, stripes, and muted paisley prints, in addition to solids. Broad, solid "power stripes" are fine. Just be sure you shun polka dots, pictures (the heads of hunting dogs, the bodies of naked ladies, and the like), and silly sporting images (golf clubs, polo mallets). Ditch the tie with the Bart-and-Lisa-Simpson print.

Take the extra time to knot your tie carefully. For quite a while now, fashion has favored a small, tight knot, and most newer ties are cut at just the right length to accommodate this knot—they're too short for the old-fashioned "full Windsor" knot. Just remember: The tied necktie should not extend below your trouser belt.

Shoes and Socks

Shoes: Wear black only (with a dark-blue or gray suit), and always well polished, with heels that are in good repair.

Heed these eternal verities: Managers tend toward lace-up wing tips, while accountants favor tasseled slip-on dress shoes. If you're going for a "creative" position—advertising copy writer, say, or anything in the design field—you might want a pair of those costly Italian loafers.

Wing tips can feel solid and substantial, but for some people they seem downright cloddish. If the style feels too heavy, wear a conservative slip-on dress shoe.

Socks: Especially if you choose a slip-on shoe with a low vamp, you must be attentive to your socks. The color of your socks should always complement your suit and should be long enough to permit you to cross your legs without showing hairy, bare skin.

All Accessories Included

You may equip yourself with the following:

➤ **An attaché case.** Carry a simple and slim attaché case or a neat portfolio, if this is more appropriate to your profession.

➤ **A handkerchief.** Use a plain white cotton or linen handkerchief.

➤ **A belt.** Make sure that it's leather and that it matches or complements your shoes. Avoid bizarre or oversize buckles—the cavalry look (Union *or* Confederate), the cowboy look, or the Hell's Angel look.

➤ **A decorative *pocket square*.** Tuck (don't fold) it into your suit pocket. Avoid the matching tie-and-pocket-square look, which hasn't been fashionable since the OPEC oil embargo.

➤ **Suspenders (or braces).** They reached the height of their popularity in the late 1980s as tokens of "manly" financial achievement. They are seen somewhat less frequently these days; be aware that some interviewers may find them pretentious.

➤ **Jewelry.** Restrict yourself to simple cuff links (if your shirt has French cuffs) and a wedding band (if you're married). Shun necklaces, stick pins, bracelets, and pinky rings.

Talk the Talk

A **pocket square** is a decorative handkerchief intended to be tucked into the breast pocket of a suit. It's neither for wiping nor blowing.

Don't Call Us ...

Of late, earrings have graced the lobes of many an unlikely male wearer. Like most bold cultural statements, however, they turn off as many people as they impress and should never be worn to an interview.

For Women Only

While women have a greater range of interview dressing choices than men, they are also under greater economic pressure to invest in current fashions. A man can wear a two- or three-year-old suit without raising any eyebrows—provided, of course, the suit is in impeccable condition—but a woman's interview attire must be much more current. This is, without doubt, a blatant double standard. It's also simply the way things are.

The Suit du Jour

A suit is appropriate for most white-collar interview situations. The good news is that your suit doesn't have to be a severely cut imitation of a man's two piece. Although a charcoal-gray suit with a white blouse is perhaps the safest interview combination, solids, pinstripes, and muted plaids in a variety of colors are all acceptable.

In contrast to men's wear, all-natural fabrics may not be the wisest choice for a women's suit. Garments woven of wool or linen wrinkle readily; therefore, consider natural-synthetic blends. If you are committed to an all-natural fabric, however, choose wool.

Hemlines rise and fall from season to season. The "career women" you see on *Melrose Place* typically wear skirts that are way too short and sexy for the real-world office. You and the interviewer will be most comfortable if you opt for a skirt that's longer than one you would wear on a social occasion.

Clincher

Make-up for an interview is governed by a single simple rule: Less is more. In this situation, the best look is *au natural*. This means minimal make-up carefully applied. If you're comfortable without lipstick, avoid it. If you do use it, apply a subdued shade sparingly.

Blouses and Neckwear

Long-sleeved blouses are most desirable, and it is a good move to show a quarter- to a half-inch of cuff beyond your jacket sleeve; this is typically interpreted as a token of professionalism and authority. Avoid short-sleeved blouses, and shun sleeveless blouses entirely.

For the blouse, a natural fabric is best, especially cotton or silk. Women may choose from a spectrum of colors, but white and pale blue are the most universally accepted colors in the business world. A fresh variation on this conservative theme is pearl gray or the deeper shades of blue.

Simple styles are best. While a front-tie bow is always appropriate, a button-down collar, though a bit severe, appeals to interviewers in conservative companies or industries.

Feel free to accent your interview outfit with a scarf. Wear something you love, but avoid the matching scarf-and-blouse look or oversize polka dots (small ones are fine). Ideally, choose pure silk in a color and pattern that complement your suit.

Heels and Hosiery

A closed-toe pump with a one-inch heel is the safe choice for an interview. Avoid very high heels, which may make your walk less self-assured. Choose shoes that complement your suit and accessories.

When it comes to hosiery, the key word is *unobtrusive*. Wear neutral or skin tones.

And the Accessories

Briefcase or purse? You may carry one, not both. A briefcase projects more authority than a purse. Why not put the essential contents of your purse in a small clutch bag, that you can store in the briefcase?

As with just about every other item of dress, women can choose from a wide range of belts, belt materials, and belt styles, as long as they match or complement the shoes. Be aware that although snakeskin, alligator, and lizard belts may be attractive, you might come up against an interviewer who feels strongly about certain environmental issues. Wear the skin of an endangered or near-endangered species, and you'll lose before you've uttered a word.

With jewelry, less is more. Wedding bands and engagement rings are always fine, but avoid wearing rings on multiple fingers. Shun thumb rings, and while small, discreet earrings are quite acceptable, jewelry that pierces any other part of the body is taboo.

There's nothing wrong with accenting your ensemble with a fine necklace, but don't wear fake pearls or gaudy costume jewelry. The same is true of bracelets. Don't wear charm bracelets or jewelry with your initials engraved on it. Many interviewers find charm bracelets too "cute" or juvenile, and with engraved jewelry, women run the same risk as men who wear monogrammed shirts: Some find it vulgar. And never wear an ankle bracelet to an interview.

Clincher

You know that your stockings will run at the most inopportune moment, so keep an extra pair of pantyhose or stockings in your briefcase or purse.

Don't Call Us ...

Long, dangling earrings make distracting jangling noises, swing around, tickle your neck, and may even catch on clothing. Avoid them.

The Least You Need to Know

➤ An important part of interview preparation is discovering the "uniform" prevailing at the target employer.

➤ Dressing "comfortably" for a job interview requires, in part, dressing appropriately for the field or industry. Be aware that dressing effectively for a job interview may require some compromise of individual expression.

➤ Dress *a little* conservatively, aim a notch above how you expect the interviewer to be dressed, and dress appropriately for the position you seek, not the position you currently have.

➤ Good personal grooming and hygiene are just as important as the perfect outfit.

Part 2
Being There

I'll leave it to the reader to judge whether this book has "heart," but I can tell you that it does have a heart—and the seven chapters of this section are it. No book can give you a set of effective cut-and-dried interview scripts to memorize, but you can develop and hone the intellectual, expressive, and emotional tools you'll need to excel in the employment interview. This is precisely what this section is designed to help you do.

Look here for advice on how to make use of the precious minutes just prior to the interview; for guidance on making the most of the crucial opening moments of the meeting, including how to become fluent in positive body language; for ways to become a dynamic listener; and for strategies to help you answer many interview questions—both the usual and the unusual. You'll also find ways to take control of the interview, together with strategies for negotiating salary effectively and profitably.

Reception Room Savvy

It is *the* longest elevator ride. Up, up, up, with many painful stops before you reach your floor. "Killing Me Softly" hums irritatingly from an unseen loudspeaker somewhere in the elevator car. At last, the doors glide open. The reception desk peeks out from behind a huddle of leafy potted plants. A corporate logo stands in relief against the wall behind the receptionist. You announce yourself to her, then take a seat on a chrome-frame chair upholstered in a nubby material that is even more irritating than the elevator music.

You wait.

You're not looking forward to this.

You're still waiting.

There *must* be something to do with this 5- or 10-minute span besides keeping tabs on the butterflies in your stomach.

This chapter offers some ideas.

Clincher

Use this time. If there's some good company literature in the reception area, read it (see "Reception Room Research," later in the chapter). If you have any work-related reading material stuffed in your attaché, read it. As a last resort, peruse other reading matter available in the reception area, but pick up something related to your field: If you're in business, go for the *Fortune* instead of that two-year-old *People*.

"Punctual": That Means On Time

Interviews go sour for any number of reasons. The natural tendency is to blame failure on the interviewee, who, after all, is the person on the spot, the performer. But it takes (at least) two to interview, and, often, it is the interviewer who does his job poorly. It usually starts with a very basic problem: Many interviewers don't make the time or the effort to figure out exactly what it is they want from the prospective employee. A staggering number of interviews, therefore, just plain drift.

Still, you can bet that there's *one* thing even the vaguest and most vacant employer wants—for his employees to show up on time. Interview performance is in large part a subjective matter and, therefore, can be difficult to assess. But every interview begins with an *objective* test that's all-too-easy to evaluate. Either you're there on time or you're not.

Chapter 4, "Get Set," stressed the importance of knowing where to go, how to get there, and how long it will take. Move heaven and earth to arrive on time.

Is Early Bad?

Aim to arrive 10 minutes before your scheduled interview time. If you're even earlier, use your extra time to scope out the reception area resources. We'll look at this in a later section called "Reception Room Research."

When the Employer Is Late

"I'm here. Where is *she?"* you say to yourself, smoldering, then stewing, then finally steaming.

What should you do when the employer is late?

First, be certain your appointment knows you've arrived. If a receptionist is present, check in. If there is no receptionist, wait until precisely the appointed minute, and then knock on the office door. If the receptionist is away from his or her post, wait no more than a minute past the appointed time. If a door is available for the knocking, knock. If a phone is within easy reach, dial your party's extension. If you don't know it, dial "0." Never go behind the receptionist's desk to use the phone. Use it only if it's clearly meant to be available to visitors.

Of course, "late" is a relative term. For you, it means a minute past the agreed-on hour. For the employer, it's a matter of opinion—and yours doesn't count for much.

Here's what I would do:

➤ At seven minutes past the scheduled hour, ask the receptionist (if there is one) if she's had any word from Mr. Smith: "My appointment was scheduled for ten. Have you had any word from Mr. Smith?" This will confirm that the reception- ist has, indeed, announced you. It might also move the receptionist to buzz Mr. Smith with a reminder. If the answer is "No. No word. He'll call you when he's ready." Say thanks and return to your seat.

➤ At 17 minutes past the mark, *ask* the receptionist to check in with your appoint- ment: "He's really pretty late. Would you mind checking in with him?"

➤ If a half hour goes by without the employer having materialized, take out a sheet of paper from your attaché—or ask the receptionist for one—and write a *polite* note: "Dear Mr. Smith: It's 10:35, and I assume that you've been unexpect- edly and unavoidably detained. Perhaps we'd better reschedule our meeting. I'm at 555-5555. I'll check in with you later this afternoon." Sign the note, fold it in half, inscribe it clearly with Mr. Smith's name, and hand it to the receptionist. In a *polite* voice that betrays absolutely no trace of irritation, ask him or her, "Please be certain that Mr. Smith gets this note. We'll have to reschedule our appointment. Thanks very much."

Keep this situation in perspective. You have every right to be angry if an employer is late for your interview, especially if he does not call to explain the situation. But anger will do you no good when the interviewer finally does show up. The last thing you want to do is go into an interview with a chip on your shoulder. Forgive, forget, and get on with the interview. That said, you may want to keep this incident in the back of your mind as *you* decide whether to accept an offer from a boss who thinks nothing of keeping you waiting.

The Receptionist: A Friend In Deed

Want a friend on the inside? Make an ally of the receptionist. This is not difficult. Receptionists, alas, are accustomed to being treated like waiting- room furniture. They are most often regarded as fixtures, someone to speak at—not with—in order to get to the person the visitor *really* wants to see.

Clincher

Don't assume that the reception- ist, the low person on the cor- porate totem pole, couldn't possibly have any company wis- dom to impart. He or she sees everyone who comes and goes and, in many offices, handles most of the phone traffic. Make use of this asset by treating him or her courteously.

Your approach should be different. Try this:

You: Good morning! Sarah Livingston to see Mr. Thomas.

Receptionist: Please have a seat. I'll tell him you're here.

You: Thanks. And your name is ...?

Receptionist (pauses a beat, slightly surprised by the question): Jane Reynolds.

You: Hi, Jane. I'm interviewing with Mr. Thomas. How's he doing this morning?

Receptionist: Oh ... he's okay. You know, always rushed. Pressured.

You: Oh. Anything unusual?

Receptionist: Well, I know they're all uptight about the big sales meeting. Happens every year. Always a crunch ... Look, I'd better tell him you're here.

You: Thanks, Jane. Nice to meet you.

Receptionist: Well, good luck!

Most interviewees would never think of having such a conversation. And that's just the point. You don't want to be like *most* interviewees. You want to set yourself apart and give yourself an edge. A brief exchange like this may accomplish three things:

1. It encourages the first gatekeeper to help you. This help might be nothing more than a pleasant voice announcing you to Mr. Thomas. A polite "Ms. Sarah Livingston is here for your meeting" will put Mr. Thomas in a more receptive frame of mind than a barked, "Your 10 o'clock is here." Moreover, if Mr. Thomas doesn't answer when buzzed, a friendly receptionist may help track him down.

Don't Call Us ...

Avoid anything that looks or sounds flirtatious, patronizing, or condescending. You are a professional, and the receptionist is a professional. Speak and act accordingly.

2. You might obtain a sliver of inside information, at least something that could help you adjust the pitch of your presentation to Mr. Thomas's mood. Even more important is a tidbit that makes you look *really* on the ball: "Mr. Thomas, I'm so pleased that you set up this meeting—especially when you're so busy with your sales meetings. I know what *that's* like." What a great way to begin an interview!

3. If the receptionist knows who you are, he or she is that much more likely to expedite your subsequent follow-up calls: "Hi, Jane. This is Sarah Livingston. Could you put me through to Mr. Thomas?"

Pit Stop

You don't need a degree in physiology to know how you feel when you get nervous. Even if you aren't urgently moved to do so, it is wise to pay a visit to the restroom before going to the interview:

➤ **Do what you must.** Once you've done whatever you have to do, take the opportunity to wash your hands and dry them thoroughly. Get rid of sweaty palms in preparation for the initial hand-shake. If you don't have make-up to worry about, splash a little cold water on your face. This will tone down any nervous flush, as well as wake you up. (Be careful not to get your suit, shirt, or blouse wet.)

➤ **Look in the mirror.** Now, take a look in the mirror and make sure everything's perfect: tie straight? no dandruff on your shoulders? everything buttoned correctly? shoes tied? Make certain you have no smudges on your face, no lipstick gone astray, no food between your teeth.

Even more important, take a good look at yourself. Smile. Smile again. Smile a third time. Keep that smile on your face when you return to the waiting area and when you walk into the interview.

Clincher

Nervous? Of course you are. Try putting your hands on the rest-room wall and leaning forward as if you were being frisked by the police. (You've seen it on cop shows: "Hands on the wall! Face forward and spread 'em!") Push hard against the wall, as if you were trying to push it down. Grunt as you push. This maneu-ver contracts various muscles and reduces anxiety.

Reception Room Research

Isn't it great when things work out in the organized and orderly way I've described it in this book? You decide to send a cover letter and resumé to Acme Widgets, so you go to the library to do the research (see Chapter 2, "On Your Mark," for suggestions), and when you're called for an interview, you're 100-percent prepared—fully versed in the who, what, and where of Acme Widgets.

Things *can* work out this way. And then again, what if this happens: It's 9:30 on Wednesday morning, and a company you just sent a shot-in-the-dark cold letter to calls you for an interview. They want you there at 11:30. Today.

Without time to prepare, do you:

A. Wing it and hope for the best?

B. Say you have another appointment and try to reschedule?

C. Just say *no?*

Out of these three, B is probably your most productive choice. But what if the employer replies that he's in a hurry? "We need somebody right away. I've got a lot of candidates waiting in line, and I just don't know if I can squeeze you in any later." Or what if this is just too great an opportunity to risk putting off?

Then skip A through C and proceed directly to Plan D: Tell the employer that you'll reschedule your other appointment and that you'll be there at 11:30 sharp. Get any necessary directions, and be certain to ask if the office has a reception area (because you'll have to use it for quick research): "Is there a reception area I'll be going to?" Thank the employer, then hang up.

Now—if the employer has answered that you will be reporting to a reception area—rush like mad to get to the office at least 20 minutes before the appointed time. A half hour is even better. Survey the lobby or waiting area for such company literature as:

➤ Annual reports

➤ Monthly newsletters

➤ Product catalogs

➤ Product/service brochures or leaflets

Don't Call Us ...

Be careful about how you deploy your research knowledge, whether it's based on long-term study or reception-area cramming. Don't just trot out the facts; doing so may make you sound overly rehearsed and insincere or may quickly get you in over your head. Work the information into the conversation as naturally and as seamlessly as possible.

If you don't see anything on the end tables and brochure racks, ask the receptionist, "Do you have any brochures that give a capsule description of Acme Widgets? Anything I could read while I'm waiting?" And while you're talking to him or her, be sure to say that you are very early for the appointment. You don't have to explain why you're so early, but do ask not to be announced just yet: "Please don't announce me yet. I don't want to interrupt Mr. Thomas."

Now, use your time to sit down and read. This is crash research, and you're looking for precious hooks to hang the upcoming conversation on:

➤ **Major products or services.** Scan the literature for these. What are the firm's "flagship" products or services? What makes them special?

➤ **Big events.** Newsletters may mention recent sales conferences, conventions, and the like. What products, services, or issues were key in these events?

➤ **Hot trends.** Look to the literature for identification and discussion of hot-button topics.

➤ **Pressing problems.** The literature may cite industry problems, regulatory difficulties, and the like.

Butterflies Are Free

Just about every how-to-interview book you'll come across admits that fear and nervousness are part of the picture. But, usually, the upshot of the discussion is, in effect, *you'll just have to live with the feelings:* "Everybody feels nervous. You're not alone."

True enough, but not much help when your heart is pounding, your mouth is as dry as old cotton, and you feel like you're going to puke.

Let's not gloss over the sensations of fear. You probably remember reading about the "fight-or-flight" response in a high school health or biology class—how, faced with a threat to survival, the organism gears up for combat or escape: the heartbeat accelerates, the digestive system shuts down, the muscles tense up, the senses become more narrowly focused. Now, as a civilized human being on the lip of the twenty-first century, you can tell yourself that you aren't really facing a life-and-death situation: No saber-toothed tiger is about to storm your cave.

And you'd be right. But will this knowledge calm you down? Probably not. Although it's true that you're not fighting for your life, you *are* fighting for your livelihood. Face it: A lot *does* ride on a job interview. Whatever any particular interview might mean to you—a step up the career ladder, a raise in pay, or the ability to make next month's rent—it's always about getting something you need or something you want (not to mention something your family needs or wants, too). No wonder you're scared.

But don't just *tolerate* or *live with* the fear. Do what champion athletes, great musicians, top-flight race-car drivers, and star actors do. *Use* your fear. Feel it, harness it to energize you, to sharpen your mind, reflexes, senses, and sensibilities.

How do you do this? Follow the example of the pros in any field. Prepare as fully as you can. They make it their business to learn how to take the hurdles, how to hit C above high C with the clarity of crystal, how to speed through to the groove at Indianapolis, how to find the heart and soul of Prince Hamlet. Do the same in your field.

CPR

Unfortunately, whether due to anxiety or some other cause, you may feel too ill to perform effectively at the interview. If at all possible, call in and reschedule the interview. If the employer is seriously interested in you, he will comply. But, in any case, it's usually better to risk losing this particular interview at this particular time than it is to create a bad impression that may remain with this employer permanently, barring you from ever getting hired by him.

If you become ill just before or during the interview, excuse yourself and go to the restroom. If you cannot compose yourself, return to the interviewer and explain that you have been fighting the flu (or some other common ailment), that you thought it would go away, but that you feel too ill to continue the interview: "I don't want to expose you to the risk of catching my flu. I would greatly appreciate it if we could reschedule, so that I could perform for you at my best."

Heroics will not be appreciated at an interview. No employer wants to have a meeting with a ghostly apparition who is obviously suffering. Nor does an interviewer wish to be closeted with someone who is sneezing and hacking. Your most effective move is to bid for a new interview date.

Afraid Because We Run

The great American philosopher and psychologist William James declared that we do not run because we are afraid, but that we are afraid because we run. Likewise, much of the fear you feel in an interview situation comes not from actually being scared, but from your interpretation of your physical reaction to the interview. Sound confusing? Well, when the anxiety and stress of the interview (just like the stress of running) kick in, your heart beats faster, your muscles tense up, and—voilà!—you feel fear (or at least you think you do). And, as a result, your heart beats faster still, your muscles grow even tenser, and butterflies beget yet more butterflies.

Getting a Handle on Nerves

Here are five little exercises to help you ease your nerves just *before* an interview:

1. Grab the sides of the seat of your chair and pull up while silently counting to five. Repeat as often as you like.

2. Put your hands together at right angles to one another, the thumbs gently interlocking. Now press your palms together as tightly as you can. Repeat as necessary.

3. Close your eyes and concentrate on relaxing each muscle in your body. Start with your toes and work your way up, moving on to the next set of muscles only after the previous set is relaxed. When you get to your chest, inhale deeply and slowly. Then focus on your back. Relax it. Lay your head back and relax your neck muscles.

4. Once you are physically relaxed, visualize a peaceful natural scene: a waterfall, waves lapping at a beach, tall pines waving against a blue sky.

5. Take the focus off yourself. Think about your "audience"—the interviewer—and how you will *help* him by sharing your knowledge and offering him a chance to hire you—which would, in turn, greatly improve his department or his company.

Faking It with Body Language

These exercises work. Try them. But if it is true that we are afraid because we run, by far the wisest thing to do is to stop running. In the next chapter, we'll explore the subject of body language. For now, be aware of the kinds of body language that signal fear:

➤ Leg swinging, foot tapping, or "piston leg"—poising your foot on your toes and pumping your leg up and down

➤ Hair twirling

➤ Hand wringing or other nervous hand movements

➤ Lip licking

➤ Finger or nail biting

➤ Touching the mouth or nose

Concentrate on eliminating such body language, not only because it sends negative signals to the interviewer, but because your own awareness of such movements—even on a less than fully conscious level—will stoke the fires of fear: "I'm pumping my leg and twirling my hair. I must be terrified!"

"But," you say, "I *feel* fear, and it's not just because my foot is tapping. If I weren't scared, I wouldn't tap!"

Well, maybe it's all just a matter of your interpretation. Then again, this theory probably isn't going to make you feel any better when you're in the thick of the interview. So what do you do? Fake it. An interview is a performance. It's the theater. Fake it. Act. Perform.

The Least You Need to Know

➤ Move heaven and earth to ensure that you are on time. If the employer is late, do not yield to anger; it won't help you when he finally does show up.

➤ Use waiting time effectively, either to practice subtle relaxation exercises or to do last-minute "reception room research."

➤ Don't overlook the receptionist. Engage him or her as an ally. Be careful, however, not to patronize or flirt.

➤ Recognize that nervousness is part of interviewing. Try to harness your nervous energy. Don't let the physical dimension of anxiety make the anxiety worse.

Chapter 7

Shall We Dance?

In This Chapter

➤ How to make your entrance

➤ A winning handshake

➤ Listening and waiting

➤ Jump-starting the interview by taking the lead

➤ Establishing, developing, and maintaining rapport

➤ Body language

A dance? But isn't an interview about two (or more) people *talking?*

Theoretically, it is. But, practically considered, an interview is about *communicating,* and the communicating begins before a single word is spoken. In fact, decades of research have shown that, in any act of communication, 65 to 85 percent of the message is conveyed nonverbally. Maybe even more. This is true even when an audience has assembled to "hear" a speech. In study after study, audience members are shown to respond more strongly to the speaker's facial expressions, posture, and hand gestures than to her words.

This chapter shows you how to think of the interview as a dance—a meeting of would-be partners who move and maneuver about one another, communicating in a language of words and nonwords. It suggests strategies for avoiding bruised toes and making the experience seem effortless.

Howdy

"He (or she) really knows how to make an entrance!"

How many times have you heard something like that? Doubtless often enough so that it's become a cliché, and you don't think much about what it means. Nevertheless, entering a room makes a powerful statement about who you are and who you think you are. Difficult—or unnatural—as it may seem to make a positive "first impression," it's a lot easier to do that than to try to undo a faulty first impression. In fact, you may well not have the opportunity even to try.

Walk Tall

Just as deeper voices tend to convey greater authority than high-pitched voices, so tall folks tend to command greater authority than short people. This isn't fair, and it's awfully superficial, but it's the way things are. Now, of course, this doesn't mean that short people with high voices can't become top-flight executives (behold Ross Perot), but, *on first impression*, height makes an impact.

Should you wear lifts in your shoes? Not necessarily. Short women can wear higher heels, but it's not wise to go overboard here. The more effective way to add height is to walk tall. Don't enter cringing, stooped, or slouching. Concentrate on maintaining an erect posture as you enter the room forthrightly and without hesitation. The message you want to deliver is nonverbal, but it *can* be put into words: *I know how to carry myself.*

Don't Call Us ...

While a grim visage or an outright scowl is the worst interview look, avoid going to the extreme of a forced, plastic smile. Try to think of something pleasant—a quiet natural scene, perhaps, or a strain of your favorite music—and walk into the interview with *that* smile. Easy does it.

Smile When You Say That

Walking tall doesn't mean coming on like John Wayne, tight-lipped and impassive. Walk in smiling. The greetings that begin the meeting should also be delivered with a smile. The last public speaker to win an audience over without cracking a smile was Sir Winston Churchill, but he was a world leader, and, besides, there was a war on. You probably have neither of these circumstances, so it'll be a lot easier for you to win your audience with a smile than with a look of grim determination or abject fear.

Look 'Em in the Eye

As soon as you walk into the room, target the principal interviewer and look him or her in the eyes. This communicates instant energy. You've probably heard people talk about the "sparkle" in someone's eye.

Actually, we *all* have a sparkle in our eyes; it's just rarely noticed because most people don't make full eye contact when they meet or speak. *You*, too, have the sparkle. Exploit it. Come across as a live wire from the very beginning.

If you fail to make eye contact, you will, at the very least, fail to "connect" with the other person. Worse, you may be perceived as awkwardly shy, not self-confident, or even evasive ("What's she hiding? Why can't she look me in the eye?").

Some Heart in a Handshake

In the old days (at least as I remember them) fathers spent time with their sons (not their daughters, back then) explaining the vital importance of a good, solid handshake. "Son, this is important!"

Quaint, you say?

We like to think of ourselves as "civilized" and "sophisticated," which translates into "intellectual" and "verbal." But physical touch and physical warmth continue to make a powerful *human* impression, and I'll bet that most of us remember the handshake of some individual we have met—because it was exceptionally warm and powerful, or perhaps, colder and deader than any cold, dead fish. Either way, it made an impression.

There is no mystery about delivering a hearty handshake:

1. Try to go in with dry palms. It's a good idea to carry a handkerchief with you and use it to wipe your hands before you enter the interview room.

2. Deliver a full, *moderately* tight grip.

3. Hold the other person's hand a few fractions of a second longer than you are naturally inclined to do.

4. While holding the other person's hand, look him or her in the eyes.

5. Start talking *before* you let go: "It's great to meet you" or "Glad to be here."

Don't Call Us ...

Gentlemen, avoid shaking hands extra gently with women. Use the same *moderately* firm grip you deliver to another man. In a business context, an excessively soft handshake is likely to be perceived as patronizing or chauvinistic.

Please Wait to Be Seated

Avoid the embarrassing slapstick of musical chairs by restraining yourself from rushing to find a seat. Wait. Smile. Not only is it more polite to be the last one seated, but it also gives you a few seconds to be looked up to—literally. Standing in a room in which the others are seated gives you an air of authority, however temporary.

When you do sit, try to avoid sofas or overly soft chairs. You want a chair that keeps you upright and that allows you to maintain erect posture. You don't want to be seen sinking or slumping or getting swallowed up in an overstuffed piece of furniture.

Let Your Partner Lead (if He Can)

The interview is a performance, and while the entrance is an important part of the show, the play's opening speech should not be yours. Let the interviewer(s) speak first.

And *listen*. That's not as easy—or, at least, as passive as it sounds. In fact, effective listening is a *skilled activity* that is complex enough to warrant its own chapter, which comes right after this one.

Enduring the Silence

But what happens if the interview *remains* nonverbal? There is no guarantee that the interviewer will be a self-starter—or will even be prepared. Many an interview has begun with a "How are you today?" only to peter out instantly into silence. It is also possible that you've come up against a kind of "stress interviewer," who purposely uses silence to make you uncomfortable and to see how you'll react. In most industries, it is far less likely that you are facing a stress interviewer than one who is simply unprepared; however, don't rule out silence as a deliberate interviewer ploy, especially if the job you're going after involves heavy client contact, sales, or negotiation.

A few minutes of silence will seem to you an eternity, and you will have difficulty resisting the impulse to fill the silence—with anything. But, before you rush in, try to determine whether the interviewer's silence is a form of evaluation or a plea for help. If the interviewer looks down, aside, or slightly away from you, or if she seems to be looking over some papers (your resumé, perhaps), endure the silence. Here's how:

Clincher

Always frame your leading questions in a gentle, helpful tone of voice. The last thing you want is to convey the impression that you are trying to put the *interviewer* on the spot.

➤ Don't get nervous. You might become self-conscious, and start feeling that the interviewer is focusing in on some flaw in your appearance or demeanor. Banish these thoughts. Your self-consciousness will start you fidgeting, adjusting clothing, clearing your throat, and generally *looking* nervous, perhaps even scared.

➤ Try to keep your eyes focused on the interviewer. Don't glare, but do look on with a calm, yet anticipatory gaze.

➤ Maintain your calm by silently counting the seconds that elapse during the silence: *one elephant, two elephant, three elephant …*

Filling the Silence

It is time to fill the silence when you see that the interviewer is asking for your help. Does the interviewer seem shy? Is *he* looking at you with anticipation—looking *at* you, not down, not aside, not at papers on his desk; eyes wide open, eyebrows arched, lips slightly parted (not tightly shut), as if he is about to speak or, more precisely, to respond to something you say. These are signals of expectation. It is time to take the lead.

Taking the Lead

Offer help—take the lead—by focusing on the interviewer's needs rather than on your own. This is *not* the time to start trotting out your credentials and qualifications, but to ask *leading* questions. You'll find a lot of excellent interview questions to ask in Part 3, but, for now, just be prepared to ask a variation on the salesperson's familiar opening gambit: "How may I help you?"

Actually, most salespeople make the mistake of approaching a silent customer with "May I help you?" Starting out instead with *"How* may I help you?" is more effective because it subtly compels the customer to focus his response, to tell the salesperson *how* she can help. Try asking the silent but expectant interviewer, "How would you like to see me fit into your organization?" Or: "How would you like me to function to increase sales (or cut downtime, or reduce costs, or accelerate response time, or whatever else you believe speaks most directly to the interviewer's needs)?" Then build on the interviewer's response.

Rapport Builders

Rapport is a relationship of mutual trust or emotional affinity. Typically, rapport develops over a long association between friends, between spouses, between business partners, between teachers and students. But, in the course of an interview, you don't have much time to develop rapport, though it's crucially important that you do.

Magic Words: "We," "Us," and "Our"

Perhaps the fastest way of creating rapport is to *will* it into being through a few magic words. You *need* magic, because rapport is nothing less than a magical transformation of an *I* and a *you* into a *we*.

How do you do this? What are the magic words? They are *we, us,* and *our* instead of *I, me,* and *you*.

Here's how the magic works:

> **You:** What do you see as your greatest need in the such-and-such area?

> **Interviewer:** Definitely fulfillment—getting the orders out on time.

You: I understand. Working together, *we* could solve that problem. I accomplished X, Y, and Z at Acme Widget, and I believe *we* could apply some of those solutions here.

More Words and Phrases to Use

We, *us*, and *our* are words of inclusion, cooperation, coordination, and alliance—the very essence of rapport. Other words that contribute to these values and feelings are …

brainstorm	offer
collaborate	open mind
collaborative	synergy
confer	team
cooperate	team player
cooperative	team up
good listener	together
huddle	work together

Try to use these words early in the interview. You can develop rapport further by choosing additional phrases from these five categories:

1. **Phrases that convey urgent energy:**

    "We could address that immediately …"

    "That is something I'd get right on …"

    "It could be accomplished in [time frame] …"

    "Don't worry. Together, we can handle this …"

    "I can see how important this is to you …"

2. **Phrases to convey understanding:**

    "I appreciate your position …"

    "I understand the situation we will be in …"

    "Let me make certain that I understand you …"

    "We understand one another …"

    "We speak the same language …"

3. **Phrases that promote a calm, controlled atmosphere:**

"Let's talk this over so that we ..."

"Perhaps we could agree ..."

"It was my impression that ..."

4. **Phrases to head off confrontation:**

"Let me explain my thinking ...

"We could look into alternatives ..."

"I believe we could come to an understanding ..."

"We should be able to agree ..."

5. **Phrases for self-defense:**

"Here is the way I saw it ..."

"It was a mistake, but, under the circumstances ..."

"It was my feeling at the time ..."

"I wish I had had the benefit of my present hindsight ..."

"Here is how I thought it should be done ..."

"Let me explain my reasons ..."

Rapport Busters

Magic? Well, if rapport is magic, it's also a spell that's all too easily broken. Rapport requires concentration on the part of the interviewer and the interviewee, and that's not always possible. While you may be able to focus on this job prospect as something of great interest and value to you, the interviewer—even though he knows he needs help—may regard the necessity of interviewing as an unwelcome interruption of the "real business" of his day. As a result, he may get distracted. Your task is to keep him on track by constantly and continually appealing to his self-interest.

Interruptions and Distractions

An interview punctuated by phone calls and people sticking their heads in the door with this or that request can be infuriating, frustrating, demoralizing, and even heart-breaking. Or, you can use this formidable rapport buster to your advantage.

Let's say you're stuck with a rude interviewer who takes calls every few minutes, maybe even *makes* a call or two, allows others to walk in to deliver or pick up papers, and so on. Your blood begins to boil. You feel like saying to her: "Look, I don't need this. If I wanted to be treated rudely, I'd take a ride on the subway. Good day to you, ma'am!"

But you say nothing of the kind. Instead, you offer rapport-creating sympathy: "Wow! You really *are* busy. It certainly looks like you really do need some help here."

Chances are, she'll put down that phone, *really* look at you for the first time, shake her head, and say, "I'm just swamped. Up to my eyeballs. Yes. I *do* need help. Let's see if I can get someone to take these calls for now …"

CPR

If you are interrupted and the interviewer is obviously distracted, the loss of contact with her may deflate you, de-energize you, or take the wind out of your sails. Loss of drive and focus is a serious interview crisis. You need to act decisively to recover. Keep the following in mind:

1. Don't take the interviewer's distraction personally. She didn't plan to ignore you.

2. Try to engage the interviewer within whatever is distracting her. If she's getting one call after another, empathize with the pressure she's under: "You really *are* busy around here, aren't you? It looks like you can use all the able help you can get."

3. Give her the time and space she needs: "Please, go ahead and attend to that call. I've blocked out ample time for this meeting."

4. Do not apologize. *You're* not intruding.

5. Don't suggest rescheduling. It's best for you to ride out the distractions. If the interviewer suggests rescheduling, however, cooperate fully (taking care not to make any appointment that may conflict with your other commitments).

6. Don't give up.

Sore Spots

I keep reading that dentists, throughout their profession, suffer from an unusually high rate of depression, even suicidal behavior. Maybe that's because it's awfully hard to create rapport when you are probing a person's mouth with a pointy stainless-steel instrument, trying to find the tooth that *really* hurts.

When an interviewer hits a sore spot, rapport can likewise crumble. In an interview situation, you will have to maintain—perhaps by force—an open mind. You will have to suspend your particular sensitivities and biases. Resist knee-jerk responses to remarks or innuendoes that rub you the wrong way. If something bewildering or unpleasant is thrown your way, respond with a calm "I'm not sure I understand what you mean by that" rather than something harsher. Or just let it pass.

No place is perfect. No boss is perfect. And it is also true that some places and some bosses are so very far from perfect as to be perfectly horrible. But try to make your final decisions on your own turf, away from the interview venue, rather than in the interview and on the spur of the moment.

If an interviewer attacks you at a weak point—a past failure, for example—do whatever you can to preserve rapport by turning the attack to your advantage. Chapters 9, 10, and 21 suggest strategies for doing just this. In general, when a failure or other sore spot is probed, don't panic, don't shy away, don't offer excuses. Instead, *explain* your failure and *describe what you learned* from it.

Words and Phrases to Avoid

Don't risk torpedoing rapport with ill-chosen words and phrases. Avoid the following:

1. **Language that is abrasive:**

    "You don't understand ..."

    "I'm right ..."

    "What exactly are you driving at ...?"

    "You're wrong ..."

    "You're mistaken ..."

    "What kind of suggestion is that ...?"

    "I resent ..."

2. **Language that dodges responsibility:**

    "It wasn't my fault ..."

    "That wasn't my responsibility ..."

    "I knew nothing about that ..."

    "It wasn't my business ..."

    "So-and-so should have done such-and-such ..."

3. **Pointless or superfluous language:**

    "Sort of ..."

    "More or less ..."

    "Kind of ..."

    "I guess ..."

    "If you know what I mean ..."

"What I'm really trying to say is ..."

"You know" (as in, "I was considered a team player, you know.")

"Right?" (as in, "You can't expect success that way, right?")

"You understand?" (as in, "That was the only way to accomplish the task, you understand?")

"Like" (as in, "I will do that, like, immediately.")

Body Language: Eloquence Without Words

We began with the body language of your entrance and first impression. Don't neglect this key aspect of your performance as the interview progresses.

Energize the Interview with "Relaxed Energy"

We've all heard the term "nervous energy." That is not what you want to convey in an interview—foot tapping, eyes darting, fingers drumming. Instead, you want to create an impression of relaxed energy, a combination of enthusiasm and confidence—what might be summed up in the word *poise*. The following will help you achieve the relaxed energy of poise.

How to Breathe

We all have breathing patterns that are natural and comfortable for us. When we become upset or nervous, breathing typically becomes shallower, shorter, and faster. This is noticeable not only to you, but, most likely, to any astute interviewer. Fortunately, you can train yourself to breathe slowly and deeply, even when you are nervous. It takes some thought, but it can be done, and doing so will benefit you in two ways: (1) It will keep your nervousness from being broadcast, and in turn, (2) It will also make you feel less nervous. Remember William James in Chapter 6, "Reception Room Savvy,": We are afraid *because* we run.

Don't Hand 'Em Your Head

For better or worse, your head and face "speak" body language with great eloquence. Here's the basic vocabulary:

➤ Tilting your head to one side indicates interest and close listening.

➤ Scratching your head indicates confusion or disbelief.

➤ Lip biting signals anxiety.

➤ A slightly out-thrust chin conveys confidence; a boldly out-thrust chin will probably be interpreted as arrogance.

➤ A lowered chin conveys defensiveness or insecurity.

➤ Narrowing your eyes communicates disagreement, resentment, anger, or disapproval. Marked narrowing may suggest puzzlement.

➤ Avoidance of eye contact conveys insincerity, fear, evasiveness, or, at the very least, lack of interest.

➤ A steady stare suggests at the very least an arrogant need to control; at worst, vacant staring just seems weird.

➤ Raising your eyebrows indicates surprise—or disbelief.

➤ Peering over the top of your glasses suggests doubt and disbelief.

Handy Advice

Next to the head and face, the hands are the most fluent conveyors of body language. You can use them consciously to help harness or drain off nervous energy. For example, you may want to take notes during the interview. You may also want to gesture with your hand to drive home various verbal points.

It's important, however, that you don't let your hands and arms get out of control, gesture too broadly, or fidget. Be aware of the following signs and signals:

➤ Open hands, palms up, suggest honesty and openness.

➤ Crossing your arms in front of your chest communicates defiance, defensiveness, resistance, aggressiveness, or a closed mind.

➤ Rubbing the back of your head or neck suggests frustration or impatience.

➤ Rubbing your eyes, ears, or the side of your nose indicates doubt.

➤ Hand wringing is a strong sign of anxiety.

➤ Rubbing your hands together communicates positive expectancy.

➤ Holding the fingers of the hand steeple-fashion conveys confidence.

Don't Call Us ...

Avoid sighing. It will be interpreted as a sign of either distress or boredom.

Clincher

Taking notes can be an interview asset, but always ask the interviewer's permission first (some find note-taking distracting). Don't become so absorbed in taking notes that you break off contact with the interviewer; *use* the notes as a means of organizing your thoughts and questions so that you can provide intelligent feedback to the interviewer.

As with head movements, head position, and facial expression, do not hold or repeat any single gesture for a significant length of time. Whatever subtleties of body language you aim to convey, your main object, before all else, is to look alive!

The Least You Need to Know

➤ A great deal of your message—at least 65 to 85 percent—is communicated nonverbally, through body language, and this communication begins with your entrance into the room.

➤ Avoid appearing overanxious: Don't scramble for your seat, and don't rush to fill awkward silences. Know when to endure silence and when to take the lead.

➤ Building rapport—a feeling of trust and mutual interest—with the interviewer is vital; it is established through verbal *and* nonverbal means. Pay attention to the words you use as well as your body language.

Chapter 8

Listen Carefully

In This Chapter

➤ Don't just perform—interact

➤ When to be silent and when to speak

➤ How to be an active listener

➤ Forging a bond of common interest with the interviewer

➤ Focusing the interview on key themes

➤ Interpreting the interviewer's body language

Thinking about the interview as a *performance* is mostly a good thing. It gives you a feeling of greater control. More important, it allows you to prepare, to rehearse, to set specific goals concerning just what it is that you wish to communicate. Thinking this way, however, does have a serious shortcoming if it causes you to neglect the interactive aspect of interviewing, the give-and-take between you and the interviewer. The truth is that star performers on stage do not simply "broadcast" to their audiences, but learn to "read the house," to pick up on the signals the audience sends their way. They respond, in give-and-take fashion, to the needs of the audience. On stage at the interview, you need to develop a similar skill. It's called *listening*, and this chapter suggests techniques for persuading with your ears.

The Lively Art of Listening

An employment interview is a highly interesting situation. Although it's all too true that *you* are on the spot, your task is to keep your own focus not on yourself, but on the needs of those interviewing you. Even as you concentrate on presenting yourself, answering questions, asking questions, and reviewing your qualifications and accomplishments, you need to give the interviewer plenty of room to speak, to respond, to comment, to interact with you, and to let his needs be known.

The Skinny

The mere presence of a listener helps the speaker direct his or her communication toward a goal.

Clincher

"We have two ears and one mouth so that we may hear twice as much as we speak."

—Epictetus (a.d. 55–135)

Interviewing is a lively art. If it required nothing more than a performance, in the strictest sense of the word, you could just mail in a videotape of your spiel and rise or fall by that. But interviewing presupposes at least two living, breathing human beings exchanging thoughts, proposing and reacting, offering and taking.

Practicing Lively Restraint

Every grade-school class has at least one superstudent, a little boy or girl who cannot resist raising a hand to answer each and every question or to comment whenever the teacher pauses for a breath. Well, just wait till you find yourself on the interview hot seat. In your eagerness to keep the conversation going, to parade your knowledge before the inquisitors, to answer questions before their mouths have even closed, you will discover sudden kinship with the overanxious hand raiser back in the fourth grade.

Don't get me wrong. If you sit in an interview as dumb as a log, you won't get the job. But it's also a great mistake to launch into a stiff, overly rehearsed presentation. Even if what you spew out is mighty impressive, the interviewer will probably see you as inflexible—and then, you're just dead in the water. To an employer, *inflexible* is synonymous with *bad fit*.

The little lad in grade four couldn't help himself. He was a child, after all, anxious to please the grownups. But you are an adult, and you should be able to control yourself—to adjust to a regular rhythm of giving and taking, of talking and listening.

This does not mean that you should bite your tongue and sit on your hands. Make a conscious effort to appear as if you are enjoying the conversation—that you are intensely interested in what the interviewer is saying to you. Keep your self-restraint lively. Smile. Nod when appropriate. React.

Becoming a Mirror

React.

Stand-up comics express failure in the most dire terms. If his routine fails to elicit the requisite yuks, the comic will moan over his after-show martini: "I *died* up there tonight. I just *died*."

And so you know what it feels like to say something in the anticipation of a certain response, only to receive nothing but stone-faced silence. Know this, too: The interviewer will be disappointed, even pained and embarrassed, if you fail to react appropriately to what she says. Like you, the interviewer feels as if she is performing. She does not want to "die up there," and it is definitely not in your best interest to let her come away from your interview with *any* negative feelings. Don't *let* her die.

This does not mean synthesizing obviously phony responses to each and every thing the interviewer says, but it does require that you bear in mind this basic principle: *Demonstrate that you are listening—really listening—by mirroring the speaker's message.*

Clincher

Show, don't tell. It's more important to demonstrate that you hear and understand what the interviewer expresses to you than to tell him absolutely everything you believe he should know about you.

If the speaker is excited about something, get excited, too. If he expresses delight, smile in return. If he raises an issue that is clearly of critical importance to him, focus your gaze, bring your hand thoughtfully to your chin—*show* that the subject is of critical importance to you, too.

Stoking the Fire and Stroking the Speaker

You need not limit your "mirroring" to nonverbal cues. Lively restraint does not mean keeping silent. Respond to important points in the interviewer's conversation with words and phrases that add fuel to the dialogue.

Words and phrases that keep the dialogue going include:

Clincher

Your object is to give the interviewer the feeling that you are *worth* talking to. Some people enjoy talking, period—dialogue, monologue, it's all the same to them. But most folks would rather engage in conversation with a person who enjoys and responds to their words.

accurate	evaluate
additional	extraordinary
consider	fertile
correct	further
opportunity	positive
right	productive

"Can we discuss that further?"	"Can you explain that further?"
"I agree"	"Take into account ..."
"I appreciate that"	"Tell me more"
"I hadn't thought about it that way"	"That's a concern of mine, too"
"I see"	"That's interesting"
"I understand"	"We should discuss ..."
"It's an issue we face"	"Yes"
"Can we pursue that further?"	

Punctuate your listening with such language, but avoid bringing the conversation to a halt with such negative expressions as:

"Absolutely not"	"That's not the way I do it"
"Couldn't possibly"	"That's settled"
"No" or "No way"	"You're mistaken"
"That can't be done"	"You're wrong"

His Interest in You = Your Interest in Him

Does lively restraint and active listening mean always agreeing with the interviewer and his point of view?

Of course not. It is a mistake to check your opinions and ideas at the interviewer's door. But you should consider *suspending* them long enough to hear the interviewer out, to learn what interests him, what concerns him, what he needs, what he wants. Then, introduce your opinions and ideas, whenever possible, from a foundation of common interest. Here's how to do it.

Clincher

Listening is a gift you exchange with the interviewer.

You walk into an interview believing that Task A is important and that the best approach to Task A is through Method 1 and Method 2. The conversation turns to Task A, which, like you, the interviewer thinks is important, but he believes that the best approach is through Methods 2 and 3. Now, you can choose not to express your opinion, and just agree with the interviewer; you can choose to disagree; or you can choose to agree as much as possible, then, taking off from this common ground, explain how and where your opinions differ:

Interviewer: Task A is crucial to our operation. The approach I favor is Method 2 and Method 3.

You: I certainly agree with you that Task A is extremely important to achieving our goals. I also favor Method 2, but have you considered using Method 1 instead of Method 3?

Interviewer: Why should I?

You: Well, these are the benefits I've found …

Focus on the Interviewer's Needs, Not Your Own

Your goal is not to come across as a mindless "yes person," but always to express yourself in a way that exhibits your interest in the interviewer—*his* needs, *his* concerns—even when you are discussing your own point of view. To whatever degree possible, take your cues from the interviewer.

Be certain that the ideas and opinions you express are relevant to the needs and concerns the interviewer expresses. This begins with an understanding of who the interviewer is. Let's say you're a well-qualified accountant with experience in management and accounting software. If you know that the interviewer is primarily concerned with management issues, don't show off your expertise in software. Focus on management. Demonstrate a good fit from the start.

Stalking the Main Thought

Do you remember how your high school English teacher struggled to get you to focus the essays you wrote? "State your theme! Begin each paragraph with a topic sentence! And make sure your paragraphs support your theme."

That was good advice. Starting with a clear, strong statement of theme keeps your writing focused and makes your essay far more persuasive. Nobody enjoys reading a pointless, meandering essay. It's frustrating and a waste of time.

Frustrating and a waste of time. That's *not* how you want your interviewer to feel about her exchange with you. Take a hint, then, from your high school English teacher. Just as you developed a theme for your essays, identify and develop a main thought (or several) in the interview.

Pounce and Develop

The dynamics of an ordinary conversation can be fascinating. You're riding the commuter train to work. The fellow seated next to you strikes up a conversation. To be polite—although you'd just as soon keep reading your paper—you respond. And so it goes for the next two or three stops. Then, suddenly, he says something that strikes a

Clincher

Please pay careful attention to "Tune In and Turn On," later in this chapter. People send non-verbal signals when they talk about something important to them. Learn to recognize these body language accents to help you "read" the interviewer's needs and priorities.

chord—that *interests* you—and the entire conversation takes on direction and purpose. It has acquired a theme, a main thought. You're almost sorry when the train pulls into Grand Central.

It's even more exciting, of course, when interviews click like that, and you can increase the chances of this happening by consciously looking for a main thought to spark and fuel the interview. Ideally, the main thought should come from the interviewer. It should be an idea, a concern, a need, or a problem he expresses and that you jump on:

> **Interviewer:** Cash flow is always a *very* big problem for us.

> **You:** I understand completely. I contend with cash flow problems daily in my current position, and the issue really interests me. Exactly what kind of problems are you struggling with?

Don't count on this ideal situation coming to pass, however. You can't rely on your interviewer to say anything worth building a conversation on, any more than you can count on your commuter train buddy to come up with the kernel of a great conversation. Go to your interview armed with a few strong main thoughts on which to build a unified interview.

What You Can Afford to Forget

It's easy to feel overwhelmed when you're preparing for an interview. There is *so* much to remember!

The Skinny

Six out of every fourteen workers in the United States actively fear that they are in danger of losing their jobs.

Or is there?

Let's return to the subject of conversation. If you felt that you had to pack everything you know into every conversation you had, you would be too swamped ever to utter a word. Well, an interview is a conversation—a *very* important conversation, to be sure, but a conversation nonetheless, and you are not responsible for packing your entire life experience into it.

But how do you decide just what you can afford to forget?

Prepare for the interview by formulating some main thoughts: the themes, ideas, and issues that you believe are absolutely necessary to orchestrate an interview with a point.

The Dynamic Listening Concept

Here are two interviewing *don'ts:*

1. Don't turn the interview into a monologue resembling a rehearsed presentation.

2. Don't restrain yourself so much that you appear to be a passive listener, without ideas and opinions.

How do you avoid these two extremes? Practice *dynamic listening,* which is neither monologue nor passive reception and reaction.

> **Talk the Talk**
>
> **Dynamic listening** is listening with your mind and imagination, not just with your ears. It is based on identifying the interests you have in common with the speaker and responding to the speaker's themes so that the conversation is energized by active give and take.

Use Your Self-Interest

So far, I've pleaded with you for almost superhuman selflessness. *Focus on the* interviewer's *needs, not your own.* Although the interviewer does care about his needs above all else, your focusing on his needs and interests does *not* require you to abandon your own. On the contrary, in many respects, your self-interest will most likely coincide with the interviewer's. If this weren't the case, your resumé or cold call or query letter probably wouldn't even have produced an interview.

So, you've got something in common. Use this assumption to explore the interviewer's self-interest.

Connect with Your Own Interests

Let's go back to that remark about cash flow, which you pounced on as the kernel of a main thought:

> **Interviewer:** Cash flow is always a *very* big problem for us.

I'll bet that cash flow is a problem for you, too. Think about it. What does a cash flow problem *feel* like? Connect with the urgency of this issue. You have strong feelings about it. The interviewer has strong feelings about it. Strong feelings are the basis of not just a conversation, but a relationship. Connect with those feelings and let them drive your remarks. I'm *not* saying that you should complain to the interviewer about how you're always broke! All I'm saying is that you should harness your personal feelings and passion to energize your business-focused remarks:

> **You:** I agree. Cash flow is an urgent issue and one that I am eager to tackle. We need to formulate creative strategies for turning receivables into cash, and we need to be relentless about it.

Tune In and Turn On

In the preceding chapter, we considered issues of body language—*your* body language. But nonverbal communication works both ways, and knowing how to pick up on and respond to the interviewer's nonverbal cues is a valuable listening skill.

Body Language Works Both Ways

The very signals that you may or may not nonverbally broadcast *to* the interviewer are the same ones to watch for *from* the interviewer:

➤ If the interviewer tilts her head to one side, you can assume that she is listening intently to what you are saying and is interested. This is a *buy signal* and suggests that you should continue in the current vein.

Talk the Talk

A **buy signal** is a term salespeople will be familiar with. It is a verbal or nonverbal cue that suggests your "prospect" is responding positively to what you are saying—or selling.

➤ Head scratching indicates confusion or disbelief. Don't panic. Instead, pause, and ask a question: "Am I making myself clear enough here?" Or: "I'm not sure I'm making myself clear. Let me put it another way …"

➤ Lip biting is an indication of anxiety. This may suggest that an issue you've brought up has touched a nerve. It may also signal concern about something that has come up in the conversation. If you are aware that an area is sensitive, you will have to exercise judgment as to whether to move on quickly to another topic or express your understanding of the sensitive nature of the issue: "I realize that this is an area that causes anxiety, but I think it's an important issue to explore."

➤ Look out for an interviewer who rubs the back of his head or neck. This gesture signals frustration and impatience. Probably the best thing to do is move on to another topic as gracefully as possible: "But, of course, that's not nearly as important as XYZ." Alternatively, you can pause and ask the interviewer where *he* wants to go: "If you like, I can share more about my qualifications as XYZ, or we can move on to ABC."

➤ An interviewer who lowers his chin markedly is broadcasting feelings of defensiveness. It is possible that something you've said has been interpreted as a criticism. Make a soothing remark: "Of course, I recognize that each department has its own management style. I am prepared to be flexible."

➤ When an interviewer nods up and down, take it as a buy signal. Keep the conversation going.

➤ If something you say elicits a head shake from side to side, be aware that what you have said is being rejected. This is an obvious enough signal for you to respond to directly. "I sense that you don't agree with me on this point. What part of my position gives you trouble?" A question like this will keep the conversation from grinding to a halt, and it will also demonstrate your acute powers of perception.

➤ Interpret a narrowing of the eyes as you would a side-to-side head shake. Again, it is possible to respond directly: "I feel that we're not in agreement on this point. Can you tell me what disturbs you about what I've said?"

➤ A severe narrowing of the eyes suggests puzzlement rather than disagreement. Pause. Then offer: "I'd like to be very clear on this point. Let me put what I've said another way."

➤ Raised eyebrows indicate surprise—or out-and-out disbelief. Meet this head on: "I know this is hard to believe, but ..." An interviewer who peers over the top of her glasses is also signaling doubt and disbelief.

➤ Avoidance of eye contact can be difficult to interpret. If eye contact has been tenuous or nonexistent from the start of the interview, the interviewer is probably shy and uncomfortable. The best response is for you to be friendly and to take the lead. However, if eye contact drops off during the interview, you are losing the interviewer's interest. Take quick action: "I can say more about ABC, but perhaps I should move on to XYZ. Shall I?"

➤ An interviewer who stares intently at you is probably trying to be intimidating, to see how you'll react to pressure. Do your best to ignore this tactic.

Watch Him Breathe

It may sound crazy, but you can actually learn something by observing the interviewer's breathing pattern. Of course, if there's nothing out of the ordinary about his breathing, then there is simply no message there. But if his breathing pattern changes noticeably, you can assume that the interviewer is reacting to something in the conversation.

Look for signs of breathlessness—the shallow, rapid breathing patterns typical of anxiety. Respond with reassurance: "Of course, that's a problem we can solve." Look for the caught breath, a sudden intake of air that indicates the interviewer's eagerness to say something. Pause—and let him speak.

The most serious breathing signal to watch for is the sigh. This suggests frustration or boredom. It is a signal that you should move on to another topic.

You Have More Time Than the Speaker—Use It

All good conversation has a rhythm to it, and a successful interview, as good conversation, is no exception. If good conversation is about give and take, then someone is always giving while the other is taking. Right? One great advantage to being the taker, or listener, rather than the speaker is that you can be thinking—faster than the other person is speaking. The listener always has more time than the speaker. Use that time to prepare thoughtful responses and thoughtful questions—questions that will lead the interview into new territory.

The End

In general, you should constantly try to fuel the conversation and keep it going, but, as the old saw goes, all good things must come to an end. So, be aware of the verbal and nonverbal signs that the meeting is coming to a close. These include:

➤ Phrases beginning with "Well, it's been …" Or: "I want to thank you …" Or: "Is there anything else you'd like me to know about …"

➤ The interviewer rising from his chair

➤ The interviewer eyeing the door

➤ The interviewer looking at his watch

Of course, the interviewer may simply tell you that "We've come to the end of our time," or something like that.

Whatever the signal, now is the time to ask those "Questions to Close the Sale," described in Chapter 13, "Questions You Should Always Ask." Do not seek to prolong the interview beyond this. A big part of making a successful impression is knowing *when* the impression has been made. As old-time sales folk are fond of saying, "Once you've made the sale, it's time to shut your mouth."

The Least You Need to Know

➤ Come to the interview well prepared, but don't rehearse to the point that you deliver a formal presentation. The interview is, in part, a performance, but it is also a live, interactive exchange.

➤ Practice dynamic listening so that you can identify the interviewer's concerns and issues as well as the concerns and issues you have in common.

➤ Be attentive to the nonverbal as well as the verbal cues the interviewer gives. Read his body language and respond accordingly.

Chapter 9

Laid off, were we???

How to Answer the Questions Everybody Asks

In This Chapter

➤ How to speak the language of business

➤ Keeping answers upbeat and positive

➤ The three major kinds of questions interviewers always ask

➤ Translating experience into skills

➤ Evading the salary issue

Picture, if you will, the bookstore shelf from which you picked up this book. Undoubtedly, you'll remember seeing a million and one books on interviewing, and, of those, a sizable number promising you the "best answers," the "surefire answers," or just *"the* answers" to the most frequently asked interview questions.

But are you really going to pore over hundreds of questions and answers, commit them to memory, then spout them at the interview?

No. The best plan of attack is to use the questions and answers that follow as a starting point—use them to inspire and provoke your own thoughts, not as holy writ or as a cheat sheet.

First, Speak the Language of Business

Do you want to know how to make yourself heard in the world of business? Here's the answer in a single sentence: *Speak the language of business.*

Regardless of where the particular business is located or what the particular business does, business speaks with but a single tongue: the language of money. To the degree that you can do so, frame all of your answers to interview questions in terms of money: money you'll make for the prospective employer, money you'll save him, money you have made for other employers, money you've saved them, and so on.

The Answers You Should Always Give

Of course, it is not possible to quantify each and every answer, but it is possible to quantify more of them than you might think, and even those that don't lend themselves to direct dollars-and-cents answers usually allow *indirect* money responses:

> **Interviewer:** How many projects can you take on at one time?
>
> **You:** Of course, that depends on the nature and scope of the projects, but, in general, I'm a great believer in parallel processing and efficiently getting more than one thing accomplished at a time.

You could stop here, but don't.

> … I'm a great believer in parallel processing and efficiently getting more than one thing accomplished at a time. This has a significant positive impact on the bottom line.

That's translating the answer into the language of business—money—at least indirectly. If you have some figures at your command, you're in even better shape. Continue:

The Skinny

Never overlook small business in your job search. Eighty percent of all private businesses employ 50 people or fewer. It is this 80 percent that generates two-thirds of all new jobs.

> … This has a significant positive impact on the bottom line. In my current position, I'd estimate that parallel processing cuts turnaround times by at least 30 percent, and time, of course, is money.

You haven't given a literal dollars-and-cents response, but you've provided the context in which the interviewer can draw his own conclusions.

Beyond speaking the language of business—answering directly or indirectly in terms of dollars and cents— keep your answers upbeat. This does not mean spouting empty boasts or painting inanely rosy pictures, but, rather, always casting your responses in the best possible light.

> **Interviewer:** Cash flow is critical with us, but we're really plagued by slow-paying customers. What has your experience been with this problem?

Here's one response:

> **You:** I hear you! It's a really tough problem for us, too. Well, what can you do? That's the way things are.

And it's a bad one. Instead, empathize. It's also helpful to be honest about facing problems, but it's fatal in an interview to *leave* the conversation at that. In your answers, never run away from a problem or difficult issue, but embrace it as an opportunity:

> **You:** I hear you! It's a really tough problem for us, too. But I look at it not only as a challenge, but as an opportunity to actually build closer relationships with customers. My approach to slow payment is to find ways to help that customer pay. You see, my assumption is that he really does want to pay, and so far as cash flow management goes, I see my job as working with the customer to help him do what he really wants to do. Ideally, I'd like to make the collection process part and parcel of satisfying the customer.

The Answers You Should Never Give

It's a fact of life: There are more wrong answers to any particular question than right ones. Obviously, listing a bunch of wrong answers is an instructional approach doomed to futility, so I won't do that. But here are more general guidelines for what to *avoid* in answering questions:

➤ **Avoid one-word or one-sentence answers.** Indeed, avoid any answers that end conversation. Effective salespeople know that the best way to pitch their goods is to ask the prospect questions, to keep the conversation going. The more time the prospect invests in considering the proposition, the greater the chance of making the sale. Take your cue from the effective salesperson, and give answers that spark rather than conclude conversation.

➤ **Avoid negative answers.** In the misguided belief that admitting errors and discussing shortcomings is a demonstration of self-critical honesty that the interviewer will admire, many job candidates actually dwell on problems and disasters. If you cannot cast a problem into a positive, productive light, avoid discussing it.

Clincher

The interviewer will judge your answers to her questions, but what she'll remember on an emotional level is the conversation as a whole. Was it stimulating? Did it have energy? Was it consistently interesting?

➤ **Avoid transparently glib answers.** Answers like "Sure, I can do that. No problem!" don't ring true. Make your responses as positive as basic honesty will allow.

➤ **Avoid answers that criticize your present employer, colleagues, or supervisor.** Some interviewers may actually bait you into such responses. Don't take the bait.

➤ **Avoid wrong answers.** Does this seem self-evident? What I mean is, don't BS. Perhaps you remember Cliff Clavin, the mailman who was a regular on the television sitcom *Cheers*. He gave nothing *but* wrong answers. They were funny, because, absurd as they were, these fictions were offered as factual responses to factual questions. Of course, they wouldn't have been so funny if a job offer had depended on them. If you are asked a question that calls for a factual response— "What is the capital of Ethiopia?"—and you don't know the answer, don't make one up. Look the interviewer in the eye and respond, "You've got me there." Or: "I don't know the answer to that one."

Questions of Ability and Suitability

Most interview questions, however, are not factual. They are usually qualitative probes, efforts to gauge your "fit" with the job in three areas:

1. Ability and suitability
2. Employability
3. Affordability

Of these, the first is usually of greatest concern to the potential employer.

Sell Skill, Not Experience

The most common opening question is also the worst possible question anyone can ask you.

What can you tell me about yourself?

The danger of questions this broad is that they are simply overwhelming, and your mind is swamped by a vast white blank. This is one question you can almost count on getting asked. Be prepared for it. Answer in two parts. The first is a simple formula:

1. "My name is _____."
2. "I've worked for *x* years as a [job title]."
3. "Currently, I'm a [job title] at [company]."

4. "Before that, I was [job title] at [company]."

5. "I love the challenge of my work, especially the major strengths I offer, which include [A, B, and C]."

With that out of the way, swing into the second part, which is a question *you* ask: "But what would you like to know about me that would be most relevant to you and to what the company needs?" This will help focus the obviously unfocused (that is, typical) interviewer and should keep the conversation from grinding to a halt.

You can also count on being asked questions that attempt to zero in on your experience and qualifications:

➤ "Give me an idea of your experience."

➤ "List a few of your most important qualifications."

➤ "What are your strong points?"

➤ "So what, exactly, do you do at [current company]?"

➤ "What makes you think you're qualified for this job?"

Talk the Talk

Skills are the intellectual and creative tools you carry with you and offer an employer. Skills that can be applied to a number of different jobs and work environments are called **transferable skills**.

All of these questions and others like them can be answered in a similar way. Translate them from the passive terms of mere experience—how you passed time the last few years—into the dynamic terms of skill. That is, frame your answers not in terms of what you have *done*, but what you *are*. This tells the prospective employer what you *will do* for him. Don't evade the stated question, but translate it in order to get at the more important underlying question, which has to do with your *skills*.

> My management of A, B, and C for XYZ Company not only brought in X dollars last quarter, but has allowed me to develop skills in D, E, F, and G. These are what I bring to the table.

Clincher

Emphasize your transferable skills—the skills that are a part of you rather than the job; the skills you carry with you and apply to whatever you do.

To frame this as a response to "So what, exactly, do you do at [current company]?" for example, begin by stating your current job title, then continue with "My management of A, B, and C …"

Answer with Achievement

Your answers to questions concerning experience or qualifications should cover at least two dimensions—skill, which we've just discussed, and achievement. Achievement is the "backup," the supporting evidence, for the skills you describe. The response we just discussed emphasizes skills, but uses achievement to back up the claim: "My management of A, B, and C for XYZ Company not only brought in *x* dollars last quarter …" The revenue generated is the achievement that demonstrates the skill.

Achievement should not be defined in personal terms—"My sales record gave me a deep sense of satisfaction"—but in terms of benefit to the employer. To the extent that it is possible to do so, express this in dollars and cents:

> As a manager for XYZ Company, I developed innovations in A, B, and C, which the company has adopted organization-wide. We estimate that the innovations I introduced save the company *x* percent in costs for fulfilling each order.

Thus far, we have emphasized translating vague questions into specific responses that highlight your skills and achievements. It's possible, however, that the interviewer will be more specific. Be prepared—and be thankful. After all, a good question makes it that much easier for you to exhibit yourself at your best:

> What have been your three most significant accomplishments in your current position?

Make certain that you walk into the interview armed with specifics. This question is a strong cue to prompt you to offer your interview kit (see Chapter 4, "Get Set") and launch into a major discussion of achievements:

> I've brought some material with me that speaks directly to that. I've had many opportunities at XYZ Company, but I think my most enduring contributions to the company have been …

Play it by ear. If the interviewer is buying what you are selling, don't limit yourself to the arbitrary three-accomplishment limit she has set. Ask permission to continue: "Would you like me to go on?"

Navigating the Minefield

The flip side of questions about your experience, qualifications, skills, and achievements are questions about what you don't know, what you've failed to achieve, what mistakes you've made, and what your weak points are. Don't evade these, but don't let them dominate the meeting, either. Use them as springboards to demonstrate your strength of character and your resourcefulness.

Most interviewers are naturally polite. They will not come out and ask you to describe your "five weakest points," but will probably say something like "Are there any areas in which you feel you could use improvement?" Or: "Is there any aspect of the field you wish you had more experience in?" Be careful that such disarming questions don't press your insecurity button, unleashing a stream of self-doubt: "You know, now that you mention it, I've never really understood how such-and-such works. The procedure is just something I usually guess at and hope for the best. So far, so good." Face the question, but frame it in as many positives as possible:

> I've developed considerable proficiency with Y and have reduced typical turn-around time by *x* percent, but I've also reached the conclusion that, if I had more experience in Z, I could cut the time even closer to the bone. I am working on this now.

Notice that this response begins with a positive (proficiency) and ends with a positive (self-improvement), thereby framing the negative element. Nevertheless, it is possible that an interviewer will seize on whatever negative you offer: "So you're telling me that you're weak in Z?" Don't deny it, but don't agree, either. Keep framing your response in positives:

> No, what I'm saying is that I've brought Y to new levels of efficiency for our firm, but I've come to believe that we could go even further. In order to do that, I'm aware that I've got to learn more about the complexities of Z. It's an area of growth I've defined for myself.

Questions of Employability

I've written enough books to have reached a few conclusions about what publishers want and don't want. Actually, I believe I can express what they want in a single sentence: *They want to publish something entirely new that's worked well before.*

Employers are a lot like book publishers. They, too, want "new blood"—fresh ideas, fresh perspectives, fresh ambition—provided the "fresh" candidate can prove that she's worked well in the past. Employers want some assurance that they are buying a pack of solutions, not a peck of problems. This can lead you into a nasty Catch-22 situation:

1. You are available for hire. (Yippee!)

2. This means you either left or intend to leave your present job. (Uh-oh.)

Clincher

In answering why-did-you-leave or why-do-you-want-to-leave questions, it's extremely important that you convey straightforward, open honesty with your body language. Maintain eye contact throughout your response. Avoid bringing your hands anywhere near your face or neck. Don't fidget. You're under suspicion until you deliver a good, positive reason for changing jobs.

3. If you were happy with your current employer (or if he were happy with you?), you wouldn't be talking to me. (A-ha!)

So the interviewer is at best wary, at worst suspicious. He will ask questions that are variations on "Why did you leave (or do you want to leave) your present job?"

I Want to Grow

The classic response to the why-did-you-leave question is some version of "I want to grow." This is not a bad response, as far as it goes. To be sure, it is better than *any* negative reason:

➤ "My boss is a jerk."
➤ "My supervisor is uncreative. I just can't stand it."
➤ "I'm bored stiff."
➤ "I don't make enough money to put food on the table."

And it is preferable to reasons that may be interpreted as frivolous, such as "I want an office with a window."

"I want to grow" is okay, as far as it goes. But it doesn't go far enough.

Here's what to do to make the answer go farther. Instead of allowing the interviewer's question to focus your response on why you want to leave or have left an employer, refocus your response on why you want to *move* to the prospective employer.

Let's say your current job bores you and has limited potential for growth. You could answer, honestly enough, "I just don't get enough challenges at ABC Company," but try instead to shift from the old company, which the prospective employer doesn't really care about, to the prospective employer's firm: "I am eager to take on more challenges, and that is what I believe I will find with your firm. I want an opportunity to apply my skills where I can really make a difference in the future of the company." Not only does this answer transform a gripe into a laudable, positive motive, it adds the dimension of what's-in-it-for-the-employer.

"Laid Off, You Say?"

If a voluntary move from one job to another is eyed with suspicion, how high will a *layoff* raise the interviewer's eyebrows?

Strictly speaking, getting laid off is not your fault; it is loss of a job because of circumstances beyond your control. Nevertheless, some prospective employers will feel that, had you really been valuable to your former employer, the company wouldn't have dumped you. Fault or no fault, you've got some negative baggage to deal with.

First, don't be the one to raise the issue, but if it comes up, be certain to have an answer ready that takes the heat off of you:

➤ "As you may know, we merged with XYZ Company, and a 30 percent staff cut was ordered across the board. Unfortunately, my position duplicated one at XYZ, held by a fellow with seniority over me. So, I became one of the 30 percent to go."

➤ "Sales were off by 25 percent at ABC Corporation and management tightened its belt. I became one of the 150 out of 600 staffers who were laid off."

The Stickiest Wicket: You Got Fired

Make no mistake, this is a hard one. Getting laid off may not be your fault, but—at least as far as your former employer was concerned—getting fired is.

As with getting laid off, don't volunteer the information that you were fired. Keep your resumé noncommittal, and if the interviewer asks you why you left your last job, you might explain that your approach differed from management's, and then go on to detail the positive aspects of "your approach." This may satisfy the interviewer, and it is one way to put your involuntary termination in a positive perspective.

There is also another way. People make mistakes, and, if it is clear that the mistake you made has resulted in learning and growth, employers are often willing to forgive and forget, provided that you explain events clearly and forthrightly and put them in the best possible light: "Mr. Smith, I have to say that my termination was my fault. I had personal problems at the time, which are now completely resolved. But, at the time, I was frequently

Talk the Talk

A **layoff** is the termination of an employee for reasons unrelated to his or her performance or behavior. Layoffs are usually the result of economic reversals, or mergers (in which certain departments or individuals become "superfluous").

Don't Call Us …

Make certain that the circumstances "beyond your control" you cite as the cause of your layoff really were beyond your control. It's okay to say that you were laid off because sales dropped dramatically at your firm—as long as you weren't in the sales department.

Clincher

Should you be honest? Provided you do not dwell on the negative, yes. In the first place, telling the truth is right, whereas lying is wrong, and, in the second place, lying in an interview is always grounds for summary dismissal—maybe not today, maybe not tomorrow, but sooner or later.

late. My supervisor—with whom I am still very much on speaking terms—was under orders to reduce the workforce in any case, and, quite honestly, my attendance record at the time gave him the reason he needed to let me go."

Unless you can make an airtight case that you were fired unjustly, never blame other people for what happened to you. Demonstrate that you understand how you failed and, more importantly, how you will avoid repeating the failure. You learned from the experience, and the prospective employer will reap the benefits of what you learned. Nevertheless, don't wallow in remorse, and, if possible, end by putting your firing in a mitigating context. Try to find out how many others were fired, laid off, or even left voluntarily during the period in which you were dismissed. End your answer with, "I'm one of 34 people who have left so far this year."

CPR

This may be painful for you, but give it some thought. Contact the employer who fired you. Ask him what he intends to say about you now. "Mr. Harris, I'm in the process of looking for a new job, and I'd like to see how I stand with you. If you are asked as part of a pre- or post-employment reference check, how would you describe the circumstances of my leaving the company? Would you say that I was fired? Would you say that I was laid off? Would you say that I resigned? My problem is that, every time I tell a prospective employer about my termination, I blow another shot at a paycheck." This may persuade your former employer to use less pejorative terminology in describing your departure from his company. If he is willing to cooperate, you may be able to skirt the entire issue of having been fired.

Questions of Affordability

None of the potential employer's questions mean much of anything if he concludes that he can't afford to hire you. If we were all truly rational beings, the issue of compensation would be settled from the get-go. You'd walk in the interviewer's door, shake hands, exchange greetings, and say, "Good morning, Ms. Jones. You'll have to pay me *x* dollars per year. Can you swing that?" Then you'd settle down to the *rest* of the interview.

But it doesn't work like that. A cardinal rule of salary negotiation is that the first person to mention an actual figure is thereby thrust into the weaker position. So, nerve-wracking as it may be, your objective in the interview is to avoid being the first to bring up a figure.

"How Much Are You Looking For?"

When asked how much "you're looking for," you are confronted with a dilemma. Giving a figure that's too high may take you out of the running. And if you pin yourself down to a bargain-basement figure, then get hired, you'll kick yourself each and every day you come to work.

The solution, then, is to avoid stating a figure. Instead, itemize the skills, talents, abilities, and responsibilities the target position entails: "If I understand the full scope of the position, my responsibilities would include so-and-so and such-and-such. Given this, what figure did you have in mind for a person with my qualifications in a key position like this one?"

Another useful reply: "I expect a salary appropriate to my qualifications and demonstrated abilities. What figure did you have in mind?" Or: "What salary range has been authorized for this position?"

If the interviewer presses—"Come, now. Don't try to evade the question"—propose as broad and as vague a salary range as possible: "I'm looking for a starting salary in the upper thirties." You'll find more advice on calculating an appropriate salary range in Chapter 12, "Money Talk."

Don't Call Us ...

Why not just make up a figure when you're asked about your salary? You know, *lie*. Well (aside from the fact that it's wrong to lie), because you might get caught. The target employer probably won't take positive steps to verify your salary, but she might make it a condition of employment to see your last payroll stub or your W2. What if this request comes *after* you've given notice to your current employer? You can't afford to get caught in a lie like this.

"How Much Are You Making Now?"

This question is more difficult than the previous one to sidestep or creatively expand upon. You can't avoid answering it, but you can frame your response so that it doesn't cage you in: "I'm earning $35,000, but I'm not certain that helps you evaluate what I'm worth, since the two jobs differ significantly in their responsibilities." Unless you are happy with your present salary, fashion a reply that provides the information requested, but that divorces your salary expectations from your current salary level. The interviewer is looking for a ceiling-setting precedent. Don't let him have one.

On the surface, this is a factual question. You know what your salary is, after all. But don't be too hasty about responding. Be certain that the figure you furnish is the absolute maximum you can honestly report. Take into consideration all perks and benefits, including insurance, profit-sharing, bonuses, commissions, stock options, vacation, and so on.

The Least You Need to Know

➤ Try to translate your interview answers into the "language of business": dollars and cents and things that either produce or save dollars and cents.

➤ Don't evade questions that probe negative issues, but always frame the answer in the most positive terms possible.

➤ Keep all your answers positive and upbeat.

➤ Find ways to answer questions about experience in terms of your skills and qualifications; shift the focus from what you have *done* to what you are capable of *doing*.

Are you
GAY???

Chapter 10

... And the Questions Almost Nobody Asks (But Just Might Ask You)

In This Chapter

➤ Answering problem-solving questions

➤ Answering behavior-centered questions

➤ Answering unrelated or unexpected questions

➤ Handling illegal, inappropriate, or offensive questions

If you stop reading right now, you'll come away from this book in danger of under-estimating what an interviewer can throw at you. Yes, it's true, an overwhelming majority of interviewers are poorly prepared and desperately in need of your guidance, but let's not overlook the significant minority that actually does give serious thought to the interview process. Although these interviewers ask the tough questions, you're probably better off dealing with one of them than with any of those unfocused types who haven't devoted enough time or energy to sorting out what they want and need. A challenging interview is an opportunity to excel, and this chapter gives you some suggestions for doing just that.

Problems, Problems, Problems

The previous chapter dealt mainly with informational questions, emphasizing the presentation of qualifications and skills. But you may also encounter hypothetical questions, questions that paint a quick problem scenario and ask, "What would you do?"

Expecting the Unexpected

You cannot know in advance exactly which *problem-solving questions* you will be asked—or even if you will be asked such questions—so you should try to prepare yourself for any possible circumstance. Take the following three initial steps:

1. Decide whether it is likely that you *will* be asked problem-solving questions. If the job calls for creativity, for thinking on your feet, for resourcefulness, for, in short, problem solving, expect that you will be put to the test.

2. Once you decide that problem-solving questions are likely, review what you know about the prospective employer in order to anticipate probable areas of questioning.

Let's pause a moment before going on to point number 3. It isn't as difficult as it may at first seem to guess what kinds of problem-solving questions you're likely to encounter. For example, if you are interviewing for a position primarily in sales, expect to be asked to *sell* something:

> **Interviewer:** Do you like my fountain pen?
>
> **You:** Yes …
>
> **Interviewer:** Good. Sell me this pen.

If you are interviewing for a supervisory or management position, expect to be asked some hard-hitting personnel questions:

> **Interviewer:** I am your administrative assistant. I consistently fail to complete assignments on time. Fire me.

Management candidates may also be asked very direct problem-solving questions:

> **Interviewer:** We have an ongoing problem with _____. Solve it.

Any interviewer may ask this one:

> **Interviewer:** If you were sitting in my seat, and I were in yours, what would you ask me?

So stretch your mind muscle *before* the interview and think of some likely problem-solving questions. Then proceed to step 3:

3. Formulate a strategy for dealing with problem-solving questions.

Strategies for Answering Problem-Solving Questions

The strategy for answering informational questions is simple: Do everything you can to give the right answer. With problem-solving questions, however, you must shift your strategy from the end (a "right" answer) to the means (how you come up with the answer). Problem-solving questions are less about answers than they are about processes, methods, approaches, and attitudes. Accordingly, you should do all you can to impress the interviewer with your problem-solving ability.

You first need to listen carefully to what is being said. Having done this, you are not completely on your own. Be certain next to *ask* questions in order to define and clarify what the interviewer is looking for.

From here, a prudent next step is to tell the interviewer that your first problem-solving action would be to gather all the necessary information: data. Then proceed to a description of how you would use the data to formulate possible solutions to the problem. Finally, pull your answer together by listing the available options and then choosing among them. Explain the basis of your choice in terms of:

➤ The nature and objectives of the position for which you are applying

➤ The nature and objectives of the prospective employer's company or department

Clincher

In posing a problem-solving question, the interviewer is not looking for the "right" answer, but rather, wants to see how you handle the question, how you respond, and how you approach the problem. Don't second-guess yourself. Take the problem and work with it as best you can, fully exposing the *process* by which you reach your conclusions.

Have Fun with It

If this looks like hard work, it is. But it is also creative work, with a strong element of make-believe. Try to run with the problem. *Show enthusiasm* for the task of solving the problem. Telling the interviewer at the outset that you would begin by gathering data is ample demonstration of your care and prudence. Having established this, it is best to cast aside timidity and move as boldly toward an answer as possible, explaining your actions every step of the way.

For Example ...

Let's try this strategy on the sales question:

>**Interviewer:** Do you like my fountain pen?
>
>**You:** Yes ...
>
>**Interviewer:** Good. Sell me this pen.

Now, you could just try to be charming and persuasive, extolling the qualities, value, and benefits of the pen and why the "customer" would want to own it. While such a performance might display some fine qualities, it's not really what the interviewer is looking for. He doesn't *really* want to buy his own pen. He wants to *see* how you go about selling it. So, *show* him. Here's how:

➤ Ask questions. "What's the intended market for this pen?" Then follow up with your own answer. Let's say it's one of those fancy "writing instruments" named after a mountain in Switzerland. What does this tell you about the market? Having assessed the market, secure the interviewer's agreement with your assessment.

➤ Explore the features of the pen. Define its benefits—the "good things" it does for the owner. Define its value—price versus beauty, durability, writing quality, and so on. Ask the interviewer if he feels that you should include any other features and benefits.

➤ Explain how you would obtain full data concerning market, features, benefits, and value. Options include focus groups, questionnaires, direct-mail surveys, and so on.

➤ Explain briefly how you would use the data to formulate marketing plan options.

➤ Paint a quick but vivid picture of just who the prospective customer is, and, based on this, choose one of the options you have named.

"Tell Me About a Time When You ..."

Related to questions that attempt to assess your problem-solving skills are those that try to plumb your character. Behavior-centered questions usually begin with "Tell me about a time when you ..." or some variation on that opening.

Strategies for Answering Behavior-Related Questions

Common sense, more than anything else, should help you anticipate what traits of character, habits of conduct, and attitudes will be most appealing and most important to a prospective employer. Modify common sense with what you know about the issues of concern to the employer and the industry. For example, if you are applying for a position as credit manager for a firm, it's a safe bet that the prospective employer will be looking for evidence of prudence combined with flexibility. If you are going after a sales job, the sales manager will want to see evidence of a positive, persuasive personality. If the prospective position involves a lot of customer service, you'll probably be asked about "the time you had to deal with an irate customer." And so on.

Here's the basic strategy:

1. Anticipate and define your desirable traits of character and habits of conduct, both in general and as specifically relevant to the needs of the industry or prospective employer.

2. Come prepared with a repertoire of stories about your experience that demonstrate a range of desirable traits and habits of conduct.

3. Listen carefully to the question.

4. Don't feel compelled to jump right into your answer. Ask clarifying questions first.

5. Tell a story. (See step 2, above.)

6. Conclude by explaining what you intended your story to illustrate. Don't rely on the imagination and perception of the interviewer. Drive the point home.

7. Ask for feedback: "Does this tell you what you need to know?"

Talk the Talk

Behavior-related questions are aimed at assessing a candidate's character, attitude, and personality traits by asking for an account of how the candidate handled certain challenging situations.

The Skinny

Ideally, the exemplary stories you tell at an interview should be directly job-related; however, you might also talk about relevant experiences outside the job—how you formulated an innovative fund-raising project for the PTA, for example.

Stirring Memories

Let's return to step 2 for a moment. Nothing is more frustrating—or more common—than the experience of going through an interview, riding the elevator down to the lobby floor, and, as each floor goes *ding*, thinking of some story or anecdote you *should* have mentioned. Look, you're only human, and it's difficult to dredge up your entire professional life within the space of the few seconds between the asking of the

Clincher

Many apparently behavior-related questions are really little more than ordinary informational questions phrased in a slightly different way. Asking a clarifying question will help ensure that you give the kind of answer the interviewer wants. To the question "Tell me about a time when you faced a major problem at work," you might respond: "Do you want me to discuss the major problems I deal with in my current position?"

question and the anticipation of the answer. The solution to this problem, as step 2 suggests, is to do your dredging at home, before you come to the interview. It's wise to prepare professional "war stories" that answer and illustrate as many of the following questions as possible. They all begin with: *Tell me about the time you …*

➤ coped with a difficult personnel situation.

➤ creatively solved a problem.

➤ made a big mistake.

➤ made a difficult decision.

➤ had to deal with an irate customer.

➤ persuaded key personnel to your point of view.

➤ made a great sale.

➤ blew a great sale.

➤ conquered a major obstacle.

➤ had to take a calculated risk.

➤ had to make a decision based on limited information.

➤ had to fire a good friend.

While you shouldn't dodge a negative question—"Tell me about the time you blew a great sale"—don't get bogged down in it. If you relate a negative anecdote about yourself, be sure to conclude by talking about what you learned from the experience and how it strengthened you. For example, conclude by discussing how blowing that sale has made you a much better salesperson: "It taught me some hard lessons about what *not* to do!"

The Truth of Fiction

What do you do if you can't come up with a true-life anecdote to cover each of the likely questions? You could make something up—and hope that you aren't caught in the lie—but a better strategy is to offer a hypothetical example:

Interviewer: Tell me about the time you had to fire a good friend.

You: Fortunately, that situation has never come up. But I could tell you how I *would* handle such a situation, if it ever did arise.

Secure the interviewer's permission and proceed to weave your fiction.

Outta Left Field

A certain type of interviewer relishes asking the unexpected, off-the-wall question. You can almost see him smack his lips and rub his hands to-gether. Sometimes this is motivated by ego—a desire to be seen as wild, crazy, unpredictable, and cool, really cool. But there may well be method to the inter-viewer's madness. At least 50 percent of the rea-son for asking a question from left field is to see how you will react. If the wacky question stuns you into silence, you lose big points. If, on the other hand, you take the question in your stride—even if you can't come up with an imme-diate answer—you'll get at least half credit for it.

The subjects of from-left-field questions range from deceptively obvious ethical issues to riddles: "Why are manhole covers round?" Answer: "Two equally sized circles won't fit through each other; if the manhole were any other shape, its cover could fall through it." Think about it.

Alternative answers to Manhole Cover Question include: 1. Because most of the people who go through manholes are round. 2; Because it's cheaper to make round covers than rectangular, triangular, square, pentagonal, hexagonal, or octagonal covers.

The Skinny

Most questions from–left-field are attempts to probe character and self-image. Some are intended to see how your mind works, while others are attempts to guess how you'll fit into the prevailing workplace environ-ment. A sense of humor is almost always welcome.

The following is an ethical question bounced off the wall, which Arlene S. Hirsch dis-cusses in her book *Interviewing* (Wiley, 1996). The manager of a new and aggressive high-tech company paints this scenario for a candidate: "We are sending you on assignment to Carmel, California. You have an unlimited expense account. What kind of car are you going to rent?"

The knee-jerk response is to be prudent, conserva-tive, modest, and "save the company money" with a no-frills compact. But if the prospective employer wants somebody who responds reflex-ively, she could hire an earthworm. Hirsch points out that the three most "successful" answers were Porsche, Ferrari, and Jaguar. The candidate who suggested a sensible Honda Accord lost, as did the one who opted for an expensive (but too conser-vative) Mercedes-Benz. *Think*. You are represent-ing a young, aggressive company in a highly competitive field. You are not driving to Podunk,

Clincher

The key to answering off-the-wall questions is to be prepared to give *reasons* for your answers. The interviewer is probably inter-ested more in process and rationale than result.

but to Carmel, a Pacific Coast town of unconventional multimillionaires whose former mayor was Clint Eastwood. The best answer reflects an awareness of image and situational context, not a one-dimensional grasp of simple corporate ethics.

The "Desert Island" Scenario

A favorite off-the-wall question is the desert island scenario: "If you could take only three things with you on a desert island, what would they be?" Some interviewers might make an effort to update this classic: "Recently, scientists have found evidence of life on Europa, a moon of Jupiter. What three things would you take on a trip to Europa?" But, of course, the question is really the same.

How you answer the desert island question says as much about you as it does about your understanding of the prospective position. If the position calls for a great deal of creative imagination, your take-along list might include a copy of *Moby Dick,* your sketch pad, and a boat (or spaceship) to get you home when you were ready to leave. If the position calls for nothing but feet-on-the-ground practicality, specify a supply of water (or oxygen), an expert on desert (or extraterrestrial) life, and that reliable boat (or spaceship).

Don't Call Us ...

Don't allow small talk to lead you blindly into controversial topics, and don't let it lead you into unwise revelations:

Interviewer: Is it still raining outside?

You: Yes, thank goodness. I hope the rain washes out some of that pollen. My allergies are killing me.

Maybe the interviewer is a fellow sufferer and will commiserate with you. On the other hand, maybe she sees a string of sick days in your future, as your work piles up and languishes on your desk.

Strategies for Answering Questions (What's This Have to Do with Work?)

A minority of interviewers plunge right into the interview with some hard-hitting questions—"This company has a serious problem with ... How will you fix it?"—but most interviews begin with small talk, and the smallest of small talk is about the weather: "Is it still raining outside?"

What motivates such a question? Perhaps it is a way of breaking the ice, of putting both candidate and interviewer at ease. Perhaps it is part of a plan to see what kind of person you are. ("Yes," you answer, "it's *still* raining, and I can't stand it." Now you've revealed what an essentially negative person you are. That was a mistake.) But, most likely, small-talk questions are born of the interviewer's temporary blankness of mind, the natural inertia that besets most conversations at the beginning.

But this does not mean that you can afford to neglect small-talk questions. Respond to small talk politely—to show that you're a likable person who is easy to be around—and respond positively:

Interviewer: Is it still raining outside?

You: Yes. It's been a dry month, and we really need the rain.
   Or
   Yes, and the air is nice and clean. Very refreshing.

Don't amplify and elaborate on the small talk so that it takes over the interview:

Interviewer: Is it still raining outside?

You: Yes, it is. We've had almost an inch of rain this month, and we're not even past the second week. I wonder what it's going to be like come fall. I'd hate to see the river rise. I guess I'd better invest in a sump pump, just to be on the safe side. Have you ever bought a sump pump? I suppose I'd better take a look at *Consumer's Report* ...

Most likely, small-talk questions are not part of the interviewer's artful design to reveal your character; still, you should be wary of apparently innocent questions that can elicit damning answers. For example:

Interviewer: Did you have any trouble finding our office?

You: I'll say! I was really confused.

Congratulations! You've just told your prospective employer that you lack the competence to navigate city streets. Even if you did have a hard time finding the office, just answer: "No. Your directions were perfectly clear."

Or this:

Interviewer: I saw you drive up in a Ripsaw 2000. How do like that car?

You: It was the worst purchasing decision I ever made. I was lucky it got me to this interview ...

Now you've come off as somebody who can't even make a successful personal purchase. Just tell him you like the car fine, even if it's a lemon.

In general, answer *all* small-talk questions positively. If you're in from out of town and the interviewer asks how you like living in Podunk, respond that it is very pretty this time of year, even if you really think it's the armpit of the northern hemisphere.

Questions You Don't Have to Answer (and How Not to Answer Them)

Employers are forbidden by law to make hiring decisions based in any way on marital status, sexual orientation, age, ethnic background or national origin, race, religious

Talk the Talk

A **bona fide occupational qualification (BFOQ)** is an employment criterion that permits discrimination based on personal attributes in certain cases; for example, a women's bathingsuit manufacturer needs to hire models for its catalog. No men need apply. A delivery company needs drivers capable of lifting 80 pounds. The applicant who is disabled by a chronically bad back and is therefore incapable of repeated heavy lifting may legally be rejected.

beliefs, gender, or disabilities. There are exceptions, in cases where a *bona fide occupational qualification (BFOQ)* can be demonstrated, but, in general, these personal characteristics and attributes are protected by law. So it follows that most questions concerning your marital status, sexual orientation, age, or ethnic or national origins are either blatantly illegal or tread on very shaky ground.

So, what are you going to do if one of these taboo questions is asked? Take offense? Invoke the law? With justification, you could do either. However, you'll probably end up alienating the interviewer and losing the job. Could you subsequently sue on the grounds of discrimination? Probably. But it's expensive, difficult, and extremely time-consuming to litigate issues of discrimination. That the papers and TV occasionally report million-dollar discrimination-in-hiring settlements should tip you off as to just how rare such judgments are. If they were common, they wouldn't be news. No, such profitable legal victories are the exceptions—and besides, do you want to sit in court, or do you want to get a job?

In general, if you feel comfortable answering a question—even a possibly illegal or certainly inappropriate question—answer it. But if you find that you cannot answer, respond with a few *ifs*. For example, to the question "Are you married?" you might reply, "I'm not sure what you wish to learn from that question. If you're concerned about how much time I can afford to spend on the job, you should know that I am a professional, and I keep my professional life separate from my private life. I intend to devote as much time as necessary to be successful at my job."

Marital Status and Family Plans

You might not be asked the marital status question so directly. Some employers troll for this information with such innocent-sounding inquiries as "Where does your husband (or wife) work?" or "What next-of-kin do we contact in case of an emergency?" The best strategy is simply to answer these questions (although you *could* finesse the second question by replying that you will "supply that information after you are on board"; it is, in fact, illegal to ask for next-of-kin information before hiring).

"Do you plan to have children?" This question is almost exclusively directed at women. You might ask the interviewer to "Explain what bearing this has on the position. I'm not sure I understand the relevance of the question." If it seems to you that a *yes* will jeopardize your shot at the job, you might also simply answer *no*. It's only a word, and it does not legally bind you to remain childless. If you really do want children and feel you must be up-front about it, answer positively: "Yes, eventually, I want a family. However, those plans are directly dependent on the success of my career."

Sexual Orientation

It is not likely that you will be asked point-blank "What is your sexual orientation?" However, you might be asked about your marital status in a way that is designed to ascertain this information: "So you've *never* been married?"

There's no graceful way to respond to questions such as these. Either reply to indirect questions as neutrally—and calmly—as possible, or quietly offer: "I don't think that question is appropriate."

Age

"How old are you?" is a patently illegal question. It may also be asked in some less direct ways: "You've had a very long career, Mr. Smith. Are you sure you're up on the new technologies?" The best way to respond is to turn your age to your advantage. Translate *time* into experience, skill, expertise, and seasoned judgment: "Now that I'm in my forties, I've had more than a quarter-century of experience in the widget industry."

Ethnic Background or National Origin

An employer may simply ask "Where were you born?" Or the question may be couched as polite or ignorant curiosity: "So many consonants in your name! What is it? Polish? Czech?"

Answer directly, but, in so doing, politely flush the interviewer out of hiding: "It's Czech. Are you concerned that where I was born will have some bearing on how well I can do this job? I'd like to put any possible doubts to rest."

Race

Your race is probably evident in your appearance; however, you may be asked something like "Do you think you'll have a problem working for a black woman?" Or "Many of the staff here are Latino. Can you handle that?"

Questions like these are insensitive, crude, and provocative, but deliver your answer calmly and without skipping a beat: "Of course, I have no problem with that. I am a team player who enjoys working with people, period. I have no problems with any race—people are people."

113

Religion

You may be asked directly whether you believe in God, or, less sweepingly, "What church do you attend?" If you *want* to answer, keep your response general: "I worship regularly, but I make it a practice not to involve any of my personal beliefs in my work." If you prefer, respond calmly and evenly: "My personal spiritual beliefs are very important to me, but I don't let them get involved with my professional life, and I make it a practice not to discuss them." This is an especially good response if you have no religious beliefs or beliefs that some may think unconventional.

Disability

"Are you disabled?" The question is illegal, but answer it honestly—with a positive spin: "No, I am not disabled. I *am* in a wheelchair, but that does not disable me in any way from managing a customer service department."

The Least You Need to Know

➤ Unexpected and challenging questions often relate to problem solving, behavior and attitude, issues apparently unrelated to the job, and personal attributes and beliefs.

➤ In answering problem-solving and behavior-related questions, focus on the process rather than on the final answer. The interviewer is most interested in how you think.

➤ Don't evade answering negative questions (for example, those concerning mistakes you made), but conclude your answer on the most positive note possible.

➤ Even if a question is inappropriate or downright illegal, look for a positive way to answer it. Keep your options open.

Take Control and Start Selling Yourself

As you already know, you *will* be asked questions at an interview. You'll also probably find yourself in an office on the visitor's side of the desk. The interviewer, of course, will be seated behind the desk, in the position of possession and authority. Despite both of these conditions, however, you should try to take control of the interview. This is the most effective way of presenting yourself: taking control of the interview without *seeming* to. This is also how a successful salesperson manages a sale: She listens to the customer, makes it clear that the customer's concerns are all-important and that what she is selling will address those concerns, but then she guides the customer, carefully shaping his actions toward the decision to buy. In this chapter, I'll suggest ways you can apply such selling techniques to the employment interview.

Don't Just Navigate If You Can Steer

So far, we have looked at two dimensions of the interview:

1. The interview as a *performance*, for which you prepare with research and imagination in an effort to reduce the amount of spontaneity required

2. The interview as an *interaction*, a give-and-take between you and the interviewer

   Now, for the third dimension:

3. The interview as a *sale*, in which you subtly take control in order to guide the interviewer into making the decision to offer you a position

Clincher

The beauty of taking the initiative is that you don't *have* to be right. Merely raising intelligent issues and demonstrating knowledge of the company and its concerns will help to begin the "sale."

To be sure, candidates have been hired as a result of interviews that reflect only one or two of these three aspects, just as three-engine jet airliners have, in a pinch, flown to safety after one or even two engines have failed. The passengers survived, the cargo was delivered, but that's hardly the optimum way to fly. Your best chance for success is to understand and use all three dimensions of the interview to your advantage. Don't just navigate; take hold of the wheel and *steer*.

Persuading with Your Ears

Steering, however, means nothing unless you have a destination. Where do you want the interview to take you? Here's where: from being a stranger to the interviewer to becoming somebody the interviewer's organization has "gotta have."

Assuming you've encountered a reasonably competent interviewer—and that is a rather large assumption—the step you must take before you can begin to steer along this course is to locate the road. Forgive me, but at this point the analogy falters. Were you behind the wheel of a real vehicle, you'd rely mainly on your eyes; in the interview, you'll find the road with your ears. Listen to what the interviewer says about his or her company, its needs, its goals, its problems. Listen to what the interviewer says he or she needs. Then respond to what you hear. Now you have begun the transformation from a stranger looking for a job to a potential partner willing to pitch in and solve problems.

Striking Sparks

Your success in getting the interviewer's attention through active listening depends, in large part, on how forthcoming the interviewer is in expressing what she needs and wants from you. If she fails to express this, you must take the initiative. In

Chapter 8, "Listen Carefully," we discussed the techniques of active listening. Use them here, and be prepared to augment them with the following moves:

➤ Demonstrate that you are listening, ensure that you are understanding, and keep the conversation going by frequently underscoring the interviewer's most important points. Do this by repeating and rephrasing them: "What I hear you saying is …" or "If I'm understanding you correctly …"

➤ If the interviewer is still not forthcoming with the information you need in order to build the conversation, take an even more direct approach: "Ms. Thomas, may I ask *you* a question?" Ms. Thomas will answer, "Of course!" Then you must draw on your research and preparation: "It seems to me that the company's operations have been wholly dependent on X, Y, and Z. Has any consideration been given to adding A and B to the mix?" This will not only impress Ms. Thomas, but it will relieve her of the burden of carrying the entire interview. Even more, it will demonstrate your knowledge of the company and the industry.

> **Don't Call Us …**
>
> Maybe you're not so sure you've got what the target employer is looking for, but this is neither the time nor place to give voice to your doubts. Go ahead and assume that what you bring to the table is exactly what the interviewer wants. You can deal with any lingering doubts *after* you get an offer and before you accept the job.

Another incentive that may move the interviewer off the dime is to remind her of why you're sitting in her office. I don't mean that you should offer something like, "Hey, you remember, I'm here about the so-and-so job." Instead, remind her of why she called you in for an interview.

But how do *you* know why?

Assume there's only one possible answer: You were called because, based on your resume or other materials, the interviewer believes that you're very likely the right person for the job. Get her attention with a reminder of that fact: "Good morning, Ms. Thomas. I'm thrilled to be here, since it seemed to me that my qualifications so closely coincided with what you need." Or: "I'm very excited about being here. What I have to offer seems to me a perfect match for this company."

Fanning the Flames

"No man is an island," the poet John Donne proclaimed some three centuries ago. You know people, and people know you. You take an interest in a number of human beings other than yourself, and some of them take an interest in you.

Why?

You have something to offer one another. That's the reason strangers become acquaintances and why acquaintances become friends. It happens every day. You know you can do it, because you *have* done it. True, in the case of a job interview, you must develop the other person's interest in a very specific direction, by demonstrating your potential value as a member of the prospective employer's team. And while acquaintances have the luxury of time—for casual conversations, lazy lunches, and cozy visits—in an interview, you have only a matter of minutes to reveal common interests and goals; therefore, make an effort to turn everything you say into an expression of accomplishment, achievement, or qualification.

Keep the conversation as specific as possible. "I'm a super salesman" will get you nowhere, but the following is highly persuasive: "As a salesman, I make it my business to discover and understand what each of my customers wants and needs. For this reason, I was responsible for *x* dollars in widget sales last quarter."

Transforming Interest into Involvement

Persuasion is not simply hammering away at the interviewer. It is an interactive process. Monitor the interviewer's responses to what you are saying. Watch his body language (see "Tune In and Turn On" in Chapter 8) and listen for "buy signals," indications that the interviewer's interest in you is high or increasing. These include some obvious ones:

➤ "That interests me."

➤ "I like that."

➤ "Great!"

➤ "Terrific!"

➤ "Sounds good to me."

But it's the rare interview that produces anything so direct. Usually, buy signals emerge more neutrally, as requests for additional information:

➤ "Tell me more about ..."

➤ "Can you be more specific about ..."

➤ "Please explain ..."

➤ "I'd like to hear more ..."

➤ "Can we return to ...?"

➤ "Let's not leave that point yet ..."

However the buy signal is expressed, it indicates that you've pressed the right button. Once you elicit a buy signal, swoop down on whatever it was that produced the positive response.

Let's say you're interviewing for a position as an executive assistant. You've just said, "I specialize in handling the details and anticipating needs, so that you can be more efficient." Wow! It was just the right thing to say, because the interviewer responds with a buy signal: "Can you tell me more about that?"

Now, if you hem, haw, and are unable to tell him more, the buy signal will simply evaporate. Your claim will suddenly seem nothing more than so much hot air. It's time to get specific. Don't *praise* yourself any further, *list* some of the great things you do:

> I approach the task actively. For example, I maintain active "hot files" in which I track the issues of most immediate importance and ensure that the relevant documents are instantly accessible. On day one, I would want to work with you to develop a list of hot topics and hot contacts—the issues and the people who must be given your immediate attention.

But don't leave it at this. Listing skills or accomplishments are valuable. It's like the list of product features in a merchandise ad. To move the sale toward a successful conclusion, however, you must translate the product *features* into product *benefits*—what your skills will do for the employer:

> Really, I see the most important aspect of my position as a kind of contact manager. The most important benefit I provide is giving you more *useful* time. My goal is to give you the time you need.

Clincher

For many of us, an interview is an uncomfortable experience, even when it's going well. It's natural to want to get it over with. You may even dread being asked for additional information. But the fact is that *any* request for more information is an expression of interest and, therefore, a buy signal. Treasure it.

Talk the Talk

As marketing people define it, a product **feature** is an attribute of the product; for example, a high-speed micro-processor that makes one PC faster than another. A product **benefit** is something good a product or its features do (or are perceived to do) for the buyer; for example, the high-speed processor on that new PC makes you feel more productive. The benefit of the processor—a perceived increase in productivity—may justify the buyer spending more money for it.

119

Notice that the example I've chosen here is a candidate for an entry-level or near-entry-level position, an executive assistant. The point is that even an entry-level position can be defined in terms of benefits for the employer. If you have more experience, however, and are moving from one position up to another, devote more discussion to your actual track record, your accomplishments. But even when you do this, point out the benefits you offer:

> I brought in revenues of *x* dollars, and I learned how to increase the number of closed sales—consistently and dependably. I want to use what I've learned to increase the productivity of your sales force.

It shouldn't be difficult to decide just what employer benefits you wish to emphasize. Define what you do—or propose to do in the prospective position—and in doing so, make sure you reveal the specific benefits you can offer the interviewer and his company. You want the interviewer to feel that he *must* have the benefits you're offering. So, for example, a candidate for an executive assistant position should understand that the "must-have" benefit he can most readily offer the prospective employer is time. A candidate for the position of sales manager should understand that the "must-have" she offers is increased and more efficient sales (that is, more sales that cost less to close).

Getting Action

Most job candidates take a fatalistic view of the interview, which, on the surface, seems realistic as well as emotionally sound: *I've done my best, presented my skills. Now it's in the hands of the interviewer.*

But no successful salesperson would think this way; and, remember, the third leg of the stool on which the interview will either stand or fall is *selling*. A salesperson does not make the pitch only to walk out the door. He attempts to *close* the sale by prompting the prospect to action.

This can be done in a perfectly cloddish manner: "Duh, well, do I get the job? Huh? Huh? Huh?"

Besides being, well, stupid, such a "close" leaves the possibility of a negative answer wide open. An effective salesperson asks plenty of questions, but tries to limit them to those that prompt a *yes*. You might direct the interviewer toward a positive conclusion by asking something like this:

> Based on what I've told you, don't you think I could give you all that you need in this position?

Clincher

Want to develop the interviewer's involvement with you? Bring up the subject of revenue—revenue you will generate and cash you will save the company.

Sure, a *no* is still possible, but, by defining a set of conditions—"what I've told you" and "all that you need"—you've at least directed the interviewer toward a *yes*.

But trust your instincts and how you sense the interview has gone. If you don't feel that you've adequately connected with the interviewer, direct him differently:

> Mr. Smith, this has been a pleasure, and I believe I have a great deal to give to this company. But, please, tell me, is there anything I haven't addressed to your satisfaction? What could I tell you that would prompt you to make an offer?

Many candidates find it difficult to "close the sale," not because they lack the skills the position requires, but because it is emotionally difficult to take responsibility for bringing the interview to some firm conclusion. But closure is the objective of the interview—a specific action, preferably an offer of employment.

This may actually happen. It may also come to pass that the interviewer tells you, right then and there, that "it just doesn't look like we're right for each other" or words to similar effect. More likely, however, the alternative either to an immediate hire or rejection is an announcement that the whole matter must now be reviewed by "The Committee" (or a similar body), or that the company still has several other candidates to meet before notifying those chosen for a second round of interviews. In this case, do not fail first to thank the interviewer and then to ask when you should expect to hear from him. This is at least some form of closure. A push toward action—even if it's nothing more than an estimated decision time—conveys a degree of urgency without making you look overanxious or desperate. It leaves the interviewer aware that you are important and valuable and that you are well aware of your own importance and value.

Reading the Interviewer

In Chapter 9, I pointed out that although every company needs certain basics from each employee, each company also has its own specific needs, problems, and desires. You learn about these by preparing carefully for the interview and discovering as much as you can about the target employer. Yet what this simple formula leaves out is the interviewer as an individual. He, too, has specific needs, problems, and desires, not all of which correspond with those of his company.

It may be impossible to find out anything about the interviewer in advance. If you are interviewing with a small firm, it's likely that the owner or CEO will meet with you personally. Perhaps you

The Skinny

According to the U.S. Department of Labor, about two-thirds of jobs get filled through such informal ways as word-of-mouth, the influence of relatives and friends, and so on. Networking is an attempt to give some structure to such informal means of finding employment, thereby increasing your odds of landing a job.

121

can uncover some background on her through articles in industry newsletters or in informational/promotional material distributed by the company. If you're interviewing with a larger organization, you still may be able to find published material on the relevant department head, who could be the person responsible for interviewing you. Make use of your network. Maybe you know someone who knows someone who knows the interviewer, and can tell you what to expect.

If you can ascertain little or nothing about the interviewer beforehand, you'll have to do your best to size her up during the course of the interview itself. Below, I discuss some common interviewer types to look out for, and tips on dealing with them.

Victor Vague

He is the interviewer you are most likely to encounter. Although I haven't mentioned him by name, I've been talking a good deal about him, because it's a safe bet that you'll meet one day.

Don't Call Us ...

The "Tell me all about yourself" opener is basically an invitation to deliver a rambling autobiography. True, the interviewer asked for it—but he doesn't really want it. Focus his request in order to discover what he really wants; then deliver it.

Victor's interviews begin in one of two ways: with small talk that, if you let him, he'll continue churning out for the balance of your visit, or with the dreaded "Tell me all about yourself" opener.

What Victor Vague needs is focus, and *you* can give it to him. Terminate the small talk by asking permission to ask a question, then launch into something you know about his company: "I read in *Widget Weekly* that you believe the biggest problem facing this industry is _____. This is a subject area that is very interesting to me. Can you say something more about how it specifically affects your company?" Then respond to Victor's answer. Try to build the foundation of the interview on that.

The "Tell me all about yourself" opener can also be focused, as we've seen in Chapter 9, by delivering a few essentials and then asking the interviewer to zero in: "But what area of my background is most relevant to *your* needs? Perhaps I can be most helpful to you discussing that."

Harried Harriet

You're eager, excited, and you've concentrated all your energy for the past two weeks on preparing for this interview. Now that you're here, the interviewer barely looks you in the eye, keeps answering the ringing phone, pauses to address issues raised by people who poke their head into her office, and, in fact, does almost everything but pay attention to you.

Your first impulse is to give in to a mixture of heartbreak, frustration, and anger. All of these feelings are justified and understandable, but they will not help you rescue this interview. Is Harriet being deliberately impolite? Purposely cruel? No. She's overworked, and the spectacle of Harried Harriet is living, breathing proof that she needs your help. When you can manage to get a word in, point this out: "You really *are* busy! It's obvious that I could be of great use to you in an environment like this."

With luck, this will get Harriet's attention. She'll put down the phone, close the door, and turn her attention to you.

Mike the Machine

Mike is someone you do not anticipate meeting in an interview. You might fear that an interviewer will be unpleasant and obnoxious, and ask questions that are too hard to answer, but you do assume that, however objectionable the person may be, he'll at least be human. But Mike the Machine never connects with you on a person-to-person level. His approach is a monotone. He ticks off one question after another, barely giving you time to develop an answer, never following up on your answers, never allowing your responses to blossom into real conversation. It's bang, bang, bang, then out the door.

How do you get through to this interviewer?

Your best hope for stopping the Machine is to throw in a few monkey wrenches. Mike the Machine is built to grind out questions. He does not expect questions in return. Try to identify an area of particular concern to Mike and/or his company, then *you* ask one or more questions concerning that area. But first you'll have to turn the question-answer tables on Mike:

> **Mike:** What experience do you have working with advertising copywriters?
>
> **You:** I can review that for you. But let me ask you first, what copywriting issues do you find most critical on a day-to-day basis?

It takes real guts to turn the tables like this, but if an interview is proceeding mechanically and unenthusiastically, you must assume that no issues of critical importance have yet been discovered, and you need both to discover them and to shake things up. And you need to do it *now*.

Ted the Techie

Ted is interested in assessing your knowledge of the nuts and bolts of the job for which you are interviewing. You cannot ignore this, of course, because the nuts and bolts are important—without them, everything just falls apart. So, satisfy his need to know by doing and saying everything you can to demonstrate your technical mastery. Be aware, however, that in spite of himself, this is not *all* Ted wants to know.

123

Although he may fail to express it, he does want to see you as a whole being, bristling with skills beyond technical know-how. Whenever possible, expand your technically oriented responses to demonstrate such skills and traits as leadership, initiative, decisiveness, ability to work well with people, and so on. Leave Ted with *more* than he asked for.

Mary the Monopolizer

I've discussed the common mistake overanxious job candidates make, of trying to fill every minute of the interview with the sound of their voice. Unfortunately, some interviewers are capable of this as well. They call *you* in for an interview, to find out who *you* are and what *you* offer, then take up *your* time with *their* words!

Deal with Mary the Monopolizer first by learning whatever you can from all those nonstop words. Listen to what she says is important to her, then use one of those points as a springboard into the conversation. Appeal directly to her self-interest and self-absorption. You may have to be slightly aggressive about it:

Mary: ... So, as I say, I really have to struggle to ensure adequate cash flow ...

You: Let me interrupt you just a moment—because what you are saying is really exciting. Cash-flow management is the chief area I've been trying to revise and streamline in my current position. I'd like to share one idea with you—and get your reaction to it. I think you'll find this quite interesting ...

You, the Problem Solver

This point has been made before, but, after our rapid review of interviewer types, it's worth repeating. There is one thing all interviewers look for and welcome, and that is *someone who'll solve their problems.* Come into the interview focused on what you can do for the interviewer, the employer, not what he can do for you. Of course, you're a job seeker. Why else would you be taking the time and trouble to show up at the interview? But just because you are a job seeker doesn't mean you have to come across as one. Instead, present yourself as a resource, somebody with skills, expertise, and accomplishments to offer.

CPR

Even if you are less than adequately prepared for the interview (for example, you haven't made an effort to discover the problems and issues that especially concern this particular company), don't give up. You can still put yourself across as a problem solver by imagining what a *problem employee* does—is frequently absent or late, needs constant supervision and correction, doesn't meet deadlines, and so forth—and then presenting yourself as exactly the opposite.

The Least You Need to Know

➤ The interview is essentially a sales situation, with you as the salesperson *and* the "merchandise."

➤ If you sense that the interview is drifting, it's critical that you take the initiative. Work to focus the interviewer.

➤ Learn to "read" the interviewer so that you can ask questions that prompt a positive response and present yourself as the answer to the employer's needs and a solution to his problems.

➤ The objective of the interview is action on the part of the interviewer—ideally, a job offer—and you should direct everything you say and do toward that objective.

Money Talk

In Chapter 7, "Shall We Dance?" we looked at some of the distractions that can bedevil an interview: ringing phones, staffers who poke their heads in the door with "urgent" problems, and so on. These you can cope with, and, really, they're less your problem than they are the interviewer's. There is, however, one monumental distraction that *you* bring along to the interview, one that you can't get away from. It's the question of salary. It just hangs there, glowering over each and every interview.

Both you and the interviewer want to raise and resolve the salary issue, so what's the problem?

You're afraid to ask for too little or too much—*either* of which can take you out of the running—and, like many folks, you're uneasy with the notion of putting a price on your own head. But, most of all, both you and the interviewer are aware that the first one to mention a salary figure puts himself in the weaker negotiating position. So the issue hangs there, staring you in the eye.

This chapter will help you do something about the salary monster.

First, Some Homework

Just because you should avoid being the first to mention a salary figure doesn't mean you should wait until you are sitting in the interviewer's office to start thinking about salary. Part of your pre-interview homework should be determining a workable and reasonable salary range.

A Cash-Need Worksheet

Let's think about those two terms: *workable* and *reasonable*. You can go about defining *workable* by determining your own minimum cash requirements. This does *not* mean the bare minimum needed for subsistence, but the least you need to feel secure and comfortable. Ultimately, only you can determine what "secure and comfortable" means, but a good rule of thumb is to figure what you need to meet all of your monthly obligations, *and* be able to put away and save at least 3 percent of your monthly income, *and* have another 10 percent (on average) that you can count on for that proverbial rainy day. Use the worksheet on the following page to figure out your monthly expenses and a workable salary.

Clincher

It's a time-honored rule of prudent personal cash management that you should have at least three months' salary in the bank to ensure that you're never just a paycheck or two from financial collapse.

What Are You Worth, Anyway?

The *reasonable* part of your homework assignment requires that you determine your "market value"—that is, the going price—in a particular industry, for someone with your qualifications and skills. Your initial job search research may have already revealed this information, but if not, consult the following:

➤ The most recent report from the *The Occupational Outlook Handbook*. Ask for it at the local office of the U.S. Department of Labor, or access it on the Internet at **www.bls.gov**.

➤ Les Krantz's *Jobs Rated Almanac* (New York: St. Martin's Press, 1999). Use it only to establish a crude salary range.

➤ Professional and trade journals in your field or industry. Look for issues that publish annual salary surveys.

➤ *National Business Employment Weekly*. It runs periodic salary surveys, and you should be able to get back issues from the publisher or at your local library.

Minimum Monthly Cash Needs Worksheet

Housing

Rent or mortgage payments	$_____
Electricity/gas	$_____
Water	$_____
Telephone	$_____
Garbage removal	$_____
Cleaning, maintenance, repairs	$_____

Food

Groceries	$_____
Eating out	$_____

Clothing

Purchase	$_____
Dry-cleaning, laundry	$_____

Automobile/Transportation

Car payments	$_____
Gas	$_____
Repairs	$_____
Public transportation (bus, train, plane)	$_____

Insurance

Auto	$_____
Medical	$_____
House and personal possessions	$_____
Life	$_____

Medical Expenses

Doctors' visits	$_____
Prescriptions	$_____
Fitness costs	$_____

Support for Other Family Members

Child care costs	$_____
Child support	$_____
Support for your parents	$_____

Charity $_____

Education $_____

Take two swings through this list. First, pencil in the minimum figures—what you absolutely need to earn to meet your expenses and achieve some level of comfort and security. In your second pass, fill in the amounts you would ideally like to earn.

continues

Minimum Monthly Cash Needs Worksheet (continued)

Pet Care	$_____
Bills and Debts (Monthly Payments)	
Credit cards	$_____
Local stores	$_____
Other	$_____
Taxes	
Federal	$_____
State	$_____
Local/property	$_____
Amusement	
Movies, video rentals, and so on	$_____
Other entertainment	$_____
Newspapers, magazines, books	$_____
Gifts	$_____
Savings/Investments	$_____
Contingency Fund	$_____
TOTAL MONTHLY AMOUNT NEEDED	$_____

Compare your workable figure with your reasonable figure. If what's workable significantly exceeds what's reasonable, you'll have to rethink your needs or your career goals or both. If, however, the two numbers are fairly close, use them to formulate your desired—workable and reasonable—salary range.

A Little Game of Chicken

Who *hasn't* seen the James Dean classic *Rebel Without a Cause?* Perhaps the film's most memorable sequence is the "chicken race," in which Dean and his rival race their jalopies to the edge of a cliff. The object is to jump out of the doomed car at the last possible second. The first to flinch—to jump—loses. (Of course, if you don't jump in time, you lose again.)

Salary negotiation is like a game of chicken. You enter the interview (supposedly) knowing what salary you need and can expect. But, who knows, maybe they're willing to offer you much more than you expect. If you blurt out a low figure—flinch—

first, you lose. But if you too insistently evade answering the interviewer's questions about salary requirements, you lose again—you probably won't get the job.

CPR

If the interviewer offers you coffee, my advice is just say no, thanks—even if you feel you could really use a cup. To begin with, you probably don't need the added anxiety caffeine may produce. More important, in an interview, with your attention tautly focused and your nerves ratcheted up about as far as they can go, a hot, dark cuppa joe is just a catastrophe waiting to happen.

That said, here's what you do if you actually spill coffee on yourself:

1. Don't try to minimize the accident. If the coffee is hot, stand up, and do what you can to get it off of you.

2. Declare, "*This* is embarrassing! Can you direct me to the washroom?" Go to the bathroom and clean yourself up as much as you can.

3. Apologize, but don't grovel and don't put yourself down: "I'm really sorry this happened. I hope I haven't stained your rug." (Do not say, "I'm such an idiot!" "I'm so clumsy!" "I can't believe how stupid I am!" or the like.)

4. Thank the interviewer for his help—even if he did nothing more than direct you to the restroom. (Actually, he'll most likely get you paper towels, make sure you didn't burn yourself, and reassure you that "it could happen to anyone." Insofar as this catastrophe empowers the interviewer by giving him an opportunity to help you, the incident is not as destructive as you might fear.)

5. Above all, get on with the interview. After apologizing, continue: "I'm okay. We were talking about so-and-so. This is what I wanted to say before I so rudely interrupted myself ..."

Putting Yourself in the Catbird Seat

This is where it gets tricky. Your primary task at the interview is to sell yourself as the answer to the employer's problems. While you're busy doing that, however, you need to remain sensitive to the signals that tell you just when it's time to get into a salary discussion. Ideally, this will come near the end of the interview.

Don't Flinch Now!

Provided that you can keep your anxiety in check, it's not terribly difficult to avoid raising the salary issue first. However, the interviewer may launch a preemptive first strike by asking you point-blank, "How much are you making now, and how much do you want?" Make certain that you have reviewed Chapter 9, "How to Answer the Questions Everybody Asks," which includes tips on evading—in order to delay—the salary issue.

Don't Call Us ...

An interviewer could actually try to pin you down to an exact salary figure. This is almost certainly the sign of a power-hungry interviewer, not of any genuine need to get an exact figure. Still, it's a power struggle you will lose if you arbitrarily fail to cooperate. If the interviewer says something like "Look, let's not play games. I really do need a firm figure from you," offer the salary range, and, if that fails, *do* volunteer a figure. Use the lower part of the *top quarter* of your range; for example, the top quarter of your original range $38,000 to $43,000 is $41,750 to $43,000. You could round that down to $41,000, or even $40,000.

Unfortunately, there is no guarantee that the avoidance techniques in Chapter 9 will work 100 percent of the time. If the employer insists on getting a figure from you, don't alienate him by persisting in evasion. But don't nail yourself to a single figure, either. Come to the interview armed with a broad salary range with which you can respond, if pressed.

Use your workable and reasonable figures to calculate the range. Let's say the workable figure you've arrived at is $36,000. Having researched the industry, you've concluded that the salary range for your target position is $33,000 to $41,000. (That's good! It suggests that your current needs correspond well with the reality of the marketplace.) Now, what do you do with these figures? Bracket the salary range you report to the prospective employer so that it interlocks with and slightly exceeds the upper range of the reasonable figures and also exceeds your own workable requirement. In this case, when the employer presses you for a figure, reply that you are looking for a salary in the low forties. If he presses you for something more precise, reply that your acceptable range is $38,000 to $43,000.

Timing Is Everything

The issue of timing has a mystical air about it. Most of us tend to feel that good timing is like a talent for wiggling your ears: Either you have it or you don't. Though good timing requires sensitivity to body language and buy signals (see Chapters 7, "Shall We Dance?" and 11, "Take Control and Start Selling Yourself"), you can guide yourself with a more basic and completely non-mystical four-step checklist.

Avoid the subject of salary *until:*

1. You're in the final interview—if there is more than one round of interviews.

2. You're satisfied that the interviewer has gotten to know you and fully understands your qualifications.

3. You feel that you've been fully informed of what the job is all about, and the duties and responsibilities it entails.

4. You're confident that the interviewer has reached the "gotta have you" stage.

A Trek from "Sorta Like" to "Gotta Have"

That last step needs some explanation. The "gotta have you" stage is the point at which the interviewer decides that you are *the* answer to his needs and the solution to his problems. At this point—and not before—is when salary negotiation should take place.

Depending on many factors—how persuasive your resumé and other supporting materials are, how desperate the employer is, the perceived fit between your background and the employer's needs, and so on—the time it takes to trek from total stranger to "sorta like you" to "gotta have you" will differ. Whatever the length of the journey, it should progress from a starting point at which the target employer doesn't know you at all (if, as is often the case, he has hardly glanced at your resumé), through a process of increasing involvement with you and commitment to you (the "sorta like" stage), to a point at which the interviewer decides: *We gotta have you.*

The buy signal that marks this stage will probably be less subtle and more direct than the buy signals of the "sorta like" stage. Maybe something like this: "I think we see eye to eye about the duties and responsibilities of the position. Now, what about salary?" Or: "I believe you can do the job we want. What salary were you looking for?" To be classified as a genuine buy signal, the request for salary information *must* be preceded by a "gotta have" statement ("I believe you can do the job …"). Without such a statement, it's just a premature request for a salary figure.

Clincher

What if the final buy signal doesn't come? In this case, it's time for you to take control by asking a question like this: "Based on what I've told you, don't you think I could give you all that you need in this position?" Review "Getting Action" in Chapter 11.

But don't jump at the buy signal, no matter how tempting. Remember, if possible, get the interviewer to be the first to mention a figure. Try this response to the buy signal/salary question: "This is the first time we've really broached the subject. Could you tell me what the authorized range is for someone with my qualifications?" Assuming the interviewer furnishes this information, you can then choose one of four options:

1. Accept the range: "The upper end of this range is certainly what I had in mind and would be acceptable to me."

2. Open negotiations by responding with your own range, the bottom end of which should overlap the top end of the interviewer's.

3. Thank the interviewer for the information, then ask for additional time to consider the figure.

4. Thank the interviewer for the information, but tell him that the range is well below what you were expecting and what you consider appropriate.

Avoid telling the interviewer that his or her offer is not even in the ballpark, unless you are prepared *not* to get the offer. If the employer's figure is substantially below your range, it is better to choose option #3: Ask for time to think over the offer.

If you really are pleased with the figures offered, you may respond with the first alternative. Just be aware that most employers don't lead with their best offer. Even if the employer is well within your ballpark, it is usually best to respond with the second option. It may capture for you a figure in a somewhat higher range.

Be aware that option #2 requires some work. It's not likely that the employer will simply cave in just because you topped his or her top range. This is the time to recapitulate and resell. Remind the interviewer of *why* you are worth top dollar. Add to this reminder a demonstration of your knowledge of the industry:

As you might imagine, I've looked through a number of industry salary surveys. The range I would find acceptable is appropriate to prevailing salaries in the industry. Since we're agreed that I have the qualifications that will more than satisfy your needs, and I can promise you that I'll be up, running, and producing for you within a week, I feel that compensation somewhat above your upper range is appropriate and fair—fair for me and, certainly, a fair value for you.

Don't Call Us ...

Don't betray yourself with negative body language. Acquire and practice—in front of a mirror—a *pleasant* poker face, one that displays neither disappointment nor hip-hip-hooray enthusiasm in response to a salary offer. Maintain near-neutral eye contact throughout the negotiation.

Clearing the Hurdles

Years ago I read a book called *Everything Is Negotiable*. An appealing title (I'm sure the book is still selling) and, actually, a helpful book. But the fact is, the book's premise is wrong. Not *everything* is negotiable.

Generally, for entry-level and lower-compensation positions, salaries tend to be rather firmly fixed, barely negotiable, or totally non-negotiable. That is a hard fact of life. As you go up in compensation, salary ranges increase in flexibility. At the very highest ranges—above $65,000—there is often considerable room for negotiation.

Let's break this down.

An entry-level position that pays $20,000 a year or less will probably offer little or no salary flexibility. For such positions, the pool of available candidates is usually large, and it makes more sense for the employer to find a person who will accept her offer rather than negotiate with someone who won't.

In the middle range between $20,000 and $65,000, there is limited room for maneuvering. It is not unusual for employers hiring in this range to negotiate as much as 15 percent above their stated salary figure. Just don't expect more.

Positions that pay more than $65,000 in annual salary are typically skilled and demanding; therefore, the candidate pool is proportionately smaller. Employers tend to be willing to spend more of what it takes to get the person they want.

With a firm grasp on reality, you can still overcome the following four major hurdles interviewers throw in the path of a salary negotiation.

"Exceeds Range Authorized"

If you're interviewing for an entry-level position, this hurdle may be immovable—that is, it's not a negotiating ploy, but a simple statement of fact: "Position Y pays *x* dollars, period." Nevertheless, you can try to negotiate a somewhat higher salary—the worst they'll say is "no."

One thing to note is that neither the "exceeds range authorized" objection to higher salary, nor any of the other three we will discuss have anything to do with your value or performance.

This objection—and the others—focus on *cost*. Unfortunately, cost is the single criterion on which most purchases are based, whether the merchandise is a bar of soap or a potential employee. Your task is to get the employer focusing on cost versus *benefit;* that is, shift his concentration from cost to *value*. Sell your special qualifications, talents, and abilities as investments in greater profitability. Sure, you may cost more than what the employer anticipated paying, but the benefits you offer also exceed what the employer anticipated. Your greater value, therefore, outweighs your greater cost:

I understand. But perhaps a higher figure could be authorized. The value my qualifications and skill represent, I think you'd agree, clearly merit a salary in the range I mentioned. Frankly, I believe that you would have difficulty hiring anyone with qualifications comparable to mine at the salary range presently authorized.

"Outside of Our Budget"

Confronted by this objection, accept and acknowledge it. Then use the *value* argument to attempt to persuade the employer to rethink his budget:

I appreciate the discipline of a budget, and I understand that you budgeted under $35,000 for the position, but I know other employers who are willing to pay more. More importantly, however, I think we're both agreed that I offer exceptional qualifications and skills. I believe my background demonstrates my absolute commitment to high standards of performance. Maybe I cost a bit more than you've budgeted for, but I'm also offering you more *value* than you bargained for. That's why I feel amply justified in asking for the $38,000.

"Others Don't Make as Much"

Attack this objection logically. When you are told that others presently employed in comparable positions at the firm don't make the salary you're asking for, remind the interviewer—politely and tactfully—that what the employer pays others is a matter between the employer and the others. Your salary concerns only the employer and you. Again, begin by appreciating and acknowledging the objection. Don't just ignore it:

I appreciate your point of view. Nevertheless, based on our conversation thus far, I understood that my salary would be based on my performance and my qualifications, and that it would not be capped by what others in the firm earn. Actually, this brings up another issue that I'd like clarified: How will I be rewarded for performance? I intend to perform exceptionally well, to give you my "personal best"—and not gauge my performance by the performance of others. So it's important to me to know whether raises will be based primarily on a cost-of-living formula, or on performance.

Do everything you can to separate yourself from limiting factors of precedents.

"But Your Salary History ..."

The best way to prevent the interviewer from using your own salary history to cap his offer is by avoiding the issue of salary history in the first place. Don't volunteer information concerning your current compensation level. This, of course, may not be possible, and if the interviewer tries to use your salary history as a precedent for setting your new salary, you need to separate the past firmly from what you are asking for now:

> Mr. Smith, I don't understand what bearing my past salary has on the work I will do for you. My history is not relevant to salary. What *is* relevant is performance and qualifications, and these we've discussed thoroughly. I believe we're agreed that I offer great value to the company. Moreover, I've looked into how this position is compensated in other organizations, and it seems to me that the figure I'm proposing is not only fair, but represents excellent value for money. Wouldn't you agree that a combination of the qualifications I offer and industry standards is a fair and appropriate way of arriving at a reasonable salary figure?

This Is Negotiable (Isn't It?)

Salary negotiation can become a single-minded tug o' war, at least until either you or the employer cuts the rope by saying no. Salary is a simple figure, all too easy for an interviewer to engrave upon her mind: *This is the number. He shall not have more! This is the number. He shall not have more!* So, at some point, it is likely that you'll hit a brick wall.

Nevertheless, there still may be room for negotiation. After all, salary is not the only part of the compensation package.

Perks Aplenty

Even if the salary figure turns out to be carved in stone, paid vacation time may be negotiable. In addition, you may be able to agree on a *flex time* arrangement that makes your day more productive and convenient. Child care and day care have emerged over the past decade as key employment issues. You may be able to negotiate for a day care allowance.

Talk the Talk

Flex time is an arrangement that allows employees to adjust their morning start and evening quitting times to suit their preferences, to accommodate family schedules, or even to avoid rush-hour traffic.

Those Bennies from Heaven

If you reach an impasse in salary negotiation, there are other nonsalary benefits you may be able to negotiate. These items include performance-based bonuses, profit-sharing plans, stock-purchase options, payment for special training and career development education, payment of professional membership dues, payment of professional subscriptions, and so on.

You might also negotiate a favorable *"golden parachute"* severance agreement: a cash payment in the event you are "let go."

Other benefits that may be negotiable include:

➤ An office of a certain size, location, and description

➤ A company car

➤ A car allowance

➤ A private parking space

Money Isn't Everything

It used to be that employee benefits—so-called "fringe benefits"—were the employer's last resort for sweetening a deal going sour. It also used to be that such benefits packages were fairly lame, fairly standard from employer to employer, and certainly a disappointing substitute for cash.

It *used* to be. Today, the cost of medical care, for example, is nothing less than terrifying, and good employer-provided medical insurance is a great benefit indeed—one that varies competitively from employer to employer. Not only should this benefit loom prominently in your evaluation of a compensation package, it can also be used as a negotiating chip. Federal law may prohibit the employer from offering you a medical plan that is better than what other employees receive, but you may be able to persuade the employer that his package is not competitive with what other employers offer. This may provide the leverage you need to return to the issue of salary and get a better offer.

Relocation Reimbursement

Relocation costs can be staggering. Let's say you have a modest house, a family of four, and you're relocating 500 miles. Expect to spend $6,000 to $12,000 just to transport your stuff. Then there are storage costs, costs for temporary living arrangements (renting an apartment or staying in a hotel), and costs associated with selling a residence and buying a new one. True, expenses for employment-related relocation are generally tax deductible (tax laws change frequently; consult your tax specialist!), but the outlay can be significant. For this reason, relocation reimbursement is an important area for negotiation:

➤ Negotiate for moving expenses.

➤ Negotiate for temporary housing expenses.

➤ Negotiate a guaranteed purchase of your former residence—the employer agrees to purchase your house at a set price if it fails to sell within an agreed-on period.

How to Win the Gulf War

The Gulf War: Not only can't you and the employer see eye to eye, but you're a million light years apart. What do you do? You could conclude the interview with a thank you, walk out the door, and continue your job search. And maybe that would be your best alternative at this particular time. But what if you really want—or really need—this job?

You have one final item left to negotiate: the future. Accept the employer's best offer now, but be explicit about the proviso that your salary will be reviewed in six months (or some other period you and the employer agree on before the interview concludes) in light of your performance. Don't let overeagerness or genuine desperation lock you into a low salary for the long term.

The Least You Need to Know

➤ Calculate your salary needs and expectations before you go into the interview.

➤ Avoid being the first to mention a salary figure; if pressed to "name your price," offer a range rather than a target figure.

➤ Try to delay the salary negotiation until the interviewer has reached the "gotta have you" stage.

➤ Overcome employer objections to your salary demands by focusing on issues of *value* rather than *cost*.

Part 3

"Do You Have Any Questions?" (You'd Better!)

The questions you ask at the interview are every bit as important as those you answer. Of course, you want to find out everything you can about the prospective employer. He may think he's hiring you, but it's a two-way street, after all. You're also deciding whether to choose him.

But the questions you ask should do more than just gather information. They must provide additional opportunities for you to sell yourself to the employer, to demonstrate your skills, your qualifications, your knowledge, and your character. The chapters in this section will help you build such double-edged questions.

Chapter 13

Questions You Should Always Ask

In This Chapter

➤ Getting the interviewer to invest time in you

➤ How to find out what the employer expects from you

➤ Guiding the interviewer through your qualifications

➤ Asking questions that make you seem like the answer to the interviewer's prayers

➤ The "official" job description versus the interviewer's version

➤ Questions that produce positive action

Is the glass half-full or half-empty? The litmus test for optimists versus pessimists—the optimist says half full, while the pessimist says half empty—applies to employment interviews as well. You can see the interview as a great opportunity involving some risk, or as a giant risk involving a slim chance at opportunity. But even the pessimist needs to realize that it's the interviewee—you, that is—who controls the gravest risk: The worst thing that can happen in an interview is that *you* fail to ask questions.

Fail to ask (good) questions, and the interviewer will assume that you are neither very bright nor very interested in his or her organization. Even worse, by not asking questions, you'll be passing up an opportunity to find out some of the things you need to know to decide whether you really want the job. Most important of all (as any sales professional will tell you), *questions*—not compelling facts or a slick pitch alone—are what make the sale. Making the "sale" depends on getting your "prospect" to respond to you in a positive manner, and thoughtful questions are critical to getting the prospect to verbalize needs and desires, as well as reservations. This chapter will get you started with some of the best questions you should ask.

Big Question #1: "Have You Had a Chance to Review My Resumé?"

As hard as it may be to believe, this is a most important question. In the first place, a staggering number of interviewers do *not* review—or even read—candidates' resumés before the interview. Understandably, few interviewers will admit this to you. Be certain to phrase the question just this way: *"Have you had a chance to review … ?"* The word "chance" communicates your sympathetic understanding that the interviewer is very busy, while "review" lets him know that you assume he has *read* the resumé, but that he may not have had an adequate opportunity to study and thoroughly *review* it. This phrasing transforms the question from challenge to opportunity—an opportunity to present your qualifications in a powerful point-by-point manner. It's also an opportunity to extend a helping hand to the interviewer—to come across, that is, as a solution rather than a problem.

Nevertheless, because interviewers are loath to admit scant familiarity with your resume, you're not likely to get a simple "No, I haven't read it" in response to this question. Odds are, the interviewer will respond with something like, "I haven't had the chance to review it as thoroughly as I'd like to." (Which may almost certainly be translated as "No, I haven't read a word of it.")

Don't be dismayed by such a response. It's not unusual; in fact, it's more the rule than the exception. Without missing a beat, and without betraying any disappointment or anxiety in your body language, simply continue: "Perhaps, then, you'll find it helpful for me to hit the highlights of my qualifications."

You'll most likely receive a positive response to this. Congratulations! You've already begun to make the sale. A positive response is the beginning of a commitment, an investment in you. You've made a big step out of the realm of "total stranger." Now, in a bright and conversational tone, review your qualifications.

Don't Call Us …

They say there is no such thing as a stupid question. I disagree. Stupid questions do exist, so be careful not to ask them. What's a "stupid question"? Any question to which you should already have the answer. For example: "So what exactly does AT&T do?"

Clincher

Pause frequently during your review to signal the interviewer that you welcome questions along the way. Remember, the more questions the interviewer asks, the greater the investment—of time and mental energy—he is making in you.

If you like, reach into your interview kit (see Chapter 4, "Get Set") and take o▢ copy of your resumé to use as the basis for this review.

Even More About Yourself

When you have concluded reviewing your qualifications, follow up with:

> Is there anything else I can tell you about my qualifications?

This is also the question you should ask if the interviewer assures you that she has read and thoroughly reviewed your resumé. In either case, it gives you an additional opportunity to present yourself in the best possible light while obtaining an even greater investment of time from the prospective employer. With each minute that passes in productive conversation, your value appreciates in the interviewer's estimation.

Big Question #2: "What Results Do You Want Me to Produce?"

Asking this question is a natural progression from the phase of displaying your qualifications. It prompts the interviewer not only to start thinking about how you will fit into her organization, but, indeed, starts her thinking of you as somebody who *could* fit into the organization. Moreover, just by asking the question, you are demonstrating that your intention is to *do* a job rather than *take* a job. The question shifts the focus from you to the subject that most concerns the interviewer: her needs and her company. You've sent the message that, for you, this job means more than collecting a salary for yourself. It means serving the company, creating profit, saving money, solving problems, and increasing productivity.

Your object is to respond point by point to whatever list of results the question elicits. Ideally, this pattern will emerge: *Here's what* you *want. Here's what I'll do.*

You can elaborate on and refine the question by going on to ask:

> What do you see as a timetable for the results you expect from my effort?

Clincher

Always try to use the word *qualifications* rather than *experience*. "Qualifications" conveys active achievement, whereas "experience" is more neutral and passive. "Qualifications" are carried with you as the *value* you offer *this* employer; "experience" is what you gave in the past, to someone else.

Not only does this question allow you to insert yourself into the strategy and operations of the organization—another move toward the status of a candidate the employer feels he has "gotta have"—it allows you to assess how reasonable and realistic the employer's expectations are. If they strike you as unrealistic, it's best not to challenge them at this point, but to allow your assessment to weigh in the balance when you are negotiating salary and when you are deciding whether to accept the offer, should an offer come.

Clincher

The ideal question is double-edged: It not only allows you to display your qualifications and show yourself at your best, it also helps you assess the job in order to determine if it's right for you.

Probing Employer Needs

The next question to develop from Big Question #2 works in two different circumstances. If it's clear to you that your qualifications mesh well with the employer's needs as they were expressed in answering Big Question #2, go on to ask:

What do you consider to be ideal qualifications for this position?

If your assessment of fit is accurate—and if you are quite lucky—the interviewer will respond with something like "Well, I'd say what you offer is pretty ideal." More likely, however, the interviewer will list some qualifications. It is then up to you to help the interviewer draw the connections between *his* list and *your* qualifications. Your objective here is to guide, not shove, the interviewer toward his own conclusions. The sense of having made up one's own mind is always a more positive and empowering experience than the feeling of having been talked into something. In response to the interviewer's list of ideal qualifications, use guiding remarks such as, "That seems similar to what I did to increase sales of widgets at Joe Blow, Inc. Wouldn't you agree?" Or: "I think you'd agree that my work with widget analysis would be valuable in that area." Or: "Managing freelancers has taught me a lot about such-and-such."

Even if you discover substantial gaps between what the interviewer identifies as ideal qualifications and what you have to offer, make guiding remarks that bridge the gaps rather than leave them gaping. For example: "My work directing freelance vendors has taught me a great deal about management" is a great deal more persuasive than "I admit I haven't managed a department, but I have worked with freelancers."

If the gulf between the interviewer's ideal and your actual qualifications is simply too broad to be bridged, consider not drawing attention to it. Focus on something else, some other item on the interviewer's list that *does* demonstrate a fit with what you have to offer. If you cannot ignore the item, respond to it as positively as possible—as an opportunity for growth: "I'm eager to develop my management skills." Don't draw attention to your lack of such skills, but emphasize your eagerness to acquire them.

One final point: If the interviewer's response is light years away from anything you expected, you will have to give serious thought to whether this job is right for you. But don't start thinking that way at the interview, and certainly bite your tongue if you're about to give voice to any doubts. The object of the interview should not be to get a job, but, rather, to excite the interviewer's interest in you and to generate an offer. Even if, during the interview, you begin to think that this job isn't for you, those two objectives remain valid. You can always ask for time to consider the offer, go home, think it over, and, if necessary, reject it. The employer's interest is something of value, even if you ultimately decide not to take the job. Why? Well, because:

> **Don't Call Us ...**
>
> Avoid making truly far-fetched or trivial connections: "Management qualifications? I've managed my 120-pound Great Dane successfully!" Or: "Management qualifications? I manage to keep my own desk in order and make sure that phone calls are returned within a half hour." Such remarks convey nothing more than sheer desperation.

➤ Another, more appropriate job with the same employer may later materialize. You've got a leg up on it if the employer is already interested in you.

➤ You may someday, in some capacity, do business with this interviewer or his company. It can't hurt to have him think highly of you.

➤ This interviewer may learn of another job, either elsewhere in the company or with a colleague in another company, that is suited to your qualifications. If you've created interest in this interviewer, you may get a positive word-of-mouth lead or referral.

All contacts with *any* prospective employer are valuable. Don't squander them. Don't throw them away.

Questions to Which YOU Are the Answer

Assuming that your qualifications have meshed, at least to some degree, with what the interviewer says he needs, it's time to ask questions that reveal you as the answer to the employer's needs. Jump in with the following:

What are the principal problems facing your staff right now?

This question has a dual purpose. First, it helps you understand the employer's problems and gives you an opportunity to define just how you will work to solve them. After all, it's easy to declare yourself a "problem solver," but if you know just what the problems are, you can address the issues specifically and, therefore, far more convincingly. The second purpose of the question is to help you discover any seriously

Don't Call Us ...

Avoid showing frustration or consternation if you discover that the interviewer's description of the job differs sharply from the "official" description. Use these differences as points of discussion. Make it clear to the interviewer that you greatly value her "inside" information.

objectionable situations at this company that might affect your decision to accept or reject an offer. The interviewer may just reveal something hopelessly intolerable.

After you ask about problems, ask this question:

How would *you* describe the duties of this job?

It should be posed as written, with the emphasis on the "you." You are not asking for a job description. You should have already done your homework and gathered a solid idea of what the job is about—at least *officially* about. But you'll often find that the interviewer's ideas about the nature of the job differ significantly from the official version. She may even offer something like this: "Well, I know the job description says that duties include A, B, and C, but really, D is very important. You've got to be good at D."

Even if the interviewer's description harmonizes with the official description, by getting her perspective, you may get a better handle on which functions are *perceived* as most important and, therefore, really *are* the most important. Such insight will help you decide whether to accept an offer and will also give you the opportunity to emphasize or reemphasize appropriate skills and qualifications: "I'm glad to hear that you consider client contact such a major part of this position. That's the function I place the highest premium on. You build business one client at a time. There are no shortcuts."

Personalize the questioning by asking this one next:

Can you describe a typical day here?

The interviewer may be taken aback at first, but this question invites the kind of informal, straightforward, and concrete response that should get beyond a dry recitation of duties. If it makes the interviewer think, it may also stimulate her, which will give her good feelings about you.

If the preceding question produces a lively response, lead into this boldly hands-on query:

What would my first project be?

This demonstrates your intense interest in and thorough engagement with the position. It also prompts the interviewer to begin thinking of you as one of the team. In order to answer the question, she will have to imagine you on the job.

The cliché about "climbing the ladder of success" is overused precisely because there is so much truth to it. Few careers are built on lateral moves. Typically, you progress upward, through increasing levels of skill and responsibility. You may, therefore, find yourself interviewing for a position that requires skills you don't yet possess. In this case, once you have established your otherwise sound fit with the organization, you might ask:

> What type of training will I receive?

Be careful to ask this in a way that doesn't suggest feelings of inadequacy. Your point is that you want to prepare yourself to do the best possible job for the employer. Your object is to demonstrate initiative, a commitment to acquiring new skills, and an ambition to learn and grow in order to do the job at hand.

Questions to Close the Sale

When you feel that you have made your case, that you have presented what you have to offer and have shown how it all fits the employer's needs, it's time to press the interview toward a close—a *positive* close. If you're lucky, the interviewer will take the initiative for this, either with a strong buy signal—an expression of satisfaction—or by making an offer. However, if neither of these is forthcoming, ask the following:

> Based on what I've told you, don't you think I could give you all that you need in this position?

Salespeople are accustomed to asking such questions, but, admittedly, it may be hard for those of us unaccustomed to putting matters quite so bluntly. What should make it somewhat easier is the confidence that this question invites a positive response, or, more accurately, invites a train of thought that is likely to lead to a positive response.

As phrased, the question is loaded. It makes it difficult for the interviewer to answer negatively. The question doesn't just force the issue to a conclusion, it coaxes that conclusion toward a *yes*.

No guarantees, of course, and if the "closing" question produces an objection rather than the positive response you'd hoped for, do your best to address the objection. If, however, the interviewer fails to formulate an objection that you can address, prompt her:

> What do you see as my greatest strengths—and my most significant weaknesses?

This should give you an opportunity to build on the strengths, using them to resell yourself, even as you address the weaknesses. Don't make excuses, but do acknowledge the interviewer's assessment and deal with it. While you should not rush to agree with the weaknesses she may identify, do express your willingness to learn, improve, and grow.

If the interview does not conclude with an offer, find out how long you'll be waiting to hear:

> When do you expect to reach a decision?

149

The next best thing to an offer is a question that puts the interviewer on notice that you are not prepared to wait indefinitely for an answer.

The Least You Need to Know

➤ Your objective in an interview is not to get a job, but a job offer. Work toward that goal, and don't worry about whether you will ultimately accept the offer (if one is forthcoming).

➤ Ask questions that encourage lively conversation—a commitment of time and an engagement of intellect from the interviewer.

➤ Even if, midway into the interview, you realize that this job isn't for you, continue to focus on making the interview a success. *All* contacts with *any* prospective employer are valuable.

➤ Ask questions to obtain the interviewer's perspective on the duties, responsibilities, and problems the job involves. Discuss major differences between the "official" job description and the version the interviewer gives you.

➤ Be prepared to ask questions aimed at closing the sale—at moving the interviewer to positive action.

Chapter 14

Roll-Up-Your-Sleeves Questions

In This Chapter

➤ Asking questions that demonstrate your *immediate* value to the employer

➤ Inserting yourself into the employer's mission

➤ Demonstrating your bottom-line impact

➤ Sounding like a leader without stepping on any toes

➤ Making sure you get the vital information

The questions in the preceding chapter give you an opportunity to tell the employer what kind of a person you are and what kind of transferable skills and general qualifications you offer. The questions in the next chapter address issues specific to certain fields: sales, marketing, service, financial, R&D (research and development), and production. The present chapter applies to any field, but is aimed at giving you questions that demonstrate your readiness and ability to jump right in, to flatten the learning curve, to—as the saying goes—hit the ground running.

Proving That You Can Hit the Ground Running

Most of the time, you can hardly go wrong by being polite. But there is a tendency among job candidates to be politely tentative at a job interview, peppering the conversation with such phrases as "if I get the job," "if you make the decision to offer me the position," and "assuming there is an offer." It's understandable not to want to

Don't Call Us ...

Don't ask questions to which you already have the answer. If you know when the proposed start date *is*, don't ask the employer when he wants the new person in place.

appear presumptuous—or foolish—but if you are politely tentative, it's the tentative part that will come through more strongly than the politeness. Better to be a little presumptuous. Walk into the interview *assuming* you will be offered the job.

In the assumption that an offer will be made, therefore, ask questions that embody enthusiasm as well as ability and willingness:

> How soon do you want an employee in place?

If no start date has been mentioned, this is always a good roll-up-your-sleeves question. Although you should assume you will get an offer, it's still better to refer to "an employee" rather than use the personal pronoun *me*. But the real secret is in the phrasing of the question: *how soon*, not *when*. The emphasis is on speed, rapid delivery of the goods, eagerness to begin, readiness to serve. Pay special attention to the way you phrase apparently informational questions, so that each question not only secures information, but also transmits a strong, positive message about yourself.

Nothing is more hands-on than being there. It is said that people vote with their feet—that is, the strongest expression of interest, eagerness, and willingness to pitch in is an expression of action rather than mere words. Indicate that you want to *see* and *experience* the workplace for yourself:

> Can I visit the department?

Or

> Can I get a tour of the facility?

There is a great advantage in asking for a tour or visit rather than in waiting to be asked. It shows that you are excited and that you know how to take charge of a situation. Even more, of course, a plant or facility tour will tell you a lot about the job, which should help you in deciding whether to accept an offer. It may also give you an opportunity to talk to some people at the site. Not only will this teach you more about the job, but, by "spreading you around" the prospective workplace, it will give more people a stake—however small—in your candidacy. Indeed, the time the interviewer spends physically walking you around, taking you from office to office or workstation to workstation, builds up a greater investment in you and increases your value in his estimation.

> Can you tell me why this position is open?

This question serves a dual purpose. It may reveal some good or some bad things about the job. Perhaps the position is open because the current employee has been promoted—which suggests that this is a position from which it is possible to grow. On the other hand, perhaps the position is open because someone quit or was fired. Perhaps the position is thankless or a dead end.

Whatever the answer to the question, the fact that you asked it demonstrates your practicality and sense of professional reality. It shows that you look before you leap, and that you are not one to snap at the first job that comes your way. The question demonstrates your self-value without obnoxiously positioning you as "hard to get."

Depending on the response you get, you might want to follow up with something like this:

> What's turnover like in this position? How many times has the position been filled in the past five years?

If the turnover is high, ask where the previous people went. If they were promoted into other positions within the company, great; if not, the indication may be that this is not such a great position, and you may want to think twice or thrice before accepting an offer. However, high turnover also gives you a positive springboard from which to launch your candidacy. Let's say the employer responds by telling you that the job has changed hands three times in the past five years. You might respond: "That's a lot of turnover you've had to cope with. It must have been a real problem for you. I wouldn't take a job without intending to make a commitment. It's not fair to the team, or to the organization."

If the line of questioning concerning the history of the position proves fruitful, you could continue with something more provocative:

> What did you like best about the person who held this position previously?

Clincher

Take the opportunity to translate "I" and "you" into "we" or "us" as often as possible in the course of the interview conversation.

Notice that the question is phrased positively— not *what didn't you like* or even *what did and didn't you like*. Let the interviewer volunteer any positives or negatives, to which you may respond accordingly.

> **Interviewer:** Joe was a real self-starter. I liked that.

> **You:** I can appreciate how important that is in this position. That's one of the things that appeals to me about it. It's an opportunity to take charge, to see projects through to completion, to take pride and satisfaction in a project.

Should you pick up on any significant negatives about the most recent holder of the position, follow up with this:

> What would you like to see the next [job title] do differently?

This does not directly criticize an incumbent or predecessor, but it does give you an opportunity to mine leads that signal directions in which the interviewer would like you to go.

> **Interviewer:** Bill was a nice guy and a very hard worker. But I do wish he had developed a better tracking and reporting system.

> **You:** That's good to know. It's awfully important to capture vital information with each sale. That's not information we'd want to squander.

The answer is not anything as graceless as "I would do a better job than Bill," but the message is unmistakable: You agree that the task, which Bill left undone, is important. Note the use of "we," which begins to integrate you into this organization's community.

Our Mission

Employers are accustomed to hearing the candidate talk about herself at the interview. That, of course, is what is expected. But the fact is, you probably didn't get as far as the interview stage by delivering just what is expected. Somehow, your candidacy stood out from the rest. You're on a roll. Do something at the interview to stand out again.

The most effective "something" is unexpected, yet precisely what the interviewer wants. How do you arrive at such a magic formula? Stop talking about yourself, and start using your questions to address the company's *mission*. This is not only the last thing the interviewer expects you to talk about, it is the very thing of greatest concern to him—even if he never actually uses the word "mission" himself.

Talk the Talk

Mission is the more or less concise formulation of the purpose, goals, and objectives of an entire organization or department.

Your pre-interview research (see Chapter 2, "On Your Mark," and Appendix B, "Information Sources for Job Searches and Interview Preparation") should tell you something about the mission of the target organization and give you a platform from which you can address your mission-related questions. However, you will find that most such questions fall into one of three categories:

1. Line extension
2. New lines
3. Market-share growth

Line Extension

All companies produce a product(s) or service(s). A fruitful line of questioning may concern *line extension*—new products or services that are not radical departures from what the company already does, but, rather, logical developments from current lines. Asking questions about line extensions serves two purposes: First, it will let you assess how forward-looking, yet realistic, the company is—and, therefore, whether it is likely to survive, prosper, grow, and, in turn, offer you opportunity for growth. Second, it will demonstrate to the interviewer that you are inventive, imaginative, yet grounded in reality. You understand the company's product or services; you're not suggesting radical new products or services unrelated to the company as it is currently set up, but logical extensions of what the firm already does. Try something like this:

> I noticed that you've extended your line of [product A] into the [product B] market. Is line extension an important part of the company's mission?

Or

> I really admire your [product A]. Is the company planning to extend the [product A] line into [products B and C]?

New Lines

Questions in this area require more caution. If the company you're interviewing with is clearly conservative, living off long-established product/service lines, you may simply want to avoid new-line questions. However, if the company has a track record of innovation, pick up on it. Avoid storming in with a let-me-show-you-how-it's-done attitude. Instead of trotting out your new-product ideas, engage the interviewer by allowing him to talk about his brainchild:

> Acme Industries has such a stunning track record of innovation. What new product line are you most excited about?

Then, respond to the interviewer in a way that keeps the conversation going. This is a subject that the interviewer probably enjoys talking about. Show him that you're interested. Let him feel good speaking with you.

Talk the Talk

A **line extension** is a new product or service that is a continuous, logical development of the products or services a firm currently offers. For example, a maker of breakfast cereal may introduce a line of snack foods (such as chewy bars) based on the cereal.

The Skinny

New products or services typically account for 40 percent of a company's annual sales.

Market-Share Growth

If nothing else—even if the company does not define its mission in terms of line extensions or new lines—mission is usually defined in terms of making organized efforts to increase the firm's share of the existing market. Engage this issue:

> What steps are being taken to increase market share, and how does this position fit into that effort?

Being a Prophet of Profitability

Although you want to avoid making promises that are as empty as they are bold— "Hire me, and I'll make you untold millions!"—it is never amiss to ask questions aimed directly at the bottom line. Put yourself on the spot:

> How would my performance be measured?

Once this question is answered, shift briefly to an apparently selfish mode:

> Obviously, I intend to perform at top level. It will keep us profitable and competitive. But, in addition to this, how is performance usually rewarded here?

The question shows that you have the common concerns of the company uppermost in mind, but that you are also a realist when it comes to yourself. You don't want to give the interviewer the impression that you are too good to be true (and too good to be truthful). However, you do want to demonstrate that your self-interest coincides with the interests of the company.

Don't Call Us ...

Ask for a job description. Never demand one. Many employers, especially in smaller companies, do not prepare formal job descriptions. If the interviewer tells you that a job description is not available, drop the request without further comment.

Demonstrating Proficiency

At some point in the interview, insert a question or two that demonstrates sheer proficiency. If you've never been given a full, written job description, ask for one now.

> Is there a written description of this position? May I see it?

Study it quickly and offer whatever intelligent comments you can on the duties as described. Demonstrate your essential understanding of the job.

If the position for which you are interviewing involves knowledge of special procedures or techniques, try to ask questions related to these. For example:

> Do you report on a cash basis or an accrual basis?

Don't get into an argument over the merits of one versus the other. If you agree with the choice of method, discuss its merits. If you disagree, ask more questions:

> That's interesting. Why do you use that method?

If you are genuinely concerned about the firm's choice of policy or methodology, ask if there is room for flexibility:

> Is there any room for flexibility on that?

Questions That Show You're a Leader

Tread softly in this area. Questions that convey leadership may also be interpreted as challenges to existing authority. The last thing you want is to present yourself to an interviewer as a potential threat to his or her job.

Matters of Clout

A relatively nonthreatening question to assess the level of authority you'll be accorded is this one:

> Can you give me an idea of how much leeway I'll have in determining my own work objectives, schedules, and deadlines?

Anything beyond this type of question risks being too aggressive. Feel your way carefully.

Take-Charge Attitude

There is a difference between taking charge and staging an invasion. Here are two questions that demonstrate your willingness to give direction and take responsibility without stepping on any toes—or gunning for anyone's job:

> How many people would I be supervising? What are their backgrounds?

This takes up the gauntlet of responsibility while framing a question that merely asks for information. Continue:

> I'm curious as to why you are looking outside for candidates for this position rather than promoting from within. Is that something we could discuss?

Clincher

Link questions about authority and clout to questions about responsibility: "Will I be *responsible* for setting my own schedules and deadlines?" *Not* "Will I have the *authority* to set my own schedules and deadlines?"

*to this may provide just the launching pad you need to discuss the role ...hip in the position under consideration.

...ing Your Team Spirit

...on't let leadership-focused questions leave the impression that you're a loose cannon. Ask some of the following:

➤ "How would you describe your management style?"

➤ "Is there a management training program or a management development program in place? How active is it?"

➤ "Does the corporate culture here promote team building?"

Getting the answers to questions about reporting levels (see "Reporting Levels" below) is also an effective way to approach issues of leadership roles.

The Nitty-Gritty

In addition to the strategic questions—questions intended to convey as much information about you as they glean about the employer and his firm—don't leave the interview or proceed to the salary negotiating stage without having obtained a full understanding of the duties, responsibilities, and reporting levels the job entails.

Duties and Responsibilities

If no job description has been furnished, ask:

What are the chief duties and responsibilities of [job title]?

Even if a description was made available to you, it pays to ask:

Are there any duties and responsibilities listed in the job description that you see as especially critical?

And

Does the job description cover all the duties and responsibilities you think are important? Is there anything else I should know about?

Reporting Levels

Assess your relative position in the organization by nailing down an official version of the hierarchy:

To whom would I report in this position?

158

When you've secured the answer, inquire about your prospective supervisor:

And he/she reports to ...?

That should be sufficient to provide a quick sketch of the organizational structure of the department or firm. Some authorities suggest requesting a formal organizational chart, but this could be seen as an imposition. Don't make the interviewer work on your behalf.

When to Stop

Don't ask questions just to hear yourself talk. Each of your questions should either say something about yourself or obtain the vital information you need to make your decisions. Ideally, your questions will accomplish both objectives. When you sense that you've broadcast and obtained all the information that is important to you and the employer, stop asking questions. You should also stop any time the interviewer indicates that the interview is at an end.

The Least You Need to Know

➤ Ask dual-purpose questions, aimed at gathering information while broadcasting your qualifications and skills.

➤ Train yourself to walk into the interview *assuming* you will get the offer.

➤ Ask questions that always allow you to demonstrate your value to the prospective employer.

Real-World Questions

All employers look for the same things some of the time, and some employers look for the same things all of the time, but all employers don't look for the same things all of the time. Not only do certain needs and problems vary from one employer to another, but also from one industry to another. Pre-interview research will help you assess the issues specific to a company, and such research is also valuable for scoping out the needs of an industry. This chapter also suggests some key questions to raise when you interview in any of six major fields: sales, marketing, service, financial, R&D (research and development), and production.

One Size Does Not Fit All

You should not fail to ask the kinds of questions covered in the preceding two chapters. They apply to virtually any employment situation, because they relate to your transferable skills, the skills that you carry with you, rather than those required by a particular job. This said, jobs are not *all* about transferable skills. They are also very much about specialized skills and qualifications that are specifically targeted to certain tasks. Before your interview, you should certainly research these functional areas of the target position and prepare some relevant questions. Your ability to ask the right questions will, in itself, be a practical demonstration of your knowledge and qualifications. The conversation such questions may spark will not only showcase your talents, but also give you valuable additional information about the job.

If You're in Sales ...

Interviewing for a sales position is unique in that the entire interview process is an opportunity to display your sales prowess. As the interviewer sees it, if you're a good salesperson, you will succeed in selling yourself at the interview. In the interviewer's estimation, if you fail to sell yourself, you are not, *ipso facto*, a good salesperson. At some level of your consciousness, you are keenly aware of this, and, consequently, the pressure in an interview for a sales position is especially high. The emphasis is on performance, on selling yourself. And that is how it should be, but—and this is critical—not to the exclusion of other key considerations.

If you concentrate exclusively on selling yourself, on deliberately demonstrating your salesmanship at every turn, on focusing attention on yourself as merchandise, you risk coming off as self-centered, insecure, and, ultimately, unaware of a number of important realities that a sales position entails.

The questions that follow assume that you have been conducting the interview as a "sale," and that you have *answered* questions that demonstrate your aptitude for the position. Now it's your turn to ask questions that go beyond an eager—maybe overeager—desire to exhibit your skills. Ask questions that reveal your sophistication and savvy, that in some degree require the employer to sell *her* organization to *you.*

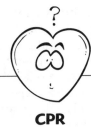

CPR

Getting into an argument is a danger inherent in discussions about the professional or technical details of a position: how a certain job is done. You may have one way of doing things, and the employer may have another. An employment interview is definitely not the time and place to get into a professional argument. If you find yourself drawn into one, step back. You won't win the argument in the course of the interview. You *may* eventually succeed in bringing about professional or procedural change, but only if you get the job. For now, stay cool: "I have to admit, Ms. Adams, that's not the way I've handled this operation in the past. I do think that my method has merit, but I'm willing to work it your way. The most important thing is that my skills should mesh with your procedures—especially if those procedures are working well for you."

and its customers, developing ongoing business rather than putting the emphasis on one isolated sale after the other? Or is it a place content to leave its sales force—and its customers—to twist slowly in the wind?

Reporting Structure

The sales professional almost always faces challenges to his integrity. Customers—especially new prospects—are typically wary. Well, that comes with the territory, and it's an important part of the sales professional's task to earn the trust and confidence of the customer, to build the business customer by customer, rather than merely sale by sale. But if integrity is the primary issue, authority is an important secondary, complicating issue. Your prospects and customers need to know that you have the *authority* to make deals, and that the deals you make are definitive. It is, therefore, vitally important for you to learn about the reporting structure of the organization that may hire you:

> To whom would I report in this position?

If necessary, follow this up with questions that clarify the reporting supervisor's level of authority.

It's quite possible that the interviewer will take her cue from your question and launch into an explanation that defines the level of your authority. If not, you must ask the clarifying question:

> The reason I'm so interested in the reporting structure is that I need to have a clear picture of just how much authority and latitude I will have to negotiate and conclude deals with customers. You know how important it is for the customer to feel that he is dealing with someone in authority, whose word is definitive. Can you address this issue?

If your hands are going to be tied, you'd better find out now.

Expectations

Let's say you went to college, got a business degree, did pretty well at that, but just barely scraped by in those Science 101 requirements. That physics course almost killed you! Now, knowing what you know about your interests and aptitude where physics is concerned, you wouldn't apply for a job as a rocket scientist. You know that you could never meet the employer's expectations.

Yet many job candidates fail to clarify issues of expectation during the interview. While this is a most consequential omission, it is an understandable one. You may fear that bringing up the subject of expectations is somehow a confession of your limitations. It's easier just to make claims and promises (truthful or not) and, for the present, assume that you'll meet them (which you'll then put off worrying about until you find yourself drowning in the job).

But the fact is that reality is ultimately more persuasive than empty claims. Frame your questions about employer expectations as positively as possible, with an assurance that you are asking the questions in order to ensure that you will satisfy the employer:

> What do you consider a good, solid level of productivity for an incoming salesperson?

Only after you have this figure, should you establish whether or not there is a *minimum* requirement:

> Do you have an absolute minimum target?

Wrap up with something like this:

> Ms. Smith, I want to make certain that I can satisfy your needs in this position. Are there any other expectations you'd like me to know
> about?

Clincher

Try to obtain a statement of expectation expressed in numbers—sales volume, units sold, clients contacted, and so forth. Vague, subjective expressions of expectation are of little help to you and may lead to mutual disappointment later.

Compensation Basis

Don't confuse questions concerning compensation basis with salary negotiation. Certainly, it's important to negotiate the level of your compensation, but it's also of crucial importance to clarify the *basis* on which that compensation is determined:

> Can we review the subject of commissions?

That question may be all you need. In addition, however, you may need to clarify:

➤ Balance between salary and commission

➤ Varying levels of commission—depending on product, price, terms, and so on

➤ Policies on splitting commissions

➤ Performance bonuses and other incentives

Don't Call Us ...

Avoid phrasing a question about expectations this way: "I want to make sure I can do the job." Never say anything that prompts the interviewer to question your ability. Instead, frame all questions regarding expectations in terms of providing satisfaction.

If You're in Marketing ...

Marketing continues to be a growth area for employment opportunity; however, few functional areas are subject to as much variation in definition and expectation as marketing. The consequences of such confusion range from a botched interview to a disastrous employment situation.

Mission

Certainly, it would be a mistake to start a marketing interview by asking, "Yes, I have a question. Just what is marketing?" It is very savvy, however, to ask *this* question:

> How would you define the mission of marketing in this organization (or department)?

It's a great question, and one you should always ask. Just don't expect the answer to measure up to the question. You will probably be shocked and dismayed by how little thought the employer has devoted to the marketing mission. But at the very least, your question will show that you are capable of thinking about something that the organization's current employees *should* be thinking about. Most importantly, the question can become a springboard to a fruitful discussion about the mission of marketing. If this discussion succeeds in raising the level of your interview above the routine, it will cause you to stand out in the interviewer's memory and give you a competitive edge over other candidates.

Relation to Other Departments

Another area of ambiguity and wide variation from organization to organization is the relation of marketing to other departments. In some firms, marketing effectively calls the shots or, at least, leads research and development (R&D), sales, advertising, and other efforts. In other firms, marketing may be little more than a reporting and analyzing service. Often, it is called in *after* R&D and production decisions have been made: "We've decided to make this widget. Now, go figure out how to market it."

The Skinny

Although job opportunities for market research analysts are plentiful, the prospects for growth and promotion are mediocre to poor in most organizations.

Establish just where marketing stands in relation to other components of the organization:

> How does marketing work with other functions here?

If necessary, sharpen the focus of the question:

> Would you say that marketing leads or follows the other departments?

Role of Innovation

That last question is a natural lead-in to the issue of innovation. You will want to determine what role innovation plays in the target company and what role marketing plays in innovation.

> Is innovation a significant part of your program?

If your pre-interview research has already revealed that innovation is a significant aspect of the firm's strategy, don't ask a superfluous question; just leap in to clarify the role of marketing in innovation:

> From what I've learned about the firm, innovation is a vital part of your corporate mission. Where does marketing fit into this? Does it lead the innovation effort? Does it follow the lead of R&D?

Reporting Structure

Marketing departments are typically either easy places in which to stick your neck out—and risk getting it chopped off—or, conversely, places in which you can find yourself buried under multiple reporting layers, your clout muffled, your chances for credit greatly compromised. Find out to whom you report, and to whom he or she reports in turn:

> To whom would I report in this position?

If You're in Service ...

Customer service is finally coming of age. For too long, too many organizations viewed the service function as a kind of necessary evil: It was something you had to provide, but it generated no revenue. Traditionally, it was classed as a support service, not a profit center. Lately, however, customer service has been seen as an important part of the *value* customers purchase. Just think of the role a reputation for good customer service plays, for example, in your decision to purchase one brand of personal computer over another. Even more, it's being looked at as an extension of the sales function: The customer-service specialist can use his or her customer contact to educate the customer about new products and accessories and to *upsell* accessories and related products.

Talk the Talk

To **upsell** is to use the customer-service function as an opportunity to offer customers accessories and other products related to their original purchase.

Mission

Precisely because the mission of customer service is in flux, you will want to ask questions that define it. Based on the answers you receive, you'll have to decide whether you can accept the challenge of a sales-oriented service operation—if that's what you're confronting—or be content with a more back-office role in organizations where customer service is strictly a support function:

> How would you define the mission of customer service in this organization?

Relation to Sales

Depending on the answer to the mission question, you may find it necessary to obtain clarification of the relationship between service and sales. Try a question like this:

> Do your customer service people do much upselling?

Then go on to a nitty-gritty question:

> What is the relation between sales and service? Is there active, ongoing communication between the departments?

The Skinny

When you ask about workload, be certain to frame your questions to focus on the needs of the employer, not on your desire to be out the door by five each day: "My concern is to have ample time with each call to ensure customer satisfaction."

Client Load

One of the hot-button issues in service is client load. Especially in high-tech industries, such as software manufacturers and makers of personal-computer hardware, customer support can be brutally time-intensive. Client load is an area you need to probe thoroughly in the course of the interview:

> What is the typical per-hour, per-representative client load?

You may define this further:

> The average customer-support call lasts how long?

And

> Typically, how long are callers put on hold?

168

If You're in Financial ...

Financial positions vary widely. If it's not clear from the job description, your major objective will be to determine to what degree the position is an accounting function—essentially financial reporting—and to what degree it is an analytical function—predictive and heavily involved in creating financial projections.

Mission

Avoid disappointment on your part or on that of the employer by asking questions that define the mission of the financial department in general and the nature of your prospective job in particular:

> Is the mission of this department primarily reporting or analytical?

Or

> Approximately what percentage of the position's responsibilities deal with financial projection, and what percentage deal with financial reporting?

Reporting Structure

In financial positions it is of critical importance to understand the reporting structure that is in place.

> To whom does this position report?

Follow up with:

> And to whom does [position's supervisor] report?

Income and growth potential are typically proportional to the degree of discretionary authority you are given. The more layers of management that stand between you and the top, the less authority you will enjoy.

Special Goals

While the mission questions should define the broad goals and objectives of the department, it would be thoughtful to add a question about any special goals. For example:

> Are there any special circumstances that call for the department to capture certain kinds of data for specialized purposes?

If You're in R&D (Research and Development) ...

Typically, interviews for R&D positions involve specialized technical issues that are beyond the scope of this book; however, you should not neglect the following, more general subject areas.

Mission

It's likely that your pre-interview research will have revealed the thrust of R&D's mission—at least in historical terms—in the target organization. If not, you could begin with:

> How would you define R&D's mission in this organization?

If you do come to the interview with some idea of the department's mission, ask questions that build on your knowledge:

> It's apparent that, historically, R&D has been involved in XYZ. Do you see that involvement continuing, or is the mission developing in different directions?

Autonomy and Reporting Structure

Creativity and accountability are not always easy to balance. Be sure to craft some questions that address issues of creative autonomy versus the department's reporting structure. Try something like this:

> How are work groups organized in this department?

You will also want to ask the usual "To whom do I report?" question.

Expectations

Clarify issues of workload and the measures by which progress and achievement are judged:

> How does the department evaluate—and reward—accomplishment?

If You're in Production ...

As is the case with R&D, the primary issues in production-oriented interviews are likely to be technical and specialized. Beyond this, the most central issues are likely to revolve around expectations.

Expectations

You don't want to leave the interview without a clear idea of what is expected in the production function in terms of volume and quality of work. Quantify expectations as much as possible:

> I understand that this position has been created to increase efficiency. What is your target increase?

Or

> What is our goal above and beyond the current rate of production?

Don't Call Us ...

Reserve comment if you discover that the employer's expectations are unrealistic. Avoid shaking your head, gasping, laughing, or muttering "Impossible!" Instead, ask the employer what she is currently achieving. Get more information. Discuss—do not judge—the employer's unrealistic expectations. Remember, you can always turn down a job offer—but only *if* the interview produces one. Don't mislead the interviewer, but do keep the discussion upbeat.

Relation to Other Departments

Ask questions to assess just where production fits into the structural picture. For example:

> What kind of input does production customarily have in new product development?

Or

> Is there a permanent liaison between production and sales?

Reporting Structure

Like customer service, production is a function in which you can either shine or be buried. To a significant degree, the fate that awaits you hinges on the reporting structure in place. Ask the usual questions:

> To whom does the person in this position report?

And

> [Job title's] supervisor reports to whom?

The Least You Need to Know

➤ Although you should not become bogged down in questions related to the details of a specific job, do tailor your questions to fit specific fields and functional areas.

➤ Real-world questions reveal your practical grasp of a field or functional area.

➤ Be careful to ensure that your nitty-gritty questions are not phrased as challenges to the interviewer. Their purpose is both to gather information and to demonstrate your grasp of the position in question.

Part 4

Special Settings and Challenging Circumstances

Most of us picture the employment interview as essentially a one-on-one meeting, strictly questions and answers. Sometimes it is just that. But often—and, these days, more often than not—the interview is a combination of variations on the traditional, one-on-one scenario.

The chapters that follow show you how to initiate an "informational interview," and how to avoid being screened out in a preliminary interview. With more and more preliminary interviewing being done on the phone, it's essential to know how to put yourself across when you're not face to face. Here, you'll find a chapter devoted to the telephone interview.

Then there are the special situation interviews, including mealtime interviews, panel interviews, sequential or serial interviews, and computer-assisted interviews. Excelling in these special circumstances requires special skills, and you'll find help acquiring them here.

Creating an Interview

You know the routine. Answer an ad or send a letter of inquiry and resumé, and, if all goes very well, you'll get a call for an interview. It's like a dance party 50 or 60 years ago: The boy's job was to ask the girl to dance. And the girl's job? She was supposed to wait until asked.

But just as all that began to change in the 1960s, so has the etiquette of the interview. You no longer have to wait for someone to respond favorably to your resumé before you secure an interview. You—yes, *you*—can take the initiative and *ask* for an interview. Here's how.

Wallflower No More

Begin by understanding this: The interview you ask for is not an employment interview, at least not directly. It is instead an *informational interview,* an attempt to collect

Talk the Talk

An **informational interview** is an interview you request in order to gather information about a particular company or an entire industry. The purpose of such an interview is to enlarge your business network, to meet potential employers, to learn from them, and to allow them to make your acquaintance. Immediate employment is not an objective of the informational interview.

information about specific careers and companies. And it's important that you approach the informational interview this way, rather than as a thinly disguised effort to "get a foot in the door" and land a job. The informational interview is a step in a process. To be sure, if you're offered a job during this interview, consider it. But don't expect it, and don't push for it. Your objectives are:

➤ Information gathering
➤ Information broadcasting

Let me explain. It's important to learn as much as you can about your target company and your target industry. The informational interview is valuable for this. But it's also important to make yourself known to the people who matter—people within potential target companies as well as within your target industry generally. Eventually, you have every reason to hope, these contacts may pay off in terms of employment, but the object is not an immediate ticket to a job.

Five Steps to an Informational Interview

The informational interview won't come to you. That's because it doesn't exist until you create it. Too many of us think of a job as something that *happens* to us, and we think of a company or an industry as a place into which we are invited. Sometimes things do work out just that way, but waiting passively for good fortune can consume a great deal of time. The informational interview is an opportunity to take control and to *make* things happen.

Step 1: Identify Your Targets

The first step is to identify your targets. You'll need to decide just what it is that interests you. Perhaps you already know; perhaps you are still looking. If you need help—or need to stimulate your career thinking—resources abound. Here are some "general outlook" books that may start your creative juices flowing:

➤ *The Adams Jobs Almanac* (Holbrook, MA: Adams Publishing, updated annually)
➤ Les Krantz, *Jobs Rated Almanac*, (New York: St. Martin's Press, 1999)
➤ *Occupational Outlook Handbook for College Graduates* (Washington, D.C.: Superintendent of Documents, U.S. Government Printing Office, updated frequently)

➤ Carter Smith, ed., *America's Fastest Growing Employers: The Complete Guide to Finding Jobs with Over 300 of America's Hottest Companies* (Holbrook, MA: Adams Publishing, 1994)

➤ U.S. Department of Labor, *Occupational Outlook Handbook* (Lincolnwood, IL: NTC Publishing Group, updated frequently)

Once you've narrowed your focus to a particular industry, start finding and reading the news concerning the target industry in the general and business press. You might contact the publicity offices of various firms in the industry. Get copies of speeches by the CEO and obtain industry-related press releases. Go to the local public library and consult *The Reader's Guide to Periodical Literature* to locate articles on the industry and on various firms and individuals involved in the industry.

Step 2: Evaluate Your Targets

After you've determined where your interests lie, you'll need to evaluate the industry and firms within the industry. You'll want to look at two dimensions:

1. Where the action is.

2. Where the action is likely to be.

Look for industries and firms that are hiring now. More specifically, look for industries and firms that are currently hiring people with your skills. Remember, however, that just because an industry is "hot"—frequently mentioned in the press, and often the topic of conversation—does not necessarily mean that jobs are plentiful. Hot industries may indeed require many new hires, but they may also be relatively closed or glutted with applicants for a few plum positions.

This brings us to the second dimension of your evaluation. The savvy investor never devotes large sums to "mature" companies—those that have done about all the growing they're going to do.

Clincher

A readily accessible way to identify growth companies, growth industries, and growth markets is to read the stock quotation pages in your daily newspaper. Track companies that show a pattern of upward movement in stock prices. These are likely to be the firms engaged in promising growth. If they are bristling with opportunity for the investor, they probably offer opportunity to the potential employee, too.

Follow this investor's lead, and look for industries and companies poised for growth and expansion in expanding markets. There is no magic formula for finding such industries and firms, and nothing takes the place of research and generally keeping your eyes and ears open. Be on the lookout for news articles on cutting-edge industries and make an effort to pick up the "buzz" on predicted growth areas.

Step 3: Identify the People with the Power to Hire You

Face it: No company will ever hire you.

Now that I have your attention, read on: No company ever hires anybody.

A *person* hires you. People hire people. You'll never get an interview with General Motors, or AT&T, or General Foods, or Microsoft. What you will get is the opportunity to speak with a human being associated with one of these firms. And the real trick is finding just the right human being among the five, ten, or twenty thousand employees who work for the typical mega-organization.

The *real* trick? Actually, it's easy to decide on the right person to talk to. Choose the one who has the authority—the clout—to hire you.

Well, where do you find him or her?

If you play by the rules, you'll dutifully go through the target firm's Human Resources department. Unfortunately, that's the one place you're sure *not* to find the person with the power to hire you. Typically, HR departments are staffed by relatively low-level folks whose principal job is to screen out unsuitable job candidates, not scout out talent.

Clincher

Don't limit your research to books, magazines, and newspapers. If your target career or industry produces something sold in retail stores, start window shopping. Look at the product or products in question, and ask the store manager or assistant manager or the cash-register clerk how the merchandise has been moving and what people say about it.

The easiest way to find the person with the clout to hire you is to apply exclusively to companies with fewer than 50 employees. Call such a place and ask for the name of the boss. That's the person who can give you a job.

But maybe you can't—or just don't want to—limit yourself to small firms. Researching the larger firms should begin to turn up names of the people in charge. Go back to the public library and look for any of the following:

➤ Daniel Starer, *Who Knows What: The Essential Business Resource Book* (New York: Henry Holt, 1992)

➤ *Contacts Influential: Commerce and Industry Directory* (San Francisco: Contacts Influential, Market Research and Development Services, updated frequently)

➤ *Standard and Poor's Register of Corporations, Directors and Executives* (Standard and Poor, updated regularly)

In addition to library research, you should build up and work your network. Ask just about everyone you know for help with identifying the person with the power to hire you at Such-and-Such Corporation. Don't give up if you don't get an answer right away. Try this: "Do you know anybody who works at Such-and-Such—or who used to work there?"

The Skinny

Since 1970, companies with 100 employees or fewer have created two out of every three jobs.

If you get a name and phone number from one of your network contacts, secure permission to use his or her name: "May I tell So-and-so that you recommended I call?"

The next step is to make the call. Explain that you are interested in scoping out career opportunities at Such-and-Such Corporation and that So-and-so recommended you call. Ask: "Who would I contact who has the authority to hire me for a [job title] position?"

Step 4: Make the Call

Once you've identified the person who can hire you, pick up the phone and bid for an in-person interview, if possible and practical. (If an in-person interview cannot be arranged—for example, if the target employer is located in another city, and you don't want to invest in the travel expenses—try to arrange for a later telephone interview.)

If you obtained the person's name from one of your contacts, make certain that you secure permission to use his or her name. You might even ask your contact to call ahead on your behalf. If, however, you obtained the name through your own research, let that be your lead-off point:

> Mr. Crawford, my name is Sarah Ferguson. I've been doing quite a bit of reading about your company, and, in just about everything I've read, your name appears prominently.

Step 5: Explain Yourself

So much for the opening sentence or two. Next? Well, don't ask for an interview. Indeed, *ask* for nothing. Instead, make an offer:

> I am the assistant controller at International Widgets, where I've been involved in upgrading our audit systems. I've been able to cut general audit turnaround time by 20 percent here, and I would be grateful for the opportunity to discuss with you how what I've learned at International might benefit Such-and-Such Corporation.

Appealing in some immediate way to your target's self-interest is a far more effective way to begin the conversation than telling him or her what *you* want.

If you're just starting out or, for some other reason, feel that you have no special information or insight to share, you can still make an offer. Offer the opportunity to help:

> Mr. Blank, Mary Wheeler suggested that you might be willing to help me with some informal advice. Mary spoke very highly of your expertise in the direct mail marketing of widgets. I've been with Acme Widgets myself for the past two years. I'm now assistant sales manager, but I would like to move into the marketing side. The move is getting a bit urgent. You may be aware—since you're apparently aware of just about everything that goes on in this industry—that Acme is beginning a down-sizing program. While I don't seem to be in immediate danger personally, I know my department is going to be reduced, along with opportunities generally.
>
> Here's how you could help me. I am hoping that we could sit down together for a few minutes—at your convenience—to discuss direct mail approaches to widget marketing. Your insights into where the industry is going and whom I should contact would mean a great deal to me. I'd also be grateful for any feedback you might have to offer on my own background and experience.

Is this request really an "offer"? After all, what does the employer get out of it? The fact is that most people welcome an opportunity to be helpful. It's not only flattering, but also gratifying. It feels good. You are offering an opportunity to feel good.

Only if your target expresses interest, either in what you have to offer or in helping you, should you set up an interview. Don't leave any loose ends here. Suggest a time for the interview: "I would be available next week, either Tuesday or Thursday morning. Would that be convenient for you?" If it isn't convenient, negotiate a time that works. Be certain to get directions to the office, including room numbers, floor, and so on.

Do not put off writing a thank-you note confirming the interview time and place. Dash one off as soon as you hang up. Although it should be friendly and informal, type it rather than hand-write it.

It would be nice if it were always this easy. Unfortunately, it's possible that your target may turn you down flat, claiming that he is too busy for a meeting. If that happens, reply politely: "I understand that you're busy …" Or: "I understand that you're not hiring at present and that your schedule doesn't give you much leeway just now." Then continue:

Don't Call Us …

Beware of offering proprietary or privileged information that belongs to your present employer! It's not only unethical, but it may be illegal and is certainly grounds for dismissal.

"Circumstances do change, however, so may I send you my resumé for your reference?"

It's unlikely that your target will say no to that. Follow through with the resumé, along with a thank-you/cover letter. Keep the tone of the letter positive so that you confirm your contact with the target employer while declining to reinforce his impression that he has rejected you. This might just be the foundation on which later contact is built.

What ARE You About?

But let's assume you're in, that you've scored at least a few minutes of face-to-face contact with someone who has the power to hire you. Congratulations!

Now what?

Offer Something

Make good on the promise that got you the interview. If you have certain insights, experience, skills, or knowledge to share, begin by sharing them. If you are "offering" an opportunity for the employer to help you, follow through and reiterate that. Whatever you do, do *not* begin by putting out your hand for employment.

The Questions to Ask

While the face-to-face phase of the informational interview should be informal, don't leave it unstructured. After thanking the person for seeing you, reiterating who recommended that you call, and reminding him of the reason for your visit—including a quick review of your situation and interests—begin the conversation. Provide a thumbnail sketch of your background. Prepare it beforehand and pare it down to no more than a three-minute presentation.

After you've presented the thumbnail sketch, open up the discussion with the following questions:

➤ How did you get started in this line of work?

> **Don't Call Us ...**
>
> Beware of renewed resistance if your conversation partner suspects you are just trying to get a foot in *his* door. Fend this off with preemptive assurance: "I want to emphasize that I am not here to hit you up for a job. At this point in my job search, I'm just looking for information—surveying the nature of the marketplace. Of course, if you know of any specific opportunities, I'd appreciate hearing about them. But I haven't come here with that expectation."

➤ What do you like most about it?

➤ What do you dislike most about it?

Then broaden the discussion:

➤ What are your views on the present state and future prospects of the industry?

➤ Can you recommend anyone else I might speak with?

Limit the Time

In a formal job interview, it's up to the interviewer to end the session. He or she decides when your time is up. In an informational interview, however, you should serve as timekeeper. Unless the conversation clearly warrants more time, try to limit the interview to no more than 15 or 20 minutes. If the other person shows any impatience, you should pick up the cue and signal that you are ready to wrap things up:

> Ms. Smith, I know you're busy, and I appreciate your having given me this time. I have just two more questions.

CPR

Televised Academy Award and Emmy Award ceremonies used to feature a set with a sweeping staircase, down which the award presenters would walk to the podium. Who could watch presenter after presenter walk down those stairs without thinking, *What if she trips?* It rarely happens, but it can happen. And when you are nervous, your feet may feel like lead and your legs may be knotted and reluctant to move. If you obviously stumble while making your entrance into the interview, it's important to get the incident behind you and the interviewer *pronto*. Neither ignore it, nor berate yourself as a clumsy, worthless oaf. Try something like this: "I always try to make a memorable entrance. Maybe I've succeeded this time." Then, offer your hand for the greeting shake: "Hello. I'm John Smith."

Don't Look for a Job Here (at Least, Not Now)

As you bring the interview to its concluding phase, reiterate that your purpose has not been to find immediate employment at this firm; nevertheless, you should ask some or all of the following questions:

➤ "Would you happen to know of any openings available now?"

➤ "Would you personally know any employers who might want to see me?"

➤ "Have you heard of any developments that might suggest a particular company would be interested in what I have to offer?"

➤ "What's the best way for me to get connected—to get into a position to hear about employment developments?"

Finally, take a leaf from the book of New York City's colorful former mayor Ed Koch. His trademark tag line was "How'm I doin'?" Ask for a similar report card on yourself:

➤ "Is my background clear to you? Do I present it effectively?"

➤ "Are my objectives clear?"

➤ "Do you think my objectives are feasible?"

If you sense that the partner in your conversation is willing to continue, you might ask a few more specific and challenging questions:

➤ "Are there certain skills or credentials I need to acquire?"

➤ "Do you see any problem areas for me, given my background?"

➤ "Is there anything in my background that is particularly appealing or strong, that I should emphasize?"

The last question is important because it ends on a positive note. Not only might it secure valuable information for you, but it will also leave this individual with an impression of you based on strengths rather than problems and areas that need improvement.

The Least You Need to Know

➤ Do not expect immediate employment from an informational interview. Its purpose is to obtain information while getting yourself known in an industry or at a company. It is but one step in a process.

➤ Do not seek informational interviews at random; research the target industry and employer beforehand.

➤ Companies never hire people. People (who work for companies) hire people. Identify and seek the person with the power to hire you.

Chapter 17

Getting Through the Gatekeeper Interview

In This Chapter

➤ What is a screening interview?

➤ Who conducts the interview?

➤ The screening interview versus the selection interview: How do they differ?

➤ Objectives of the screening interview

➤ What the screening interviewer is looking for

➤ Questions to expect and how to answer them

Officially, it may be called a preliminary interview. Internally, it's probably referred to as a screening interview. In fact, it's a *gatekeeper* interview. Its purpose is not to identify and harvest talent, but to eliminate "unacceptable" candidates in order to save the valuable time of the senior executive—the person with the power to hire you. In many large organizations, interviewing is a two-step process. First a Human Resources person screens you. If you aren't screened out, your name is sent to the person or persons who have the clout to hire you. It's up to him, her, or them to conduct an in-depth (*selection*) interview.

Screening interviews are inherently frustrating for the job candidate because the object is not so much to win as it is not to lose; that is, the object is to evade the screen. This chapter shows you how.

The First Cut—So What?

You open your morning mail. There's a letter from XYZ Corporation. Your hand trembles as you run your fingers around the edge of the envelope. Good news? Or bad? In? Or out? At last you get up the nerve to open it.

Talk the Talk

A **screening interview** is a preliminary interview typically conducted by a junior-level Human Resources staffer. Its purpose is to screen out unqualified job candidates, so that (theoretically) only qualified candidates are interviewed by the supervisors who are actually authorized to hire.

It begins with the pronoun "we." Now, that's usually bad news. Employers prefer to frame rejection in terms of a collective "we" rather than a personal and individual "I." But you read on.

No. Wait. Yes! XYZ wants to interview you! They were impressed with your resumé, your background, your qualifications. But, just another minute, the letter is *not* signed by Ms. T.J. Krumm, Manager of Sales, to whom you had addressed your cover letter and resumé, but by a Larry Larson, Human Resources Associate.

What gives?

This is your signal that you've been selected for a *screening interview*. Sure, you've made the first cut, but so what?

A Lesson from the Hippocratic Oath

Upon taking their medical degrees, many graduates still recite the Hippocratic Oath, composed by the great physician of ancient Greece, Hippocrates (ca. 460 B.C.E.–ca. 377 B.C.E.). Its initial precept is "First, do no harm."

This rule doesn't just apply to doctors; it also serves those who suddenly find themselves in a screening interview. Remember, first and foremost, the screening interviewer is looking for *negatives*—reasons to weed you out—not positive reasons to take your candidacy to the next step. Once you understand the nature of a screening interview, you'll need to adjust your objectives and interview strategy accordingly. To "do no harm," observe the following:

Talk the Talk

A **selection interview** is the in-depth interview conducted by the person or persons who have the authority to hire you. In larger organizations, this interview is often preceded by a screening interview.

➤ During in-depth interviews (or *selection interviews*), it's a good idea to take the initiative, but in the screening interview it is best to follow the interviewer's lead.

➤ Respond to questions as directly and as concisely as possible. Do not digress. Do not evade the question. Do not shoot the breeze or otherwise make small talk.

➤ Avoid introducing negatives or potential negatives. Emphasize positive qualifications, strengths, and skills.

➤ By all means, be courteous, pleasant, and polite, but don't make an extra effort to put your personality in the spotlight. Stick to the facts.

Foot in the Door (Not in the Mouth)

Stick to the facts. Let's investigate just what this means and why you should proceed this way.

First, just who is the screening interviewer, anyway?

➤ She may be a Human Resources professional, which means that she may have some training in interview methodology, but has little specialized knowledge of the field in which you are interviewing.

➤ She is probably asking questions prepared by the department or person who is actually doing the hiring. More than likely, she is following a requisition form filled out by the person or department requesting a new hire.

➤ The interviewer may not be an HR person, but a lower-level staffer in the department that is doing the hiring.

➤ He may be the assistant to the person who is actually doing the hiring.

➤ He may be a secretary or receptionist.

Whatever the screening interviewer does for a living, he or she does not have the power to hire you. He or she does have the power to screen you out and end your candidacy for the position.

What, exactly, is the screening interviewer's mission?

➤ First and foremost, to find reasons to send you packing

➤ Second, to note a solid background and promising levels of qualifications and skills

As a rule, candidates are summoned to screening interviews because a resumé, cover letter, colleague's recommendation, telephone conversation, or query letter has roused the interest of the

The Skinny

The screening interviewer's supervisors judge his performance by the volume of candidates he screens out and by the absence of complaints about unqualified candidates slipping through the initial screen.

person who actually has the power to hire—or has roused the interest of the person delegated to review incoming resumés. Since interest at this point is based on the alleged facts of the resumé or some other equivalent, the screening interviewer will likely ask questions designed to uncover inconsistencies in your background and possible discrepancies in your resumé. In other words, the screening interviewer is looking for:

> ➤ Glitches in your employment history
> ➤ Gaps in your employment history
> ➤ Evidence of lying about the "facts" you have presented

This is not a very friendly approach to the task of interviewing. Now, I'm not saying that the screening interviewer is an evil person. He has a tough job, and, in a large organization that may be flooded with job applicants—many with dubious qualifications—he may even have a worthwhile job. But it *is* just that: a job. The screening interview is mainly a clerical function. Only the most rudimentary judgment is being exercised:

> ➤ Does the candidate's background raise blatant questions about her suitability for the job?
> ➤ Is the candidate lying?

Don't Call Us ...

Bear in mind that the supervisors to whom the screening interviewer reports will never criticize him for failing to send a promising candidate up to them. (How can they criticize him for something they don't even *know* happened?) If an unqualified candidate slips through the screen, however, you can bet the screening interviewer will hear about it. Therefore, the screening interviewer is actually *motivated* to err on the side of screening out too many candidates.

Brevity

The screening interviewer's assignment is to get facts. Your objective is to get past the screening interviewer and move up to the next stage. While the screening interviewer's purpose and yours may seem to conflict, you can, in fact, find common cause. It is this: Both of you want to get through the interview quickly, efficiently, and with the facts clearly expressed.

The Challenge

The challenge in the screening interview is ...

> ➤ To provide the facts for which the interviewer is hungry
> ➤ To provide these facts clearly and without evasion (apparent or actual)

➤ To provide these facts concisely

➤ To be brief, without being terse or curt

Let's talk a little more about the last two points. Answer the interviewer's questions as fully as possible *without* digressing; that is, without going on to other subjects. Whereas the in-depth or selection interview (the interview conducted by the person who can actually hire you) resembles a conversation, in which one subject does naturally lead to another, the screening interview is strictly Q&A: question and answer. It is not a conversation.

Don't Call Us ...

Never preface your answers with "As I mentioned in my resumé ..." or "As my resumé states ..." Just answer the question, as if it were fresh.

But, in your effort at brevity, do not cut your answers so short that valuable information is omitted. Except where obviously called for, avoid simple yes or no answers. Avoid one-word answers altogether. Also, be sensitive to the essence of the screening interviewer's mission, which is confirmation of information you have already provided. So, when he asks you to tell him how long you worked for Acme Industries—an item featured prominently in the resumé he has right in front of him—be careful not to show irritation.

Painting Broad Strokes

Here is another fact you should know about the screening interviewer: He will probably never see you again—especially if he is an HR functionary. This has some important implications:

➤ He doesn't have to be concerned about how he will get along with you.

➤ He doesn't have to assess how you'll get along with others.

➤ He doesn't have to concern himself much with your personality.

➤ He doesn't have to assess your problem-solving ability.

➤ He doesn't have to probe how your mind works.

➤ He doesn't have to gauge the level of your creativity.

➤ He doesn't have to possess a specialist's knowledge of the open position.

Clincher

Be aware that while the screening interviewer's mission is overwhelmingly fact-oriented, he or she is a human being who responds to the way you act and to your appearance. Act in a polite and pleasant manner and dress appropriately, as you would in any other interview situation. See Chapter 5, "Clothes Call," for advice on appearance.

All he has to do is verify facts and, perhaps, elicit additional facts. Not only are the screener's intuitive feelings about you irrelevant to his mission, he has probably been cautioned against allowing his personal feelings to interfere with his job.

None of this means that you should come across like a machine, impersonally churning out fact after fact. Always, in any business contact situation, be polite and pleasant. Being businesslike doesn't mean you can't smile. Go ahead: Smile. Just don't waste time.

As to your personality, render it in broad strokes. Make a positive impression as a decent, friendly, outgoing, eminently cooperative person. You're not one who'll make waves. You're a team player. That's all the screening interviewer needs to know about your personality.

Say This

Difficult as it may be, you should strive to avoid overt creativity in the screening interview. Follow the interviewer's lead. Expect questions relating to:

➤ Your job history

➤ Your skills, including transferable skills

➤ Apparent inconsistencies in your resumé (i.e., lies)

➤ Work-history gaps

Be prepared to answer such questions directly and forthrightly. Being prepared means that you should have clear answers prepared and ready to trot out. Even more importantly, act preemptively by creating a resumé that is free from inconsistencies. Fill chronological gaps in your work history as fully as possible. Perhaps you were working (or job-hunting or studying or traveling), but not employed full-time for a period of five months or so. Account for this gap in print—*on your resumé*. Here are some tried-and-true tips for making your between-jobs activity sound most convincing:

➤ If you worked as a *freelancer* or an *independent contractor,* be sure to list your most important clients or projects.

➤ If you took time out for training or special study, cite where and why. If you did not attend a formal institution for this study or training, call it "independent study" or "independent training" or even "independent research," and state clearly your area of concentration and your purpose. This will probably elicit questions from the screening interviewer, but it's preferable to leaving a gap that denotes unemployment.

➤ Don't *excuse* planned employment gaps. Celebrate and capitalize on them. If you took a half year off after your last job to see the world, present this as a deliberate and worthwhile act. Talk—briefly—about what you learned, especially what you learned that may be of value to the employer.

➤ At the very least, be prepared to account for any employment gap in a positive way: "I knew that I didn't have to be desperate for a job, and I decided to take adequate time to find a position in which I could offer excellent value to the employer and in which I could grow professionally."

Confronted with a request to explain employment gaps, the last thing you want to do is blurt out something about how you "just couldn't find a job." Nor do you want to blame external circumstances: "Well, with the downturn in the economy, jobs sure got scarce." This may, in fact, be true, but it sounds like you are just whining and making excuses. Finally, don't get caught short. If you hem and haw, looking flustered or stymied, the interviewer will conclude that he has hit pay dirt: a reason to screen you out. Be prepared with a positive answer for any and all gaps or apparent inconsistencies.

Don't Say That

If you want your hand held through the screening interview, hold tightly to this phrase and concept: *positive answers only.* Answer everything in positive terms. Do not:

➤ Volunteer modesty or doubts about your skills or qualifications.

➤ Speculate on whether a particular skill or qualification is relevant to the job.

➤ Criticize your current or past employer(s).

➤ Criticize a supervisor, coworker, subordinate, or customer.

➤ Talk extensively about your family or your family responsibilities.

Clincher

If the salary range the screening interviewer mentions is significantly below what you had expected, don't comment or express disappointment. Your sole objective is to get to the next stage, the selection interview. You can always discuss salary there. You're free to reject an offer. But first you must get an offer. Keep your options open. Even if you get nothing else from the selection interview, you'll get one more contact to add to your professional network.

Don't Call Us ...

Avoid hedging your salary requirement by stating a figure, only to add, "Of course, I can be flexible on that." If you can, avoid stating a figure in the first place. If you cannot avoid this, state a range without any qualification whatsoever.

It is possible that the screening interviewer will address issues of salary: "What salary level are you looking for?" This can be a sticky situation. You know from Chapter 12, "Money Talk," that it is decidedly not to your advantage to be eager to volunteer a salary figure. You can be sure that any figure you mention in the screening interview will be passed along to the supervisor at the selection interview. That will make negotiation difficult. Even more serious, however, is the possibility that mentioning either too high or too low a figure will get you screened out, if the figure you give falls outside of the salary range authorized for the position. You have several choices:

➤ If you answered an ad for the position, and a salary range was mentioned in the ad, respond this way: "The announced salary range seems a reasonable place to begin negotiation."

➤ If no salary or salary range has been mentioned, ask for one: "What salary range has been authorized for this position?" If you get a response, respond in turn: "That certainly seems like a good place from which to negotiate."

➤ If the screening interviewer cannot or will not give you the authorized range, you may answer that you "expect a salary commensurate with my skills and qualifications and with the duties and responsibilities of the position."

➤ If the interviewer presses for a figure, respond with a salary range. See Chapter 12 for a method of calculating the range. Come to the screening interview prepared with this information—just in case.

Turn "Goodbye" into "See You Later"

The screening interviewer will signal or tell you when the interview is over. If that signal comes in the form of his asking if you have any questions, respond this way: "Yes. When might I expect to hear from you about the next step?" This communicates your understanding of the process and puts you in charge of closure of the interview. It also elicits the most positive response possible in a screening interview—a promise of further action or further communication.

Once you have the answer to your question, *thank* the interviewer and tell him that you enjoyed the experience. Without getting mushy, praise the interviewer for doing his job well: "Thank you. I enjoyed meeting with you, and I appreciate the clarity with which you conducted this interview. You gave me a great opportunity to present myself. Thanks." Leave the interviewer feeling good about what he has done. The idea is to have him associate that good feeling about *his* job and *his* judgment of you.

The Least You Need to Know

➤ In contrast to the purpose of the selection interview, which is to find new talent for the company, the objective of the screening interview is to identify and screen out "unqualified" candidates.

➤ The screening interviewer is usually a junior staffer in the target firm's Human Resources department. He or she is not a specialist in the position for which you are a candidate.

➤ The screening interviewer does not have the authority to hire you, but does have the power to screen you out.

➤ The screening interviewer is a fact verifier and, to a lesser degree, a fact-checker. He or she is not interested in you as a person.

Chapter 18

I'd like to ask you some questions...

The Telephone Interview

In This Chapter

➤ The purpose of a telephone interview

➤ Advantages and disadvantages of the telephone interview

➤ Taking control by dodging the call

➤ Preparing for the call

➤ Being prepared with a "telephone interview kit"

➤ Answering questions, overcoming fear, and projecting confidence

---

While the world of commerce has become increasingly legalistic, a rugged landscape pocked by insistent requests that you sign this waiver or that one or prepare one cover-our-rumps memo after another, it has also become less formal or, at least, less ceremonial. In many situations, faxes and e-mail, quickly dashed off, take the place of letters; while contracts, which used to require the labor of experienced legal secretaries, are now routinely altered and adapted with a few word-processor keystrokes.

The harbinger of this new immediacy is technology, and it's also worked its way into the employment interview process. In the last chapter, we discussed screening interviews, assuming that you would be physically summoned to one. These days, such preliminary interviews take place on the phone as often as they do in person. This chapter will show you how to prepare for the telephone interview and how to make the event a success.

Welcome to a Process of Elimination

Ask yourself this: Why would an employer telephone you rather than fly you in, put you up in a hotel, feed you a meal or two, and take half a day or more to sit down and converse?

Even if you've never taken an economics course in your life, you know that it's because calling would be a lot cheaper.

The Skinny

Many employers don't even conduct the telephone interviews themselves, but outsource the job to recruiting firms specializing in telephone interviews.

The Role of the Phone Interview

But that's not the whole answer. Think it all the way through. *Why* does the employer want to save money on you? Answer: The employer doesn't have sufficient interest in you to make much of an investment. At least, not yet. This is true even if an in-person interview involves no travel expenses. It still "costs" time. The employer wants to make a minimal investment—of money and time—in screening candidates, and the fact that he has chosen to call you, rather than summon you to a face-to-face, is a sure signal that this is a screening interview. A telephone call is rarely substituted for a final or selection interview. Instead, it's a common vehicle for the preliminary interview.

The Good News: It's a Signal of Interest

If this sounds pretty grim, there *is* an upside. While it's true that the telephone interview is usually a screening interview, it is also an expression of interest. You were found to be worth running through the screen, which means that you've made the first cut; you can be sure that nowhere near all of the candidates (those who answered an ad or sent in a resumé) are called. The phone call is a signal of interest.

The Bad News: It Isn't Face to Face

Many job hunters are actually relieved to take a phone interview rather than "endure" a face-to-face meeting. Sitting in the privacy of your home or office, invisible, free to fidget, unburdened by issues of appearance, body language, and eye contact, is less stressful than meeting with an interviewer in person.

But who said job hunting, in general, and interviewing, in particular, were supposed to be easy?

The fact is that the telephone, even as it allows communication, stands in the way of contact. The impression you make is blunted by the phone, which delivers nothing more than a disembodied voice. Moreover, precisely because the telephone interview is less demanding than meeting in person, you will be tempted to prepare less thoroughly for a mere telephone conversation. Such complacency is always dangerous.

Observe these rules:

➤ Understand that the telephone interview is an attempt to screen you out. Review the preceding chapter for guidance on avoiding the screen.

➤ Unless she identifies herself otherwise, understand that the person on the other end of the line is most likely a recruiter or Human Resources staffer, someone who does not have the authority to hire you, but does have the power to eliminate you from the running.

➤ Also understand that the telephone interview is an opportunity to secure an in-person interview, which may well be a final or selection interview conducted by the person who has the authority to hire you.

➤ Psych yourself up for the call. Assume that the call is a prelude to a face-to-face selection interview.

➤ Do not fixate on getting the job as the objective of the telephone interview. Focus on using the telephone interview to secure a face-to-face meeting.

Don't Call Us ...

When you answer a call, don't start speaking until you have the telephone handset to ear and mouth. Think this advice is too basic? How may times have you made a call to the firm of Dewey, Cheatham & Howe only to be greeted by a voice announcing " ... am and Howe?

Blind Side

Alexander Graham Bell patented the telephone on March 7, 1876. Within a few years, it became an indispensable instrument of everyday life. Yet, as more and more telephones were installed throughout the world, thoughtful commentators on the contemporary scene expressed fears that the telephone would create a generation of what they called "neurasthenics"—what modern psychiatrists would call neurotics and what you and I might call nervous wrecks. Why? Because the ringing phone was a cruel and capricious master, who could summon an answer at will and without warning, carrying a demand for instant answers, instant action, and instant results. Who could withstand such pressure?

Although many of us are driven crazy by nonstop phone calls, the telephone hasn't produced the mass hysteria that prognosticators anticipated. And if technology has threatened our sanity, we've used technology again to fight the threat. Many of us ignore incoming calls and let an answering machine or voice mail do the talking. (This practice has led to a new form of impending nervous exhaustion caused by overindulgence in telephone tag.) But some of us *do* actually answer the phone, and, once we've answered it, we do feel obliged to answer questions, to converse, to perform.

A Welcome Call at an Unwelcome Time

The problem is that this eagerly anticipated, possibly momentous call may come at the most awkward of times and places. Like when you're seated at your desk, with your boss hovering over you. *Ringgg!* It's a recruiter. Or it may come at a time when you are simply unprepared for it.

Clincher

Even if you reschedule a call so that you call back from the comfort of your home, consider dressing for the part. Dressing as you would for a face-to-face interview helps you to "get into character," even though the person on the other end of the line cannot see you.

Taking Surprise in Stride

Fight the impulse to render unthinking compliance. Just because the call has come in, you are under no obligation to conduct the interview right there and then. Without panic, without seeming flustered, without an air of urgency, welcome the call, but seize the opportunity to reschedule it.

➤ Reschedule so that *you* are the one who makes the call. The caller always has a psychological advantage over the one who is called.

➤ Reschedule so that you can make the call at an advantageous time and from a convenient place. If possible, make the call from your home rather than the office—especially if your office is not private.

Bidding for Time

You need not offer elaborate excuses for rescheduling the call. After all, you are a professional whose time is valuable. The easiest thing to say is that you are in a meeting: "Yes, Ms. Deacon, I look forward to speaking with you, but I'm in a meeting just now. I can call you back at 10 o'clock tomorrow. Would that work for you?" Once you have agreed on a time, be certain to get the phone number and the name of the contact person.

If the recruiter insists on calling you back, don't fight over the issue. Agree quickly, but exercise control over when that call will come. If you can arrange to take the call at home, make certain that the recruiter has that number: "I'll be working at home then, and you can reach me at 555-555-5555."

While it's unlikely that the recruiter will insist on talking to you immediately—"now or never"—it is possible. You will have to decide, first of all, if the chance of this job opportunity is worth relinquishing so much control, or whether you should reply with equal insistence: "I'm sorry. I *am* in a meeting. I would very much like to take your call, but I can't. What I *can* do is call you back in 45 minutes."

Don't Call Us ...

Avoid being overly familiar with the interviewer. Use his or her surname until you are invited to do otherwise. Do not ask permission yourself ("May I call you Al?").

A Lesson from the Boy Scouts

Maybe you'll be able to buy two days, a day, or a few hours to prepare for a callback conversation. Maybe it will be no more than 45 minutes—or now or never. The one thing you *cannot* count on is having enough time to prepare—you should be preparing even if you're only *thinking* about job hunting. Review Chapter 2, "On Your Mark," and Appendix B, "Information Sources for Job Searches and Interview Preparation," for advice on research and pre-interview preparation. Gather the information you need to make an impression as a thoroughly informed individual.

A Telephone "Interview Kit"

Beyond preparing yourself personally, assemble the following items next to the telephone or telephones you plan to use for interview purposes:

➤ Your resumé.

➤ An "executive summary" of your resumé, highlighting your most important skills, qualifications, and accomplishments.

➤ A crib sheet that gives the answers to the questions you anticipate.

➤ An up-to-date calendar listing all of your obligations; you don't want to fumble if you are asked about your availability for an in-person interview.

➤ Copies of any correspondence to or from companies you have queried or to which you have applied. Keep a separate folder for each firm. Be sure to keep copies of any relevant employment ads.

➤ A notepad, pen, and calculator.

➤ A small bottle of water. Nothing dries the mouth like a potentially life-changing telephone conversation.

Let the Caller Do the Talking (Mostly)

While you should keep up your end of the conversation, let the recruiter or company representative do most of the talking. Let him or her ask most of the questions. Follow his or her lead in the direction of the conversation. For the most part, limit your own questions to those that will illuminate and expand on what the interviewer asks. For example:

> **Interviewer:** How would you rate your problem-solving skills?
>
> **You:** Very highly. Are there any particular problems your firm is facing now? Any challenges that stand out?

Don't expect a Human Resources interviewer to answer such a return question, but the fact that you asked it suggests that you are, indeed, a roll-up-your-sleeves problem solver.

Repeatedly demonstrate that you are listening carefully and analytically. An effective technique is to give the interviewer feedback in the form of paraphrasing some of his or her key statements or questions. For example:

> **Interviewer:** How would you rate your problem-solving skills?
>
> **You:** So problem-solving is a key aspect of this position?
>
> **Interviewer:** Yes.
>
> **You:** Great! I would rate my problem-solving skills very highly. For example, in my current position …

While you're listening, take notes. This will not only help you identify topics of concern and topics for further conversation—whether it occurs now, on the phone, or later, in a face-to-face meeting—but will help you later to evaluate the company, the position, your performance, and the general situation.

Giving Answers

Because the telephone interview is usually a screening interview, it is generally best to keep your answers brief, yet thorough. How do you satisfy both requirements? Answer factually. It is, after all, facts that most interest the screening interviewer. Don't digress. Don't make small talk. Don't volunteer information beyond the scope of the question.

You might periodically vary your responses by answering a question with a question in order to sharpen the original question's focus or shift the question over to your areas of strength. For example, the interviewer asks you about your experience in customer service. You've been exclusively in sales. Here's your response:

You: Customer contact is important to the position, then?

Interviewer: Yes, it is.

You: My approach to sales has always been customer-oriented, with an emphasis on service. For example, a recent customer needed ...

In interviews for positions that involve extensive customer contact by telephone, you might encounter something more than the usual cut-and-dried, screening-interview, fact-finding/fault-finding questions. The interviewer may engage you in role play. For example, she may play the part of a disgruntled customer. Your assignment: Satisfy the customer without giving away the store.

This task is less threatening than it sounds. In any telephone role-play scenario, it's less likely that you will be judged on the basis of every word you say than on your ability to keep your

Don't Call Us ...

Avoid rushing the telephone interview—even if it's long distance, and you're paying for the call. If this opportunity isn't worth long-distance charges, should you be pursuing it at all? Also, resist your natural tendency to cut the interview short because it's hard work, makes you feel uneasy, and can even seem like an ordeal. Don't drag it out; just take whatever time is necessary.

cool, to respond in a generally creative manner, and to keep the conversation going. A significant bit of your score will also be based simply on your willingness to go along with the game.

If the interviewer comments on your role play, thank him for his suggestions, criticism, and advice. Do not defend or explain your words or actions, just make it clear that you are listening to and learning from the interviewer's comments.

Finally, consider this ploy. Answer just about every question that comes your way. But when a major question comes up toward what you sense as the impending end of the interview, defer it or defer part of it:

> I can answer A, B, and C, but D is such a large subject that it can be answered adequately only in person, with give and take. Can we set up a meeting? I'll be prepared to discuss this issue in detail, as well as anything else of interest to your firm. I'm free at the end of the week—Friday all morning. Would that be good for you?

Deferring an answer like this takes a certain amount of nerve, but no interviewer will criticize you for it. On the contrary, this maneuver will probably elicit admiration of your initiative. It might even prompt an in-person interview. Of course, if the interviewer insists on an answer over the phone, don't fight him: "Well, I'll do my best to do the issue justice." And proceed with your answer.

Don't Say "Yes," and Don't Say "No"

However you answer the telephone interviewer's questions, try to avoid giving yes or no answers or one-word responses. These say very little about your skills and qualifications. Instead of making you sound direct and forthright, excessively terse answers give the impression of evasiveness or out-and-out lack of knowledge.

Control the Voice of Fear

Maybe—just maybe—you'll encounter a telephone interviewer who will subject you to an unusual challenge, such as the role-playing exercise. More likely, however, you will experience the standard screening-interview Q&A. The interviewer has no supernatural powers, cannot read your mind, and is unable to peer into your soul. Nor does he want to. Nevertheless, in stressful situations, your voice may reveal more than you want it to. Even the most unimaginatively robotic of interviewers will probably pick up on a tone tinged with terror.

The voice of fear is insidious, because it sustains itself. As you listen to yourself speak, you, like the person on the other end of the line, also become aware of fear. As you listen to your own fearful voice, you find yourself becoming even more anxious, so that your voice becomes tighter, higher, and thinner. All you hear is fear, and you become self-conscious and distracted. You might well lose focus sufficiently to blow the call. At the very least, you're sending an unwanted message.

Achieving Control

One way to fight the voice of fear is to make sure that you are prepared for any telephone interviews that come your way. Also, take control by trying to reschedule the call, with you calling back at a time and from a place that are convenient for you.

Don't Call Us ...

Don't smoke during a phone interview. The sound of your dragging on a cigarette is very audible over the phone. What if the interviewer has strong feelings against smoking?

Beyond this, however, it's necessary to recognize that the source of much of your fear is physical, and, therefore, physical remedies will go a long way toward transforming the voice of fear into a voice of confidence and authority.

Begin with your breathing. Concentrate on taking regular, deep breaths. Don't sigh, but keep your breathing full, slow, and regular. The very act of focusing on this will help take your mind off your anxiety, and the regular breathing will in and of itself make it easier for you to speak smoothly, fluently, and without rushing.

Achieving Authority

In addition to breathing regularly, consciously try to push your voice to a lower pitch than what comes naturally. You should do this whether you are a man or a woman. Even in an era of heightened sensitivity to the benefits of diversity, men enjoy an advantage in employment situations in part because they possess lower-pitched voices, which, simply by virtue of their pitch, convey more authority and self-assurance than high-pitched voices.

An authoritative voice is also the product of pacing. Once you achieve a resonant pitch, slow the pace of your speech to match it. Take advantage of the slower pace to enunciate, opening your mouth wide to give full weight to each word.

Finally, just as it is a good idea to dress for a phone interview—to look as if you are interviewing in person—it is also useful to smile. Strange as it may seem, a smile is heard as well as seen.

Don't Call Us ...

As useful as call-waiting is, it can be thoroughly distracting during an interview call. Another advantage to *your* calling the interviewer back is that you can temporarily disable call-waiting before the interview begins. To do so, simply dial *70 + the rest of the number. Of course, even if you don't disable call-waiting, you shouldn't interrupt the interview to take the other call.

Speak into the Phone

Everything said so far is useless if the interviewer cannot hear you clearly. Position the telephone mouthpiece about one inch from your mouth, and speak directly into it. Do *not* use a speaker phone.

While you are speaking directly into the phone, make certain that background noise is kept to an absolute minimum. Background noise includes music, conversation, television, loud fans or air conditioners, and the chatter of children. It also includes such personal background noise as gum chewing and cigarette smoking.

Make a Note of This

Keep a legal pad and pen handy for taking notes. Jot down key points, but don't become so intent on your note taking that you fail to concentrate on what's actually being said. Your notes should serve two purposes:

1. They are a record of key issues and questions to study prior to a subsequent face-to-face interview. It's rather like getting the exam questions before the midterm.

2. They will help you keep focused. As a question is asked, jot down the points you want to cover. Having these down on paper will not only make your answer

more complete, but will significantly reduce your anxiety. You need to worry less about becoming confused or leaving out something important.

An added bonus of good note taking: If the interviewer is interrupted or for some reason distracted, you can jot down his last question. When the interviewer gets back on the line, you can jump in with "We were just discussing ..." or "You were asking ..." In any interview, it's always to your great advantage to be perceived as a practical problem solver.

The Least You Need to Know

➤ Most of the time, a telephone interview is a screening interview—more a process of elimination than an effort at recruitment.

➤ Your objective in a telephone interview is not to get a job, but to get an in-person interview.

➤ Feel free to reschedule calls that come at an inconvenient time. Try to arrange it so that *you* call back; the caller always has the psychological advantage over the recipient.

➤ Make it your business to be prepared for telephone interviews; create a "telephone interview kit" and make sure that it's ready, by the telephone, at all times.

➤ Give concise, factual answers. Don't wander.

➤ Take thorough notes during the telephone interview; these will be invaluable in preparing for a subsequent in-person interview.

The Internet Interview

It's Christmastime. A few stomach-churning minutes negotiating a mall parking lot, or juggling packages on a packed cross-town bus, or jostling for your shot at the toy counter, then standing on a frozen conga line at the checkout lane can transform even the most devout fan of *It's a Wonderful Life* into Ebeneezer Scrooge. Alternatively, the experience may prompt you to preserve the spirit of Christmas by forsaking the freeway, the bus, and the crowds for a few clicks of a mouse. Just you, a keyboard, a screen, the ever-obedient e-rodent, and (of course) a line of credit or two or more. Arrange your workspace right, and you don't even have to crawl out of bed. Online shopping has come of age.

If e-commerce is such a snap (or click), why not e-employment? In 1995, the Internet boasted 500 employment-related Web sites. Within three years, this number had exploded to 100,000 sites that included at least some job listings or job information. Similarly, whereas approximately 10,000 intrepid job hunters posted resumés on the Internet in 1994, by 1998, an estimated 1.2 million resumés were online. From this, the venerable career-building guru Richard Nelson Bolles estimates that at least 2 million job hunters are online during any month.

Obviously, e-employment, like e-commerce, is catching on—big time. While this hardly guarantees that you can find employment without lifting your fingers from the keyboard, e-employment is a force to be reckoned with, big already, and bound to get much bigger.

(Virtual) Reality Check

Two million job hunters online each month! Can you afford to be left out?

The short answer is no—but not because the Internet is a magic carpet to a job. No job seeker can afford to ignore the Internet because no job seeker can afford to be cut off from *any* employment-related source of information and communication. Moreover, most industries value technologically proficient people. If you can demonstrate your high-tech savvy in the very process of applying for the job, your personal stock with a prospective employer is likely to come onto the market that much higher.

Yet it is important to recognize two things:

1. Two million is a lot of people—until you put this number in the context of the current American workforce, which is about 138,000,000.

2. Two million is still a lot of people. And if 1.2 million resumés are floating around the Internet, how is yours going to get noticed?

The Skinny

Richard Nelson Bolles (*Job Hunting on the Internet*) cites this 1998 statistic: 5.5 percent of the 99 million U.S. households had done some online job hunting. Bolles estimates that perhaps 5 million people are online during a typical year specifically to do a job search.

Want some cyber advice? Always temper *virtual* reality with *real* reality.

➤ The Internet is the Wild West: free, unregulated, and largely undefined. Truth and fiction, the likely and the unlikely, the possible and the impossible, all may be accessed here, and rarely are they clearly labeled.

➤ Web-based job sites may promise anything and everything. They are not bound to deliver anything at all.

➤ A very small percentage of job hunters who post their resumés on Internet job sites find jobs this way. (This is not the fault of the Internet, however. A very small percentage of job hunters who mass-mail unsolicited resumés find jobs *that* way, either.)

➤ So-called job-posting sites are little more than electronic hoppers into which you may toss your resumé in the hope that a prospective employer will dig through and pull it out. This may actually happen, but it probably won't. However, it *certainly* won't if you don't toss the resumé in.

➤ It is quite possible to do all of your Christmas shopping online. However, given the odds against finding a job exclusively through the Internet, it is a bad idea to do all of your job hunting online. Add the Internet to your kit of job search and employment communication tools. Just don't empty out the tool box to fit it in.

Clincher

If you limit yourself to the Internet in your search for a job, the chances are that you'll be disappointed. However, the Internet is a gateway that offers access to information on a scale unparalleled in history. Do not fail to use it as a means of gathering information on your target industry, target employer, or target location. Use the Internet to help you make career decisions and to stock yourself with information to help you create more effective resumés and to perform more effectively in interviews.

What This Chapter Won't Do

This chapter won't give you the key to finding your dream job via the Internet. It won't even give you much advice on using the Internet to search for a job. For this, consult one of the Web-focused books mentioned in Appendix B, "Information Sources for Job Searches and Interview Preparation."

What This Chapter Will Do

Instead of telling you how to use the Internet to look for a job, this chapter is intended to help you use the Internet for employment-related communication, namely the Internet interview and the steps immediately preceding it and following it.

Information, Please

The Internet is a great place to scope out corporate America. The multitude of company Web sites are unique expressions of what firms great and small think about themselves or, at least, want the world to think about them. Whether you are a consumer, an investor, or a job hunter, there is a lot to be learned on the Web.

Job Boards or Dart Boards?

Many job hunters don't make a corporate Web site their first stop, however, but go instead to one of the many *job boards* that have a Web presence.

Client Load

Why do so many people look down their noses at salespeople? After all, a salesperson enables us to purchase products we want. A salesperson is the agent of a desire satisfied and the means to a better life ... yeah, sure.

Ask most folks, and they'll tell you that a salesperson is someone who, while not always deliberately dishonest, makes promises and claims that don't necessarily have a firm basis in reality.

Don't justify that impression at the interview. You can make claim after claim about your selling prowess, but if you don't base what you say in the hard ground of reality, each of your claims will be perceived as so much hot air.

For experienced salespeople, that hard ground is made of two principal substances:

1. The product itself
2. Client load

The interview is not the place to argue the merits of the product—although you could ask something like, "What do you see as the major selling points of the Acme Widget?" Instead, the interview is very much the appropriate venue for discussing client load:

> What is the average client load per salesperson?

Once you have an answer to this, continue:

> How does that typically break down in terms of contact hours?

Then, open up the question:

> What kind of support do you give your salespeople in terms of assistants, secretarial help, and customer service?

You could then explore the functional links between sales and service:

> How do sales and service function together?

This question is critical for two reasons. It not only demonstrates your strategic understanding of sales—the necessity for follow-through and customer support, which requires a strong customer-service operation—but also provides an X-ray view of the organization. Is it a place that logically and logistically supports its salespeople

The Skinny

Both retail and wholesale sales positions typically have great potential for income growth. Successful retail salespeople can expect to earn 200 percent more than their entry-level income within the same basic position after a few years. Successful wholesale salespeople can expect almost 300 percent.

Job boards may function in a few different ways. Here are examples of some of the most popular sites:

➤ America's Job Bank (www.ajb.dni.us) is a government site run jointly by the U.S. Department of Labor and some 1,800 state employment offices. Employers post jobs, to which job seekers may reply directly. They may also post their resumés (using the site's special template) on "America's Talent Bank." Neither employers nor job seekers are charged a fee.

➤ CareerPath.com is a venture of six major city newspapers from Boston, Chicago, Los Angeles, New York, San Jose, and Washington, D.C. This site draws its job postings from newspaper help wanted ads and from corporate Web sites. You can forward a resumé to specific employers for free.

➤ HotJobs.com is a genuinely interactive job board, which allows firms to post position announcements directly on the board. You, the job seeker, can program a "Personal Search Agent" to find the jobs that interest you and to e-mail them to you.

➤ Monster.com is the biggest and most popular of the job boards. It charges firms a fee to post their jobs and to gain access to its vast (over a million) bank of resumés. Job hunting is conducted through keyword searches.

➤ JobOptions.com was formerly called E-Span and is one of the oldest job boards. Job seekers find it particularly user friendly.

These are only a few of the many job boards on the Web. Sound pretty wonderful, don't they? Richard Nelson Bolles believes that such boards are about 45 percent effective in helping people find computer-related jobs, but only 2 percent effective for noncomputer-related jobs.

The lesson here? Since they are free to the job hunter, there is little reason *not* to make use of any number of job boards. Just don't be lulled into thinking that searching one or more of these and adding your resumé to their resumé banks is sufficient to serve as the sum total of your job-hunting campaign.

Talk the Talk

A **job board** is a site on the World Wide Web on which employers post job openings and job searchers reply and/or post resumés.

Corporate Gateways

Once you have targeted your job search on a particular industry or firm, turn from the job boards to the Web sites of individual corporations. You can find these either by using one of the popular Web search engines (such as Yahoo! or Google), or you can go to www.companiesonline.com, a service of Dun and Bradstreet, which contains links to the home pages of about 100,000 firms.

Think of these home pages as true corporate gateways. Many have links that will take you directly to their employment pages, where you can often find job openings explained in far greater detail than is possible in any newspaper or even industry journal want ad. Most corporate Web sites that post vacancies also allow direct communication in response to the job, either by e-mail or by allowing you to post a resumé on a special template.

The Online Resumé

This book is about interviewing, not resumé writing. Susan Ireland's *The Complete Idiot's Guide to the Perfect Resume* can help you with resumé essentials, and *Cyberspace Resume Kit* (Jist Publishing), by Mary B. Nemnich and Fred E. Jandt, is a comprehensive guide to putting your resumé online.

But since the resumé is usually a prerequisite to an Internet interview, a few words concerning options available for online resumés are useful here.

The simplest online resumé is composed in *ASCII text* (sometimes called "DOS text" or "text only"). Use this to create a bare-bones document that can be read using any e-mail program. This ensures that your target prospect will be able to open up and use the document you send. The downside is that ASCII resumés don't look very attractive. They lack special type fonts and fancy formatting.

Another option is to post your resumé on a job board or a corporate employment page using whatever template the Web site provides. Many corporations require you to use their template for online resumé posting.

Clincher

Because job announcements posted on corporate Web sites are usually more detailed than newspaper or journal want ads, it is a good idea to cross-check the corporate Web site when you find a print ad that interests you. The more information you have, the more accurately you can tailor your response. Also, if you are about to interview for a position and you haven't checked the company's Web site, do so now. Look especially for a description of the job for which you are interviewing.

Talk the Talk

ASCII text, sometimes called "DOS text" or "text only," is computer-generated text without the special formatting and font options word-processing software introduces. ASCII text is not very attractive, but you can be certain that any e-mail recipient can read it.

The most elaborate online resumés are created using HTML (HyperText Markup Language), which results in a Web page that may feature not only elaborate typefaces and beautiful formatting, but, if you like, photos, sound, video, and even links to other Web sites. Including your e-mail address in this document means that an interested employer need only click his or her mouse to get in touch with you. You may also include e-mail links to your various references—former bosses, customers, teachers, and so on.

Today, many software programs are available that make creating a personal Web site fairly simple. Professional Web designers are also willing to sell you their services. Publishing your resumé is easier and less expensive than ever before, too. In fact, it may cost you no more than you are presently paying your Internet service provider (ISP) for your Internet connection. AOL and many other commercial ISPs offer space on their Web servers for customers' Web pages. If such services aren't available from your ISP, you can do one or more of the following:

➤ Contact a Web presence provider (such as Pair Networks or Digital Landlords).

➤ Find a resumé bank that allows you to post HTML resumés on the World Wide Web with your own URL address.

➤ Use a free Web server (such as GeoCities), which allows you to post personal home pages without a fee, but in return for allowing pop-up advertising on your page.

Connecting

The road to an Internet interview often begins at much the same point as the road to a traditional, face-to-face interview. You identify an employer and job that interest you, and you make contact. Contact may consist of a phone call or a resumé. Although the resumé may be submitted the old-fashioned way, on paper via "snail mail," chances are that, if a company wants to interview you electronically, it has received your resumé electronically. Perhaps you've e-mailed it. Perhaps you've responded to a job announcement on the company's Web site and have submitted your resumé on a template carried on the site. It's even possible that the firm contacted you, after reading your resumé on one of the big job boards.

However you've done it, contact has been established. The next step is the interview.

You Have Mail!

The most common form of Internet interviewing is through e-mail. In almost all cases, this "interview" is really a pre-interview or, to put it more negatively, a pre-interview screening. Most of the time, a prospective employer will send you an e-mail message related to some point or points made in your resumé. Typically, you'll be asked to clarify or to elaborate on something.

This is your opportunity to provide more detail than you could in your resumé and, what is even more important, to provide that detail in areas that are of direct interest to the employer. Here are some tips:

Don't Call Us ...

Do not e-mail an HTML resumé to a prospective employer. Chances are that the recipient will be unable to open (and, consequently, unable to read) the document. Use ASCII text for resumés that are sent via e-mail.

➤ Strike a friendly, warm, conversational tone. Use full sentences. Proofread and spell-check your message before sending it.

➤ Be sure to answer the question or questions asked. Be succinct, and do not give vague or general answers to specific questions. Help the prospective employer understand just how you will benefit his organization.

➤ Be concrete. Provide specific details, including actual examples, whenever you can. Avoid simple yes/no responses—even if it is possible to answer a question this way. For example, if you are asked whether you have worked with Windows-based spreadsheet software, reply with some details: "I have worked with several leading accounting packages, including the latest versions of Excel and Quattro Pro. I am comfortable with both of these programs, and I am quite willing to master others." In providing detail, try to formulate a reply that fully defines your areas of expertise, but that does not give the employer an excuse to screen you out. (Note here that the reply names two specific spreadsheet programs, then goes on to convey a willingness to master *any other program* the employer may use.)

➤ Sort out your answer. Often, questions come in bundles: "Did you leave your last position to freelance?" Take this question apart before you answer it. The employer is asking you why you left your last job, and is inviting you to talk about your freelance work. Moreover, you are also being asked, in effect, if you took up freelance work *because* you left your job or if you left your job *in order to become* a freelancer. The spin you put on this point is important.

➤ Give full answers, but keep them concise. Don't ramble. Don't shoot the breeze. Seasoned sales professionals adhere to this maxim: *Once you've made the sale, stop talking.* Stay on the subject, and concentrate on the highlights. If you say more than this, you risk revealing something that may get you screened out.

The e-mail interview, or pre-interview, may be conducted in a single exchange of messages, or may become a rather conversational exchange, back and forth. If this is the case, keep it friendly, but also keep it on the level of business. Observe the following guidelines:

➤ Do not use your correspondent's first name unless you are explicitly asked to do so. Use "Ms. Smith" or "Mr. Jones." For your part, sign your e-mail message with your full name—not just your first name. And do *not* ask permission to address your correspondent by his or her first name.

➤ If your return e-mail address has a user handle—a "clever" nickname—consider changing it. How will that accounting firm hiring honcho feel about replying to a candidate whose e-mail address is "sneaker@soandso.com"?

➤ Don't degenerate into slang. Use polite, conversational English.

➤ Write complete sentences. It is all too easy to fall into a kind of digital shorthand when replying to e-mail messages: "Will get info to you ASAP." You wouldn't reply this way in a paper letter. Translate it: "I will get you the information you requested as soon as possible, certainly within the week."

➤ Write grammatically correct and properly punctuated sentences. Check your spelling. You *are* being judged.

➤ Beyond grammar, spelling, and punctuation, devote some time and care to the style of your writing. Choose words carefully. Write clearly. Your communication skills are under the microscope.

What's Next?

The measure of success for a face-to-face interview is whether or not you get a job offer. For an Internet interview, it's usually whether or not you get a follow-up interview. This may be live—an invitation to the office for a conventional face-to-face interview—or it may be yet another pre-interview, this one by telephone. (You might want to review Chapter 18, "The Telephone Interview," for advice on handling this one.)

Voice and Video

E-mail isn't the only medium through which Internet interviews may be conducted. Some—though very few—companies use voice e-mail for Internet interviewing. With this technology, one can send voice messages from one computer to another. Other firms have been using desktop videoconferencing. In contrast to the e-mail interview, videoconferencing takes place in real time, just like a phone call, but with live video added.

We can expect the use of videoconferencing to increase in the years to come, especially for remote pre-interviews. With this technology, an employer can "screen" (the pun is intentional) candidates from all over the nation or the world, without going to the expense of flying them to the head office. Moreover, multi-point conferencing allows interviewers in several locations —say the Chicago, New York, and London offices—to interview the same Cleveland-based candidate simultaneously.

Does the likely increase in videoconferencing use mean that you should run out and buy a PC- or Mac-based video camera and software? Not necessarily—although this stuff is surprisingly affordable. If you don't own the equipment, you may be asked to go to a branch office of the company, or perhaps an employment agency, a television studio, or even a local duplicating shop, where videoconferencing facilities are available.

Clincher

These days, even some portion of an in-person, face-to-face interview may include videoconferencing, perhaps to include a key interviewer who is stationed in a remote location. Be prepared.

If you are interviewed on video, prepare by careful grooming, just as you would for a conventional face-to-face. You might take a step beyond this, and use face powder to control a shiny complexion, just as TV pros do. Women usually have no trouble applying this make-up. Gentlemen may wish to solicit aid and advice from a female friend, relative, or significant other.

IRL

If you spend much time "chatting" on the Internet or communicating by e-mail, you may have run across or have even used the initials "IRL." They stand for "in real life," and it's how one e-communicator tells another that she'd like to get together, say, for a cup of coffee: "Let's meet IRL. Lunch good for you Wednesday?"

With all the job search related e-communicating you may do, never forget that the ultimate goal is to be found not online, but in real life. Put yourself across as a well-rounded human being, eager to meet other human beings, face to face, handshake to handshake, IRL.

The Least You Need to Know

➤ The Internet is an increasingly important tool for job hunting and for employment-related communication, but it should be regarded and used as only one tool among many.

➤ Job boards offer a common digital ground on which employers and job seekers may meet, but, once you have targeted a specific industry or employer, the most effective job-related sites are the corporate Web pages.

➤ An effective online resumé is almost always a prerequisite to obtaining an Internet interview.

➤ An exchange of e-mail is the most common form of Internet interviewing, which (usually) is really a process of screening prior to a face-to-face interview.

➤ When communicating via high-tech media, always remember that you are speaking to human beings with the object of obtaining a real, live, face-to-face meeting.

Chapter 20

Expecting the Unexpected

In This Chapter

➤ Surviving—and shining—in the group or panel interview

➤ Avoiding the "Ancient Mariner" syndrome in sequential interviews

➤ Turning the computer-assisted interview to your advantage

➤ Making the right impression in mealtime interviews

➤ Coping with the out-of-town interview

➤ Handling drug-test issues

The interview as performance. You enter, stage left, lines memorized, fully prepared, well rehearsed. A peachy idea!

Too bad reality doesn't always oblige. True, many interviews are the classic one-on-one (or two- or three-on-one) encounter, but there are variations on this "standard" interview format. Especially in cases where the employer is paying for your long-distance travel and lodging, expect to be interviewed by a number of people, maybe together, all at once, or maybe one after the other. The employer will be eager to get his money's worth by giving you maximum exposure. You should also anticipate more complex interview situations in large organizations and those with elaborately developed bureaucracies. This chapter will help you to prepare.

Panel Interviews

People have nightmares about stuff like this. You walk into a room, and a dozen slick-suited inquisitors put you on the spot and pin you to the wall. The *panel interview*, also called a group interview, typically consists of five to a dozen interviewers, assembled at one time and in one room, typically at a conference table, asking the candidate questions. The purpose of this mass interview is to expose the candidate to as many decision-makers as possible in a short time.

"We're Not Ganging Up on You ..."

The main object of the panel interview is probably not to expose you to stress (although there may be an element of this), but rather to allow the greatest number of decision-makers to see and talk to you at one time. In theory, this is an efficient and cost-effective interviewing strategy. In practice, it can be highly inefficient and, for you, intimidating. For what too often emerges in panel interviews is a distressingly broad spectrum of private agendas among the interviewers. Not only do different members of the "executive committee" want different things, but what one member wants may conflict with or contradict what another insists on. Sometimes, these meetings turn away from the candidate entirely and degenerate into a debate among the interviewers. This may take the pressure off you temporarily, but it's *your* show that's being stolen, and, when it comes time for the "executive committee" to review candidates, what they'll recall is a candidate who sat silently watching the debate.

Clincher

The upside of any interview challenge is that, while posing a difficulty, it gives you a chance to demonstrate your problem-solving skills by actually solving a problem.

Basking in the Barrage

If you're lucky, the group interview will proceed in an orderly fashion, with interviewers asking questions in turn. In effect, you'll be speaking to one person at a time. More likely, however, questions may come from several directions, perhaps several directions at once. It is this barrage effect that makes the panel interview so intimidating.

What do you do?

Some candidates believe that the best strategy is to try to identify the leader of the group and play to him or her. If this means responding most often to the person who asks most of the questions, well, you have little choice. However, the most talkative panel member is not necessarily the person with the power—or the most power—to hire you. Sometimes the boss keeps herself in the background, quietly listening. Worse, you risk offending other group members by directing your comments and your eye contact to a single, apparently dominant individual.

Identify a leader if you wish, but make an effort to distribute your attention and your remarks to as many members of the panel as possible. Don't leave anyone feeling frozen out.

A greater challenge is making yourself productively heard over the din of competing agendas. The most effective approach is to address the panel members as individuals, asking each what he or she wants or expects or needs from the position in question. As a result of such patient questioning—*on your part*—you may be able to define areas of consensus and address those. This, of course, is the ideal outcome. You may be unable to gather a consensus, either because your *group dynamics* skills aren't quite up to the task or, more likely, because the opposed points of view among this group are fundamentally irreconcilable. One possible outcome of a panel interview is your realization that the job these folks require is simply impossible. Better to learn that sooner than later.

> **Talk the Talk**
>
> **Group dynamics** is the systematic study of how groups operate, how members persuade one another and fail to persuade one another, how conflicts develop, and how consensus is reached.

The most brutal form of the panel interview involves a dozen questioners or even more, some of whom may actually come and go during the course of the interview. Don't let such traffic rattle you. In fact, force yourself not to think of more than one panel member at a time. You *are* playing to an audience, but you must play to them one at a time, person to person.

Sequential Interviews

In the panel interview, you stay put, and the questioners assemble before you. In a *sequential interview*, also called a serial interview, you are passed from interviewer to interviewer, to be met with privately in the office of each.

"The Rime of the Ancient Mariner" Revisited

At some point in your high school or college career, you probably read this narrative poem by the Englishman Samuel Taylor Coleridge, about the old seafarer doomed to tell his woeful tale to everyone he meets, over and over, mainly because he thoughtlessly killed an albatross. The business about the albatross may not have made much sense to you back in high school (I bet you've never even been *tempted* to kill one), but once you embark on a serial interview, you'll gain a profound insight into what it's like to be cursed and have to churn out your life story again and again. That is the principal challenge of the sequential interview: to treat each encounter as if it were absolutely fresh.

Keeping It Fresh

The easiest way to keep each interview in the sequence fresh is to begin each as if it were a screening interview, keeping your answers straightforward and factual until you feel your way into the interviewer's needs and interests. Only then should you engage in an in-depth discussion. The Ancient Mariner was obliged to pour out his heart and soul to all comers. Why make an already demanding task more difficult by imitating him? Don't *start* with your soul; focus on business first, then share your personality as each interview session ripens.

Tying It Together

While you should not comment extensively to Interviewer B on your conversation with Interviewer A, you can seek advance information from Interviewer B concerning Interviewer C. As Interviewer B wraps up his time with you—"Well, I'd better send you on your way to Ms. C"—you might take the opportunity to probe for some key company issues: "Does Ms. C share your concerns about cash flow and collections procedure?" The answer to this provides a lens to help you focus the next interview and allows you to present yourself as a problem solver who has materialized as the perfect solution to the company's problems.

A word of caution: Never criticize one interviewer to another, even mildly—"Gee, your Mr. Thomas is sort of an odd guy." To begin with, such criticism is not your province. More importantly, you don't know how Interviewer B feels about Interviewer A. They may be best friends or mentor and protégé. You could end up knocking yourself out of the running in a single stroke.

Booting Up

A growing number of employers are using computers to handle the main phase of the screening interview. Depending on your feelings about computers, this can be a daunting or offensive process, or one that is refreshingly stress-free. Some of us have an easier time relating to a non-judgmental machine than to a human being.

Multiple-Choice Scenarios

At its most basic and impersonal level, computer interviewing begins when you answer a want ad directing you to call a certain number. You call and are asked to answer a series of prerecorded multiple-choice questions, using your Touch-Tone keypad to respond. The sophisticated interviewing programs will ask you to forward your resumé or will arrange for a company callback if your answers fit a certain profile programmed into the machine's software. You may be asked to record your name and phone number, then answer multiple-choice questions relating to job title, responsibilities, years on the job, and salary. Beyond this, you may be asked *any* other kinds of questions that can be answered by multiple choice. Many of these questions are intended to gauge intelligence and aptitude.

The secret here is to answer quickly, since you are probably being timed, and to make certain you get the question right the first time. While you may be offered an opportunity to have the question repeated, requesting such a repetition may be counted against you.

Computer-assisted screening interviews are aggressively impersonal. You have every right to be aggressive in return. Take as much control as possible. If you dial a phone number in response to a want ad and find yourself confronted by Robo-Interviewer, hang up without leaving your name or a message. Either ask your telephone company to block your number from appearing on Caller ID? on your line or call back from someone else's phone. In either case, your objective is to defeat caller identification technology,

The Skinny

Despite appearances, the computer is rarely used as a substitute for human interviewers, except sometimes in the initial screening stage. Usually, the computer serves merely as a tool to gather, sort, and flag data that will help human interviewers structure useful, probing questions during a subsequent selection interview.

because at this point, you want to make an anonymous call. If asked to give your name, simply make one up, so that you can get to the questions and listen to them. Jot them down. Then, hang up without leaving your real name, phone number, or any other message. Study the questions and prepare answers to them. Now, call back from your own phone and proceed with the interview, furnishing full and accurate information.

Not all computer interviews are conducted by phone. You may be asked to come to a recruiting center or to the employer's offices, be offered a seat in front of a terminal, and be left to answer 50 or more multiple-choice questions. If you find this less stressful than talking to a person, fine; just don't relax *too* much. Remember, your responses may be timed.

Open-Ended Approaches

Computer-assisted interviewing is not limited to multiple-choice questions. You may encounter situations in which you are asked to compose, in your own words, brief narrative answers to a battery of questions. In this case, the computer is probably not being used to evaluate your responses, but is acting merely as a word processor. Your answers will be read and evaluated by human beings. It is generally advisable to keep your responses concise and to the point, but take care to use good grammar and appropriate vocabulary.

Honesty—Not Always the Best Policy

Funny thing about the computer: It invites more candor than any human interviewer. There is no living, breathing human presence to please or to displease, no one there to smile or frown at you, and the result, for many candidates, is an attitude better suited to the confessional or the psychoanalyst's couch than to a job interview. Answer the computer as you would a human interviewer. Don't confess your flaws or express your doubts. Respond as positively as truth and credibility permit. Your objective is to make yourself look great. Period.

Mealtime Interviews

The good news is this: Being asked out to lunch or dinner is a very positive sign. Indeed, you may take it as a "buy signal," a clear expression of significant interest in you. The employer is imagining you as part of the team and wants to get to know you in a setting less formal than the office. Moreover, you are justified in seeing the invitation to lunch or dinner as a gracious act: The employer sees you as a human being, not some anonymous working stiff.

Clincher

Do you want to get hired, or do you want to lay aggressive claim to your rights under the law? Sure, employers are barred from asking you potentially discriminatory questions. But if you are interested in gaining employment, you should try to answer any questions you do not find intolerable—even those that may tread the edge of what is appropriate or legal.

Getting to Know You

Waiting for the other shoe to drop?

Here's the bad news: Whether by design or simply by its nature, the mealtime interview puts you off guard. Questions that would be blatantly inappropriate in the office—conversation about spouse, kids, the kind of car you drive, the kind of home you live in, your neighborhood, your hobbies, your politics, your religious beliefs—seem more excusable, natural, even inevitable in a mealtime setting. Such questions are still improper and some may even be illegal, but, in a social setting, they are nevertheless more likely to come up.

Focusing the Conversation

If the conversation strays into the personal arena, try to answer whatever you feel comfortable with and whatever you feel creates a positive image. If the questions encroach on areas you consider inappropriate, respond firmly but politely and as inoffensively as possible:

Interviewer: So you live in the Brighton area. What church do you go to?

You: I consider religion a family matter, and I never discuss it outside of our family.

The best way to avoid having to answer a lot of questions that get too close for comfort is to steer the conversation as much as possible to matters directly related to business. However, don't dwell on the daily routine—"Do you use #1 paperclips or the premium jumbos?"—but talk about issues and trends that really excite you. Make it *interesting* business conversation.

Dangerous Passages

Openness and candor are qualities we greatly prize in our friends. But your prospective employer and colleagues, while friendly, are not your friends. Present yourself in an open and straightforward manner, but don't open up too far, confessing heavy credit card debt, say, or the fact that your spouse "just doesn't appreciate me," or that your child had a brush with a drug problem. Nor should you volunteer opinions concerning public figures, politics, religion, or morality. Your host's views may be very different from yours.

What do you do if the employer is insistent on probing areas that are inappropriate? For example: "It is very important for us to know how you stand on the issue of abortion."

➤ You can insist—gently but firmly—that your views on this subject are private and can have no bearing on your job performance.

➤ You can ask—again, gently but firmly—how the question relates to the job: "It's not clear to me how my opinions about the abortion issue relate to this job."

➤ You can claim that you have no opinion.

➤ You can state your opinion—and hope that it is the answer the employer wants to hear.

➤ You can decide that the question is so offensive that you wouldn't take the job if it were offered to you.

Your Manners

Your table manners are on display. If you eat like a pig, that fact will be duly recorded. Beyond this, your hosts, consciously or not, will take note of what and how much you order. Err on the side of modesty and moderation, ordering neither the most expensive nor the cheapest dishes. Also, this

Don't Call Us ...

One time-honored mealtime interview ploy is to offer the candidate salt and pepper. If she takes it and seasons her food without first tasting it, she flunks the test. Her host concludes that she is a person who makes hasty, thoughtless, premature decisions.

is not the time or place to experiment with new foods, especially highly spiced items. Order food familiar to you and food that is easy to eat. No lobster, please. And hold the spaghetti. They're stain bombs waiting to explode.

CPR

Despite prudence in ordering easy-to-eat foods, accidents happen. If you spill something on the table, *handle* the situation. If your host does not immediately summon a waiter, you should do it. If you spill food or drink on yourself, wipe yourself off, summon a waiter, and ask for club soda. Dab a little on the stain. This time-honored method may or may not minimize the damage to your clothing, but at least it will demonstrate that you know what to do in a minor crisis. Apologize simply and quickly to those at the table. Don't apologize profusely or at length. This is an employment interview, not a seminar on mealtime catastrophe. You might, however, poke gentle fun at yourself: "Well, I hope this job doesn't require much eating!"

If you spill food or drink on one of the interviewers, you do have a more serious problem. Chances are, the "injured party" will be gracious and a good sport, but there may be unspoken resentment, and you will certainly look foolish. Accept the catastrophe as a test of your grace under fire. Apologize quickly, then *ask* what you can do to help. Do not start wiping down your fellow diner. Suggest the club soda treatment: "Let me call the waiter over and get you some club soda for that." Do not add insult to injury by offering to *pay* for dry cleaning, but do offer help: "I have a marvelous dry cleaner. Can I send you there—or take your suit there myself?" Finally, give voice to your embarrassment: "This is *really* embarrassing. I'm very sorry." Then get on with the interview meal.

A good approach to ordering is to ask your host what he recommends.

Good manners also require you to thank your hosts. Never complain about the quality of the meal or the service. Finally, don't bat an eyelash when the bill comes. There is no question that the host—your potential employer—pays. It is vulgar and inappropriate to offer to pay.

I'll Drink to That!

The best approach to liquor during a mealtime interview is to avoid it. Even if your hosts drink, you are best advised to order sparkling water. If you feel you must have a drink, order a glass of wine or a light drink, such as a white-wine spritzer.

When You're In from Out of Town

Traveling any distance to an interview presents nagging logistical concerns. Be prepared for the unexpected. Formulate alternative plans if weather seems likely to delay your flight (a real possibility if you're interviewing in Minneapolis in January, for example). What will you do if your luggage goes astray? How will you find your way around in a strange city?

Scheduling and Logistics

At the time the interview is set up, be certain that you know:

➤ Who is responsible for arranging for travel and accommodations

➤ Who is paying for transportation and accommodations

➤ How to get from the airport to your hotel

➤ How to get from your hotel to the employer's office

➤ How long it takes to get from the hotel to the office

Make certain that you are prepared with sufficient cash and/or a major credit card to cover your out-of-pocket expenses. Always assume that your luggage *will* go astray, so bring along a fresh suit, shirt/blouse, and shoes in your carry-on luggage, just in case. Also ensure that any essential papers—such as extra copies of your resumé, letters of recommendation, and so on—are in your carry-on bag or briefcase.

Jet-Lagged

Long flights, either transoceanic or coast-to-coast, can leave you jet-lagged. If you're in for a long flight, schedule your arrival for the day before the interview, if possible.

Don't Call Us ...

No smoking. Even if the interviewer smokes, it is best not to do so yourself. These days, with antismoking legislation and escalating health-insurance premiums, no company wants to go out of the way to hire another smoker.

Clincher

If the weather looks doubtful either where you are or where you're going, call your airline. If the situation looks dicey—a storm front looming or heavy snow in the forecast—consider flying in a day early and picking up the extra day's hotel tab yourself.

At the very least, try to arrange to have time to freshen up at your hotel before the interview. This includes a shower, a change of clothes, and, if possible, a nap.

Speaking of sleep, be certain to pack your own alarm clock *and* arrange with the hotel desk for a wake-up call. Even if you are one of those lucky people who *never* oversleeps, a change of time zone can wreak havoc on your body's internal clock.

International Interviewing

The customs of international business constitute a subject vast enough for several volumes. A single word on international interviewing will have to suffice here. Take the time and the effort to learn about the culture and the protocol—particularly the business culture and protocol—of the country to which you are traveling. Actions, including apparently casual gestures that are perfectly acceptable in the States, may be vulgar or downright insulting elsewhere.

Drug Testing

You don't need me to tell you that drug abuse is a serious problem in our times. Certainly, most employers believe this, and as many as half of the *Fortune* 500 companies include some form of drug testing either during or after the hiring process. The odds are good that you may be asked to take such a test.

Is It Legal?

Being asked to take a drug test is neither an inappropriate nor an illegal question. Worse, if you indicate that you would not be willing to take a drug test, you will almost certainly be assumed guilty without a trial. ("What is she hiding?") You won't be hired.

The Skinny

While most authorities believe that 5 percent of drug tests yield false positives, some authorities place the number at a staggering 14 percent.

Sign on the Dotted Line?

If you answer that you are willing to take a drug test, the chances are only about fifty-fifty that you will actually be given one. But if you do find yourself submitting to a drug test, don't assume that, just because you're clean and sober—perhaps have never used a controlled substance in your life—you will pass the test. At least 5 percent of drug tests routinely yield false positives due to the presence of such innocuous substances as certain foods and over-the-counter as well as prescription medications.

Obviously, it's critically important that whoever performs the testing—usually an outside firm hired by the employer—fully explains the test in advance and provides you with a complete list of items that may cause false positive results. Avoid these substances if at all possible before taking the test. If you must take medications that may yield a false positive, report this fact *in writing* to the testing company, with a copy sent directly to the prospective employer.

If you are the victim of a false positive, insist on being given a backup test of a different type. Document your request in writing and be sure to send a copy of this document to the president or CEO of the firm to which you have applied.

The Least You Need to Know

➤ Although you should pay attention to everyone in a group interview, remember that you are speaking to individuals. Relate to them all, but do so one person at a time.

➤ Maintain a high level of enthusiasm and energy in sequential interviews by feeling your way into each interview session. Let the interviewer identify his or her areas of special concern, then pursue these.

➤ Answer computer-assisted interview questions quickly and as positively as possible.

➤ Don't let your guard down at mealtime interviews. While the conversation may stray to social and personal topics, remember that you are still being evaluated.

➤ Prepare for international interviewing by learning about the most important cultural—and business—customs in the target country.

➤ Employers have the legal right to ask you to take a drug test; be certain that you have some protection against possible false-positive results.

Chapter 21

"Nice to Be Here": Mastering the Mid-Life Interview

In This Chapter

➤ The aging workforce

➤ Rethinking your career at mid-life

➤ Why health is more important than youth

➤ Turning age into an asset

Comedian George Burns was born in 1896 and died 100 years later, in 1996. He remained employed in show business to the end, and in a 1995 stage appearance, greeted his audience with, "It's nice to be here." He paused to study his trademark cigar, then continued: "When you're 99 years old, it's nice to be anyplace."

Now, 99 is old. No doubt about that. But it's less old than it used to be. Right now, out of a population of 270 million, some 2 million Americans are 100 years old or older. Each national census proves that we're all living longer. In 1995, the average American life expectancy—male, female, all races—was 75.8 years. But that's from birth, and is only part of the story. If you make it to age 40, you still have 38.3 years to go. At age 50, 29.3 years. And at age 65, the so-called "traditional" retirement age, you can expect, on average, to live 17.5 more years.

Now, let's go back to that 40-year-old. According to federal law, namely the Age Discrimination in Employment Act, anyone 40 or older belongs to a "protected class" of workers who have the right to sue for age discrimination. So, these days, the government says that, at 40, you can call yourself an "older worker."

Thanks a lot, Uncle Sam!

Trouble is, at 40, you have at least half your life ahead of you —a lot of years to fill and to finance. These days, mastering the mid-life (and the later-life) interview is more important than ever. This chapter will give you a hand.

The Skinny

Economists agree that 0 percent unemployment is impossible, because, at any moment, about 4 percent of the workforce is between jobs, in transition, or otherwise briefly and temporarily unemployed; therefore, most authorities define "full employment" as 4 percent unemployment. During the late 1990s, U.S. unemployment was about 4.3 percent, just a third of a percentage point shy of theoretical full employment.

Talk the Talk

A **baby boomer** is anyone born during the sharp increase in birth rate following World War II, that is, between 1947 and 1961.

Mid-Life Crisis or Mid-Life Opportunity? (Pick One)

Well, it's finally here, a new millennium, and, at this moment in time, the American economy is more prosperous than it has ever been. *Ever.* Not only is inflation low, but employment is high. In fact, as economists define things, America is just about at full employment.

For workers, then, there must be more opportunity than ever. Right?

Right. At least, on average. Entry-level jobs are more plentiful than ever before, and many firms are committed to training, mentoring, and developing employees—up to a point. The fact is, corporate commitments begin to wear thin once an employee passes 40—so thin that the government has stepped in to protect those 40 and over. Not that this eases middle-aged anxieties any; for the "protection" given is little more than the right to sue, and if you're 40 or 50 or 60 and out of a job, can you afford the time, the cash, the effort, and the heartbreak of dragging big business to court?

Doubts and Direction

Now, before you become too depressed to read any further, there *is* good news. *Baby boomers* are moving into their 40s, 50s, and 60s, and, with this, the nation's average age is also climbing. As this trend continues, more and more candidates for each job opening will be 40 or older.

This should help ease anxieties over losing your job in middle age, but that isn't the only angst mid-life has to offer. Now is the time many of us begin to question (and doubt and even regret) the career choices we've made. Am I on the right track? Where is that track going? Have I reached my goals? Can I reach my goals? Have I set the right goals? Have I set any goals at all?

Such thoughts can be chilling. Or they can be invigorating. Before you worry about preparing for a job interview, maybe the time is right to rethink your career and retool your skills. Consider going back to school part-time. Maybe you earned a college degree in a subject you loved, only to find on graduation that the paying jobs lay outside of your field. So you compromised, jilting the love of your intellectual life. Maybe the time has now come to return to what first excited you. Just remember that, if your formal training is more than 20 years old, you'll need to update your knowledge and your skills.

Clincher

Mid-life is an ideal time to return to school, because you not only have a wealth of experience to bring added meaning to the training you will receive, but also enough work years ahead to make the investment of time, money, and effort worthwhile. Besides, employers respect mid-life learning.

Family Values

If changing career direction in mid-life is so great, why doesn't everybody just jump in and do it?

Why not? In a word: *family*.

If you have children, you are probably already struggling to juggle work and family time. Adding reeducation to the mix may seem out of the question. If you have college-age children, financial pressures are doubtless acute, with tuition payments heaped on house payments piled on top of car payments, and don't forget insurance.

It *is* possible that full-scale retraining is not a viable option for you right now. But this doesn't mean that you can't shoehorn in some significant time to devote to career development. Schedule just one hour each week for career development. Use this time to do the following:

➤ Revise your resumé. Don't just update the facts—though you must do this—but hone and sharpen the document. Think about it. How effectively does it sell what you have to offer?

➤ Have lunch with a friend or colleague outside of your workplace. Learn about what's going on in his or her shop or field.

➤ Look for relevant short-term or one-shot training seminars to attend.

➤ Invest some time reading about new developments in your field.

➤ Surf the net. Identify Web sites relevant to your interests, and devote some time to monitoring these.

Investing time is like investing money. Over the long run, small investments, made regularly and with discipline, add up and pay off. You may find that you have accumulated enough information to make a move voluntarily—or, should disaster strike rather than opportunity knock, you will be better prepared to cope with the crisis.

The Spirit Is Willing ...

Many industries are undeniably youth oriented—at least on the surface. Scratch that surface, however, and you may find that the corporate climate is not so much youth directed as it is health conscious. It is a fact of life that health is easier to maintain in youth. As we grow older, physical strength and stamina decline, but whether that decline assumes the shape of a sheer cliff or gentle slope is, in some part, very much up to you. Exercise, eat properly, get plenty of rest, and stay emotionally engaged with life, and you will retain more of the health that employers value in youth.

It has been said repeatedly in this book: At the core of most successful job interviews is the transmission of energy. If you can make the interviewer perceive you as a vibrant presence, you will deliver a highly positive impression. Keeping yourself fit and presenting yourself as such are keys to transmitting this most effective personal energy.

And this advice should be taken well beyond the interview stage. If you are to be the oldest—or among the oldest—employees in a department or a company, don't present yourself in ways that emphasize the age gap. This doesn't mean that you, at age 50, should try to present yourself like a 20-year-old. Age *does* have its perks. You may be viewed with respect for your experience. However, if you don't want to be cut out of the loop when more innovative projects come to the fore, do all that you can to keep yourself healthy and vigorous, and to present yourself that way.

To Boldly Go?

There was a time when a man—and in those days, it *was* almost always a man—"built" a career over an entire working life. Having done this, he didn't dare change careers, nor was he asked or required to do so. These days, however, the "average" worker can expect to change careers—not jobs, but *careers*—four times in his or her working life. While this means that employers no longer regard "job-hopping" or career changing with as much suspicion as they once did, it is also true that you may have trouble matching your set of skills to the level of the job for which you are interviewing. In moving from one field to another, you are not precisely a neophyte (because you have been working a long time), even though you may be a beginner in the new field. This can make for some awkward application and interview situations. To overcome problems, consider these two strategies:

➤ Get your foot in the door: Set as the objective of the interview persuading the interviewer that you are willing to take a step-down position in exchange for early performance reviews and likely promotion.

➤ Build a bridge *before* you interview. Prepare for the transition to a new field by acquiring special training or by acquiring special experience. Perhaps you can do consulting work that allows access to higher-level projects in your target field. Perhaps you can arrange for intern or volunteer work in order to build up your resumé prior to making applications and bidding for interviews.

To Square One

For most job hunters, a resumé is a prerequisite or, at least, a prelude to an interview. *The Complete Idiot's Guide to Getting the Job You Want*—by Marc (yours truly) Dorio—will help you create a winning resumé, but, for now, take note of these special tips for the mature candidate:

➤ Don't give your date of birth or age on the resumé.

Let's pause a moment. Your age is nothing to be ashamed of, but remember this: resumés are used as much to *screen out* job candidates as they are to *find* or *select* applicants. Your first object in preparing your resumé is to exclude anything that may serve to screen you out. Age is never a positive reason to hire someone, but, unfortunately, it may be a reason to screen a person out; therefore, avoid making reference to your age.

Even if you are careful not to disclose your age, many employers will look for clues. For this reason, don't include your graduation date from college. Just list the degree and the name of the school. Although you may list ten, even fifteen years of experience, put the focus on the past five.

➤ Highlight relevant, up-to-date skills, such as proficiency in certain technical areas, computer literacy, and the like.

➤ Remember the subject of "transferable skills" from Chapter 2? Don't assume that a prospective employer will recognize these

Clincher

Consider posting your resumé on the Internet or transmitting it to prospective employers via e-mail. See Chapter 19, "The Internet Interview." Use your personal e-mail address, not an address assigned by your current employer and used at work! Recent court decisions have denied employees any right to privacy with regard to e-mail sent or received via an employer's system. Your current employer may—quite legally and without your knowledge or permission—monitor your e-mail correspondence.

transferable skills—that (for example) your customer service experience at an air conditioner manufacturer will also serve you in the high-tech customer support position you've applied for. Point out, very explicitly, just how your past and current experience are directly relevant to what you hope will be your future employment. Remember, there is nothing sacred about your resumé. Revise and rewrite it specifically to suit each position you apply for.

Get Ready, Get Set

At least one important prerequisite for interview success is the same for a "mature" job candidate as it is for one just out of college: *preparation.*

Don't "wing" an interview. Spontaneity is fine, valuable, and charming—as long as you thoroughly prepare for it. Review the chapters in Parts 1 and 3 for advice on preparing for the interview.

Also be aware of the following special considerations for the candidate who is over 40:

➤ Don't worry about your age and don't bring it up. Don't allude to it or draw attention to it in any way.

➤ It is against the law for the interviewer to raise the subject of age, unless you raise it first. Hence, don't.

➤ Practice substituting such words and concepts as "experience," "achievements," "accomplishments," "successes," and "judgment" for "age" or "years on the job."

➤ Be prepared to discuss highly relevant examples of these achievements and accomplishments.

One final interview aspect to prepare for: Spend some time thinking about the negative stereotypes that are attached to older employees:

➤ They are inflexible.

➤ They are worn out, tired.

➤ They are hopelessly out of date.

Now think about what you can do, how you can look, how you can act, behave, and move, what you can wear, and what you can say to shatter these stereotypes.

CPR

What do you do if the interviewer lacks the legal savvy to avoid bringing up the issue of age? What if he asks you how old you are? Or what if he asks, "Aren't you a little old for this position?"

You would be within your rights to point out that such questions are illegal. But, then, you'd probably fail to get the job, and while this might give you grounds for litigation, do you want to spend your time and money in court or in a rewarding career?

Assuming that you still want the job—that the question doesn't simply turn you off to this employer—direct your answer away from the negative aspects of the age issue, but without obviously evading the issue. Here's how:

➤ First, quickly dismiss the negative issue: "It's not a question of age ..."

➤ Next, focus on the positive aspects of age by translating age into experience, judgment, and wisdom. Demonstrate that your years in business have raised your performance level well above the standard.

Some interview experts call this the "5/55 Rule": spend five seconds answering the negative part of the question, then invest 55 seconds in focusing on the positive. Whatever you do, *end* with the positive. That is what the interviewer will remember.

Go For It

Go into the interview with your mind made up not to hide your age, but to reveal it as an asset. The value a young person brings to a company is youth—which is really more of an asset to the employee than to the employer. It's great to be young, isn't it? But what does the employer get out of it? The benefit of inexperience? In contrast, the assets a mature employee brings to the enterprise are of greatest benefit to the employer: The wisdom and judgment born of experience, of time on the job.

Play the Age Card

Avoid "age" as a word and a concept, but sell *maturity*. Discuss specific ways in which your experience has enabled you to make faster and better decisions than younger coworkers, whose experience in the real world is no match for yours.

These days, diversity is on your side. For legal as well as purely business reasons, more and more employers are committed to increasing the ethnic, racial, gender, and age diversity of their workforce. As a mature employee, you may be just what's needed to introduce a necessary and desirable element of diversity. But there is an added bonus: Your years of experience mean that you have worked with many different types of customers, subordinates, colleagues, and bosses. As a mature worker, you are an expert on diversity.

Broadcast Positive Attitude, Positive Appearance

You are 55 years old. You keep in shape. People say you look 40. That's nice. However, they don't say you look 20. Why not? Well, because you are 55 years old.

Our years are written on our faces and hands. Eyes get crow's feet, hairlines recede, hands acquire the marks of "character." Perhaps plastic surgery and dye can trim a year here or there, but not twenty or thirty.

➤ Decide what you can change and what you cannot.

➤ Keep fit.

➤ Develop and project a winning attitude.

➤ Walk into the interview briskly. Smile. Make eye contact. Give a firm handshake. In other words, broadcast energy and good health.

Clincher

In the short term, prepare for the interview by anticipating key questions, formulating answers, and thinking of examples to share with the interviewer. In the longer term, prepare by eating well and exercising. If you are unaccustomed to exercise, consult your physician before embarking headlong on a strenuous physical fitness program.

Up to Speed

Review Chapter 5, "Clothes Call," for advice on interview dressing. Don't dress like a teenager or even a 20-year-old, but do look around you. What is fashionable *for your age*? Be stylish in clothing and haircut.

It is also important to assess the "dress code" of the company or industry in which you are interviewing. If you are bidding for a job with a new high-tech firm and you come calling dressed like an old-line banker, your look will scream *generation gap*. Get in touch with the prevailing look, then leaven it according to what makes you comfortable.

Women need to pay special attention to the amount of lipstick and other make-up they apply. As mentioned in Chapter 5, with make-up and perfume, the principle of less is more should be rigorously followed. As you age, avoid using make-up as an obvious cover-up. The effect of this is likely to be overly harsh. The object is to soften your look. It is also a good idea to avoid dark, somber-colored clothing. Choose lighter and more cheerful hues.

Watch Your Language

Learn the language of the industry, and use it. In some fields, terminology changes rapidly, and some words go quickly out of date. Know what these are and avoid them.

➤ A subject to avoid? *The Good Old Days.*

➤ An interview for a job tomorrow is no place to reminisce about the working world of yesterday.

➤ A word to avoid? *Old.*

➤ If you need a synonym, use *mature, seasoned,* or *experienced.*

> **Don't Call Us …**
>
> Like it or not, packaging is important. You have a matter of minutes to make an impression. *How you look* amplifies, for better or worse, the impact of *what you say* during those minutes. You can devote a lot of time to keeping up with the trends and technology in your field, but if you present yourself at an interview *looking* outdated, your words will have little positive effect.

Get in Touch

If you're trying to work with 20-somethings or 30-somethings, tune in to their world. What issues interest them? What books do they read? What television shows do they watch? What celebrities appeal to them? What music do they listen to?

You don't have to immerse yourself in any of these items of pop culture, and you certainly should not feign any enthusiasm you don't genuinely have. But do get in touch, so that you don't come across as a stranger in a strange land.

Add It Up

Remember: An interview works both ways. You may feel as if it's you who's under the microscope, but, really, the interview gives you, as well as the prospective employer, an opportunity to evaluate one another.

You've come to this company for an interview. Use the occasion to ask questions, to look around you, and to listen.

Do the place and the pace excite and energize you? Or does the prospect of huffing and puffing to keep up with a flock of newly minted college graduates, single, wildly ambitious, determined to work an 80-hour week, seem discouraging and daunting? Sure, it's important to be flexible, but before you say yes to a job offer, make sure that it has at least the possibility of feeling right for you.

The Least You Need to Know

➤ Despite federal law, there is, in some industries, prejudice against the mature worker; however, it is also true that the workforce as a whole is maturing.

➤ It is no longer either foolish or uncommon to rethink and revise your career in mid-life.

➤ You don't have to fake youth to get a good job, but you usually do need to present yourself as in touch with relevant current trends, in synch with current technology, generally energetic, vigorous, and in good health.

➤ Look for opportunities to present age as an asset by translating "age" into "experience," "maturity," and "sound judgment."

Part 5

On the Spot

The chapters in this section are devoted to understanding how to succeed in two of the toughest kinds of interview situations: the performance interview and the (dreaded) stress interview. Also, I deal with the most common—and thorniest—objections, doubts, and other obstacles an interviewer is likely to hurl your way. The assumption is that most "objections" are really pleas for help: The interviewer wants you *to help* her *say yes. The trick, though, is to avoid feeling discouraged or intimidated, to transform challenge into opportunity, and to use objections as points of persuasion. Read on.*

Chapter 22

Hey, You're On! The Performance Interview

In This Chapter

➤ How to prepare for an "audition"

➤ How to set up your performance

➤ The art of radiating confidence

➤ The K.I.S.S. principle

➤ Preparing for tests

➤ Doing well on psychological tests

➤ Scoring high on integrity

All jobs require performance. You have to *do* something. That's what you get paid for. In many jobs, the performance takes place over time: You do accounting, you design airplanes, you analyze the profit potential of new companies—whatever. In some jobs, however, performance can be seen and evaluated in a matter of minutes. "Do you see this pen?" the interviewer, brandishing his fountain pen, asks the hopeful salesperson. "Sell me this pen." Or the chairman of the English department asks the candidate for a teaching position at a private school "to teach a class on the poetry of Emily Dickinson." Or the customer service manager is asked to "handle" some customer service scenarios.

Even if the job you're up for does not lend itself to an audition, you may still be tested to measure aptitude, knowledge, or your psychological profile. Here's a chapter to help you perform at your best, whether in a vocational audition or on a test.

The Show on the Road

It would be comforting if I could guarantee that you will be told beforehand everything that will be expected from you during the interview. In some cases, you will be asked to prepare a "sales presentation" or to "teach a training class for widget sales personnel," but it's also possible that an audition will be sprung on you and that you'll be put on the spot.

The fact is, a demand to perform should not come as a surprise to you. Think about the nature of the job for which you are interviewing. Does it lend itself to performance on demand? *Expect* a performance component if you are interviewing for jobs that involve any of the following functions:

➤ Customer contact

➤ Customer service

➤ In-person or telephone sales

➤ Client or staff training

➤ Counseling

➤ Hands-on management

➤ Human resources

➤ Diagnosis and repair

➤ Troubleshooting

If your target position involves any of these, expect and prepare for an "audition."

Clincher

Need a reminder about just what a *network* is? Essentially, your network may consist of anyone you know who has some contact with businesses in your field of interest. See Chapter 2, "On Your Mark," for more information about networks.

Run Through Your Network

Whether or not you've been alerted to performance as a component of an upcoming interview, work your network to find out all that you can about the target company, about the interviewers, and about what you can expect at the interview. If you can obtain information on what the company is looking for, you can be certain to showcase key issues in your performance.

Let's say you're a customer service trainer. You have an interview at XYZ Company. You call everyone you know who has had any contact with XYZ, and you find out that the company is working hard to make customer service more than a department that handles complaints and warranty issues. XYZ wants customer service to work more closely with sales, to help generate direct revenue. Using this information, you plan a training demonstration that concentrates on "upselling"—the use of the customer service function to promote and sell additional products and accessories to a firm's current customers.

Play to Strengths

Some children simply avoid food they don't like, leaving it in a heap on their plate. Others wolf down their favorite stuff first, then pick at the less-relished fare. But certain kids purposely eat first what they like least, saving the food they love for last. This is a fine approach, if you've got a big enough appetite. If not, your favorite food may be left barely touched.

In preparing for a performance interview, there is a natural tendency to try to repair your weak areas. Don't know much about subject A, but excel in subject B? You'll have the urge to "cram" for subject A to the exclusion of any thought for subject B.

To a degree, the impulse to address weak areas is healthy and necessary. You don't want to be caught short, after all. But a day or two before the interview is not the time to attempt to acquire expertise you do not have. Your precious hours are better spent honing to an even sharper edge the areas of your greatest strength. If you are asked to come to the interview prepared to give a "training session" on some aspect of personnel management, work up a presentation in your strongest area. If you are big on risk management, but less interested in, say, mentoring techniques, you'd better prepare a session on risk management and leave mentoring alone. This is true even if you have not been *told* that you will be expected to make a presentation. If you suspect that an audition may be sprung on you by surprise, have your strongest area prepared to present.

Clincher

If possible, practice your presentation in front of a friend. And I do mean *friend*. This is not the time to seek out your harshest critic. Find someone who is honest, but also supportive. You want positive comment and genuinely constructive criticism.

Props

If you have been asked in advance to prepare a presentation of some sort, of course you will need to ensure that you have any necessary props available. If you need a blackboard, whiteboard, a projector, or a computer audiovisual setup, make certain—in advance—that whatever you need will be available to you. If you can conveniently carry any necessary props yourself, do so. If your presentation requires setup in advance, make certain that you are permitted to arrange and prepare whatever you need.

Even if you have not been asked in advance to prepare a presentation, it's wise to be prepared. If you have supporting material that requires a personal computer, be sure to pack a notebook or laptop in your briefcase. Imagine the strong impression you will make by an exchange like this:

> **Interviewer:** I've got something to spring on you. We'd like you to do a quick dog-and-pony show. How would you present financial data to non-financial people? Can you give us a sample presentation?

> **You:** I'd be happy to. I just happen to have some supporting material on disk. May I pull out my laptop, set it up here, and show you? Of course, if I were presenting this for real, I'd use a multimedia projector, but this will give you a good idea of how I approach a general presentation.

Carry the right equipment with you, and the interviewers will feel like you've read their minds. It's a real power trip.

CPR

What if you forget to bring a key prop to the interview? Let's back up. You shouldn't let this happen, and it won't if you make a checklist of items you *must* bring to the interview. But if your failsafe system somehow does fail, you have two choices: Either improvise without the missing item, or try to obtain the item in a hurry.

If you do improvise, you must avoid making apologies for not having brought the equipment you should have. You need to be able to perform adequately without the missing item, such that the interviewers never realize there's anything missing.

If you decide to buy a replacement for your missing item, do it fast. This, of course, may be neither practical nor even possible, and, in that case, you'll have to depend on the kindness of strangers. Ask the employer if you can use whatever item you need.

Take It Away!

Once you're on stage, cast all modesty and doubt forcibly aside. Your mission is to radiate confidence and self-assurance. Smile. Try to look as if you are enjoying yourself. Also:

➤ Pace your presentation. Don't rush.

➤ Open your mouth when you speak. Give full value to each word.

➤ Review Chapter 7, "Shall We Dance?," on body language. Be certain that you are not broadcasting mixed messages—saying one thing verbally while communicating doubt and uncertainty through your gestures.

➤ Don't waste time by digressing. Make certain you and your audience know the objectives of your presentation, then focus the presentation exclusively on those objectives.

Framing the Show

That last point bears repeating. Set up your performance by telling your audience *exactly* what you intend to achieve. You don't have time for the luxury of subtlety, and why entrust a career opportunity to the intelligence and imagination of your audience? *Tell them what you are going to do.* Think of this as half of a frame in which you set your performance. Those who have mastered the art of public speaking will tell you that one key to successful public speaking is to set the presentation in a solid frame. It works like this:

The Skinny

Tests have repeatedly shown that people respond far more to a speaker's visual presence—gestures and facial expressions—than to his or her words.

1. Tell your audience what you are going to do and say. (That's half the frame.)

2. Do and say what you said you were going to do and say. (That's the presentation.)

3. Conclude by telling your audience what you did and said. (That's the other half of the frame.)

Remember: Your goal is not so much to provoke thought among those who are reviewing your performance as it is to communicate crystal-clear and unambiguous messages. Above all else, the performance interview is about communicating. Whatever your area of expertise, whatever kind of performance you give, you are committing an act of communication. The clearer and more vivid that act, the better.

K.I.S.S.

Most of us say that we enjoy seeing movies that are "true to life." But is this really the case? Think about it. If movies were true to life, they'd be very long, tortuously meandering, intolerably complicated, full of contradictions, and mostly boring—though punctuated by a moment of excitement here and there. If movies were really true to life, nobody would pay to see them.

So, take your cue from the movies when you think about your performance. You don't have to make it *too* true to life: complex and contradictory. Instead, take the message of this acronym to heart:

Keep

It

Simple,

Stupid

Simplify the presentation, giving it a clearly stated objective, a beginning, a middle, and an end. Then, for good measure, tell your audience what you just—successfully— did. The performance in a performance interview is an artificial *demonstration*. It is not a slice of life.

Leave 'Em Wanting

Customer satisfaction is the goal of any successful business transaction, and it's also the goal of a successful employment interview. You want to leave your "customers" satisfied. But there is a paradox here. "Satisfaction" in an employment interview is not synonymous with "satiation." A successful employment interview leaves your audience wanting more. The last thing you want is an interviewer or group of interviewers feeling they've had enough of you.

Clincher

The average business speech is no more than 25 minutes long.

Keep your performance as brief as possible without skimping or seeming evasive. Stimulate the interviewers' collective appetite, don't sate it. If you exhaust or bore your audience, they won't want you back. Even worse, they may get the feeling that they have seen all that you have to offer—that you're a one-trick pony. Like an Impressionist painting, your performance should suggest more than it actually delineates and delivers. Know when to bring down the curtain.

Surprise!

Despite your best efforts, it's certainly possible that a "command performance" will take you by surprise. You may have even expected an audition and have prepared a fine presentation on subject A—only to be asked to deliver something on subject B instead.

What do you do? This *is* a tough one.

Grace Under Fire

When an employer springs a surprise demand on you, he is looking for two things:

1. How well you can think on your feet
2. How you react to pressure

That there are two objectives actually puts you at an advantage. If you can at least *act* unruffled—calm, cool, and in control—you will have successfully met challenge number two. This requires no knowledge, no expertise, no particular thought. It's an act and an attitude. Demonstrate grace under pressure, and you've automatically earned your first 50 points out of the 100 required to pass the test.

Never Apologize, Never Excuse

But it is all too easy to lose those points. This is precisely what will happen if you make apologies or excuses for your performance: "Oh. I'm not really prepared ..." Or: "I wasn't expecting to ..." Or: "This would be a lot better if I had been given some warning ..."

Don't prepare your audience for a bad show. If they *expect* to see a poor performance, they will tend to interpret whatever you show them—good, bad, or indifferent—as more or less of a disaster.

Respond to the surprise demand with pleasure: "I'd be happy to do that!" No apologies, excuses, or other qualifiers are necessary or helpful.

Test-Taking Tips

Employment-related tests come in six types:

➤ *Knowledge tests.* How much do you know in a given area?

➤ *Skills tests.* How proficient are you at certain tasks—typing or data entry, for example?

➤ *Aptitude tests.* What is your performance potential, based on natural abilities?

➤ *Career interest inventories.* What jobs interest you most?

➤ *Personality or psychological tests.* How do your traits and character stack up against those of others?

➤ *Integrity tests.* How honest and trustworthy are you?

The Skinny

Lie-detector (polygraph) tests were once popular employment screening tools. In 1988, however, federal legislation was enacted barring lie-detector tests as an adjunct to employment screening, and about half of the states severely limit the use of the polygraph in employment situations.

You may be asked to take any one or a combination of these tests.

Homework

If you know—or suspect—that you may be tested on your knowledge of a subject area, or that your skills may be tested, the best advice is to do what you did (or were supposed to do) to prepare for exams in school: Study. Review the essentials of your field of interest. If there are skills involved in what you do, practice them.

While you can't really study for psychological or integrity tests, you can prepare for them. Make a list of language that communicates positive traits:

achievement-oriented	honest
agreeable	realistically optimistic
communicative	reliable
conscientious	responsible
dependable	stable
imaginative	tolerant
intelligent	trustworthy
inventive	willing

Commit this list to memory. Choose answers that contain these and similar words. By the same token, avoid answers that contain language like this:

angry

dishonest

prejudiced

rigid

stressed out

temperamental

violent

Pop Quiz

Even if a test takes you by surprise, you can arm yourself with the test-taking skills that will help you to perform at your best:

➤ Get comfortable with computers (if you aren't already). Much testing these days takes place at a computer terminal rather than with paper and pencil.

➤ Avoid extreme or absolute answers. "Never say never," the cliché goes, and that is sound advice. Don't hem and haw with your responses, but do make them reasonable.

➤ Skip what you don't know. Play to your strengths by answering first the questions you know best. Then, as time permits, tackle the ones you are less sure of.

➤ Imagine yourself scoring high. This isn't magical thinking, but if you can picture yourself successful—a high scorer—you have a better chance of performing well.

➤ Imagine the ideal employee. Now, try to answer the test like one.

"Beating" a Psychological or Integrity Test

The single most important thing to do is always to think before responding. Beware of giving knee-jerk answers. The next, most important point concerns honesty. You should approach this issue in two ways:

➤ When asked for factual information, be absolutely honest, giving true answers about your name, your address, your background, and so on.

➤ When asked to rate yourself, always rate yourself very highly, even if you feel this is not completely honest. Never express self-doubt, even if you "honestly" have doubts about yourself and your abilities.

Beyond these basics, take four steps to psych yourself up for a psychological test:

1. Don't view the test as psychotherapy. This means that you should not plumb the depths of your soul to come up with an answer. Answer positively. Make yourself look stable and happy—whether you *feel* that way or not.

2. Related to the first step is this: Be prepared to give the answers you think the employer *wants* to get. Look at yourself from the employer's point of view. Answer as the ideal employee.

The Skinny

The most common personality tests you may encounter include Personnel Decisions, Inc.'s Employment Inventory (seeks to identify stable, responsible, motivated applicants, while weeding out those who are non-conforming or hostile); the Hogan Personnel Selection Series (seeks to measure conscientiousness while identifying hostility and "problems" with authority); the Wonderlic Personnel Test (a broad-based personality test that emphasizes measurement of the candidate's attitude toward challenge); and the Minnesota Multi-Phasic Personality Inventory (seeks to evaluate a broad spectrum of traits relevant to job performance).

Clincher

You don't have to be "you" when you answer questions on a psychological test. Instead, be—at least for the duration of the test—the person you imagine the employer wants.

3. Think of people you know who have failed in the workplace. What are they like personally? Avoid answering questions as you imagine they would.

4. Conversely, think of your friends who have succeeded in the workplace—people whose success you may even envy. How would they answer personality questions?

Integrity tests are easier to handle than personality inventories. Answer each question in a way that paints you as a 100 percent honest, trustworthy, and responsible person. Leave absolutely no room for doubt. For example, if asked if you "ever thought of stealing" from an employer, you could be honest and answer yes. Who hasn't *thought about* stealing? "Yes" is almost certainly the most honest response you could make. Unfortunately, it won't get you hired. Just answer no, no, no, you never, ever had a thought like that!

Kudos and Lumps

If your performance or test interview concludes with an on-site evaluation, critique, or commentary on how you did, listen carefully and with obvious attention. Try to maintain a pleasantly neutral expression, nodding occasionally to indicate that you are taking in all that you are being given. Do not defend yourself or make excuses. Do not argue with the evaluation. Do not protest it. But you do not have to remain silent in the face of criticism, either. Hear the interviewer out, then, instead of defending yourself, thank him for his comments. Go on to ask: "Do you have any suggestions for improving _____?"

You also need not agree with the criticism. If you believe that it's unfair or that you have been misjudged, respond this way: "I appreciate what you're saying, and I agree that I could improve my _____. However, I don't agree with you concerning _____, and I'd like to point out _____, _____, and _____."

If you are praised at the end of the session, accept the compliments with warm thanks and an expression of pleasure: "Well, thank you very much. This has been a lot of fun and very interesting for me."

If you are neither criticized nor praised, don't assume that you have failed to make an impression. Most interviewers do not rush to evaluate you or to make their opinions known. After all your hard work and sweat in the performance or test interview, you'll most likely receive nothing more than thanks and a promise that "We'll be in touch." Return the thanks, express pleasure over the event ("I really enjoyed this!"), take your leave, and do the *really* hard part: Wait.

The Least You Need to Know

➤ The performance interview is about handling stress and communicating clearly.

➤ In most performance interview situations, how you behave is even more important than what you say.

➤ The key to performing well on psychological tests and personality profiles is to imagine yourself as the ideal employee and answer the questions from that perspective.

➤ Answer questions concerning integrity in one way only: so that you seem 100 percent honest and trustworthy. Leave absolutely no room for doubt.

➤ Should you answer all questions with brutal honesty or should you give the answer you think the employer wants to get? No contest. Give the employer what he wants.

Chapter 23

You're On Fire! The Stress Interview

In This Chapter

➤ What is a stress interview?

➤ Motives for conducting a stress interview

➤ How to show that you have "the right stuff"

➤ A catalog of stress–interview strategies

➤ Typical stress questions—and how to answer them

Welcome to your worst nightmare. The stress interview is to the world of employment what freshman hazing is to military school: part rite of passage and part trial by ordeal, an attempt to assess how the candidate handles pressure, and an attempt to weed out the weak from the strong.

Stress interviewers may pose abrasive questions; adopt an unpleasant or outright hostile tone; indulge in long, uncomfortable, staring silences; rapid-fire one question after another, without giving you time to answer any of them; ask impossible, riddle-like questions; put you in an uncomfortable role-playing situation; or simply show up a half-hour late to the interview. Fortunately, few interviewers employ all the stress techniques in any one interview, and few interviews are stress interviews from start to finish. However, many interviewers employ one or two stress techniques—just to see how you'll respond—and, in certain high-pressure work environments, the stress interview is the interviewing style of choice. It pays to be prepared. This chapter will show you how.

No More Mister Nice Guy

No matter how uncomfortable—or even fearful—the prospect of an employment interview makes you, your assumption probably is that the interviewer will at least be polite. After all, he's not out for the sole purpose of shooting you down.

Or is he?

An interviewer who scowls, doesn't offer a handshake, sits down and just stares without speaking, then begins with a question like this: "What's the stupidest thing you've ever done?" can throw you for a very serious loop indeed.

Body language? What kind of impression do you think you're making now, with your mouth gaping open like that?

Stress Interview Motives

You'll have an easier time handling the *stress interview* if you understand the interviewer's motivation. It has nothing to do with you. The interviewer doesn't *know* you, after all. The stress interview is motivated by one of two things:

➤ The interviewer considers the position he is trying to fill high pressure and stressful and wants an employee who can handle whatever curves the job throws his way.

➤ The interviewer is a twisted little fellow who has heard somewhere that you can tell what a person is "really made of" if you abuse him (and besides, it's fun).

Talk the Talk

A **stress interview** is characterized by strings of difficult questions, "trick questions," demanding role-playing assignments, and even verbal harshness on the part of the interviewer— all with the objective of assessing the candidate's performance under emotional pressure.

To Beat You Silly?

Ask ourself this. Does the position in question fall into any of the following categories?

➤ High-volume customer service

➤ Customer service in a field subject to complaints (auto repair, for example)

➤ Top-level management

➤ Labor-management relations

➤ High-stakes negotiation

➤ Fast-paced negotiation (commodities trading, for example)

➤ Security or law enforcement

➤ High-pressure sales

If the job you're up for falls into one of these categories, a stress interview is a distinct possibility. More important, it's a technique the employer may well feel justified in using because of the nature of his business. If, however, the job you're interviewing for is not obviously stressful and does not fit into one of these categories, you may have just run into a misguided, unhappy interviewer who really does like to see people squirm.

His motive? To beat you silly.

Now, it's up to you to decide whether to endure such an interview or excuse yourself and leave. My preference is to keep all options open, to see what develops. But I would certainly think long and hard before accepting a job offer from an individual who uses stress interview techniques for no apparent reason.

The Skinny

According to Les Krantz's *Jobs Rated Almanac*, President of the United States is the most stressful job you can land. Firefighter comes next, followed by senior corporate executive, which comes in as just a bit more stressful than race-car driver. Stockbroker, real-estate agent, advertising account executive, and public relations executive are all among the 20 most stressful of the 250 jobs Krantz lists.

To Reveal the "Real You"?

If the target position does fall into a high-pressure category, you'll just have to accept stress interview tactics (if they are used) as part and parcel of the territory—and, if you can't take the heat, consider the possibility that this particular kitchen isn't the place for you.

Now, if you're applying for a high-pressure position, assume that the motive behind all this stress interview unpleasantness is to find out just who you are. That, at least, is what the employer believes he is looking for. Given this, your best available strategy is to oblige him. But don't just show him who you really are. Show him that "who you really are" is the very person he wants on his team.

To Let You Shine?

That certainly *sounds* like a good idea, but how do you pull it off?

To begin with, don't worry about "who you really are." Think instead about who this employer wants you to be. That he is subjecting you to a stress interview tells you that he wants you to be a person who handles stress well. So concentrate on that.

Now, the interviewer believes that his cleverly ruthless questions will reveal whether or not you have "the right stuff." The interviewer believes that he is looking for certain answers—the *right* answers—to his questions. Indeed, you probably believe this, too.

Stop believing it.

Don't Call Us ...

Address the issues the stress interviewer throws at you, but avoid matters of personality and emotion. For example, if you are asked to describe your most serious weakness, avoid discussing a personality defect; instead, tell a story about some event that shows how you overcame a weakness. Defuse emotion by focusing on acts and actions.

What the interviewer is really looking for, whether he realizes it or not, is not so much the words you give him in return for his questions, but how you behave, how you act in response to *his* questions, *his* actions, *his* behavior, and *his* demonstration of attitude. The image you manage to create and convey—of unflustered calm, stability, coolness, and the willingness to tolerate and even play along with the stress interview game—is far more impressive than any single answer you may give.

The real you? That may be the interviewer's agenda. For you, the stress interview is your finest hour: a chance to shine. Just play the part, don't respond emotionally, keep your voice slow and even, maintain eye contact, think before you speak, and don't give in to fear, nervousness, irritation, or exhaustion.

Stress Interviewer Strategies

The stress in the stress interview may be created by the interviewer's apparently hostile, certainly unpleasant demeanor. It may be heightened by long silences. The response to either of these techniques is simple: Don't react to them at all. If the interviewer is curt or unpleasant in tone, uphold your end of the conversation calmly and politely. If the interviewer is silent, you can be silent, too. Don't let your eyes wander. Just maintain a pleasantly neutral expression.

Talk the Talk

Layering is an interrogation technique that rapidly builds, piles, or "layers" one question on top of another.

Overload

Beyond these brutally simple stress tactics, the interviewer may try to overload you by heaping one question after another on you or by *layering* questions, like this:

Interviewer: Do you work well in a high-pressure environment?

You: Yes, I do.

Interviewer: Fine. Give me an example of a time when you experienced pressure.

You: (You manage to come up with an incident. After you are halfway through your story, the interviewer interrupts.)

Interviewer: Okay. I get the picture. Look, why did this situation come about?

You: (Now you have to come up with an analysis. You begin ... only to be cut off with another question.)

Interviewer: Now, when did all this happen?

You: (You pin down the date.)

Interviewer: I see. What kind of mistakes did you make in that situation? What would you have done differently?

You: (Now you've been maneuvered into saying something negative about yourself. Don't accept the negativity. Show that what you did was the best thing that could have been done in the situation.)

Interviewer: Well, what about the others? How did your supervisor create a stressful situation?

You: (This is not only overload, but entrapment. The interviewer wants to see if you'll start telling tales against your current employer. Resist the temptation.)

Interviewer: Then who was responsible for that situation?

You: (The interviewer refuses to let you off the hook. You'll have to come up with an answer.) I'd say it's just all part of doing business in a high-pressure environment. You take the pressure. You handle the pressure. Nobody goes out of their way to create the pressure. It comes with the territory.

It takes a certain amount of imagination to fire one question after another, but any interviewer can layer questions, simply by insisting on knowing the who, what, why, when, and how behind every answer you give. In answering, you have two objectives:

1. Refuse the bait tempting you to launch into negative remarks about yourself or others.

2. Answer calmly. Don't let yourself get rattled. Don't protest ("Would you give me a chance to answer?!"). Remember, what you actually say is less important in the stress interview than how you say it. The interviewer is prepared to judge behavior more than words.

Brainstorm

Another stress technique is to put you on the spot by asking questions that are off the wall and of sweeping scope:

➤ "Tell me what's wrong with my company and how you'd fix it."

➤ "I want to sell more widgets. Tell me what to do."

➤ "Why should I hire you?"

The first mistake you'll be tempted to make is to respond by remarking on the scope of the question: "That's an awfully broad question." Of course it is. Don't waste time remarking on the obvious, or worse, dropping a suggestion that the question is too big for you to answer. Pause several seconds to organize an answer. The interviewer has revved up the pace, but you don't have to keep step. Collect your thoughts and begin an answer whenever you can. Remember, the most important aspect of your answer is its tone—calm, straightforward, unrattled. *After* that comes content.

Set Up for a Fall

Finally, there is the heavy artillery of the stress interview. It begins with an innocent-sounding question:

> **Interviewer:** You are currently a [job title]?
>
> **You:** Yes.
>
> **Interviewer:** How long have you been in that position?
>
> **You:** Three years.

Hey, all of this is on your resumé. What gives? *This* gives:

> **Interviewer:** How do you account for your failure to advance?

Bang! The zinger. It's meant to make you feel bad, to tear you down, to provoke a negative, disheartened response.

Understand the game. This kind of cruel question is designed to simulate a circumstance in which, say, a client tries to tear you down. How will you handle it?

You handle it by refusing to accept the criticism, the negative appraisal the remark proposes:

> I don't see my progress as slow. The position I have is challenging and has prepared me to move on to even greater responsibility.

Twenty Stress Questions (and Answers)

Now that we've surveyed the landscape of the stress interview, let's zero in on a few of the typical questions.

1. *Tell me what your greatest weakness is.*

Stress interviewers love to ask *When-did-you-stop-beating-your-dog?* questions—that is, questions that invite negative answers. The secret to fielding these is to reject the negativity. Don't deny that you have failings. No one will believe that you are perfect. Instead, go ahead and identify a *minor* weakness or *slight* flaw, then put it in the past. Show how you overcame it: "I used to have some difficulty staying organized on the road. But then I got into the habit of making journal notes immediately after each customer call. I just learned to take the time to do it—then and there. Since then, I've always been together, in the home office or out on the road."

2. *What skills do you need to improve?*

The trouble here, once again, is that you can't simply proclaim your perfection, yet if you admit to areas that need improvement, the stress interviewer will respond like a shark to blood. Sidestep the question by redefining it: "Based on our conversation thus far, I'd say I have all the skills necessary for the position. That's what excites me about the job." You could then take the opportunity to review the highlights of your resumé.

3. *What decisions do you find especially difficult?*

If you answer this question using the terms that the question offers, you can only answer negatively. Then, the interviewer will pounce. The secret here? Reject the negative terms: "I don't find any decisions particularly 'difficult,' but it is true that some demand more thought and analysis than others. Perhaps you might call this 'difficulty.' I call it doing the job you're being paid to do."

Clincher

Asked about your "greatest weakness," offer a flaw that is really a strength in disguise: "Often, I get a little *too* focused on my work." Or: "I'm a perfectionist. I don't settle for halfway measures. Or: "Well, some people tell me that I demand too much of myself." Be careful, however, that you don't make yourself sound like a humorless grind or give the impression that you really are neurotic—a hard-driven individual who will soon burn out.

4. *How do you manage to live on an entry-level salary? You must be in debt. It must be tough.*

Here's an attempt to trick you into confessing personal problems or difficulty managing your own finances. To be sure, there may be more than a grain of truth in what the interviewer implies. Sidestep the issue nevertheless: "Have you ever met anyone my age satisfied with their salary? Sure, I want to advance. Obviously, that's one of the reasons I'm talking to you. As for now, I pay the bills, and I budget my expenses."

5. *You've been with your current employer quite a while. Why haven't you advanced with him?*

Let's assume the interviewer has struck a nerve. What he says is all too true. That doesn't mean you have to agree with the negative terms of the question. "What I like about my present position is that it is both stable and challenging. But it's true that I've grown about as much as I can in it. That's why I'm here. I'm ready to offer more

Clincher

The stress interview is not a court of law. You need not deliver yes or no answers. Bend the questions to deliver the answer you *want* to give.

to a different company." Note that this response turns the issue of salary on its head, transforming it from *"What more can I get?"* to *"What more can I offer?"*

6. *I know I can't ask how old you are, but it's apparent that you're no teenager. Shouldn't you be in a more advanced position by now?*

This is meant as a dig, a goad, something to bruise you. But you need not take it that way. Why not look at it as a compliment paid to your skills and level of achievement? "I am in this for the long haul. I'm willing to pay my dues, and that is what I've done. I've gained a great deal of experience and a solid background. I'm here to offer those assets to you."

7. *Are you a risk-taker?*

A trap for the unwary. If you simply answer yes, you open the door to questions about your prudence: "So you're careless sometimes?" Before answering any wide-open question, ask for qualification: "How would you define 'risk'? What do you see as an example of a possibly acceptable risk? I'd need to know the upside and downside. This is not a question I would answer without thorough knowledge of all the elements involved." Whether or not the interviewer pursues the question, you have demonstrated that you won't take mindless risks. You look before you leap. If the discussion of risk does continue, be sure to leave the impression that you are neither timid nor careless: "Look, I'm not interested in doing anything that would put the company at risk. Sure, there is no reward without risk, but risk can be managed, and management takes information and assessment. With the right information, I might be prepared to take certain risks."

8. *I have a "reputation" in this industry. Tell me, what's the worst thing you've heard about me?*

The last thing this person wants to hear is that you've heard nothing at all bad about him. Obviously, he relishes his tough rep. On the other hand, you certainly don't want to volunteer that you heard he was, say, an <insert organ of elimination here>. Smile: "What I've heard is that you're a tough interviewer. The word on the street was sure right on that one!"

9. *I'm considering promoting from the inside to fill this position. Why should I hire you instead?*

You'll be tempted to respond incredulously: "Why the heck did you invite me out here if you're going to promote from within?" But recognize that this question is just a particularly intimidating way of asking you to persuade this person to hire you.

Take a deep breath and review your resumé highlights, always painting yourself as the answer to the employer's needs. Having concluded this, accept the question at face value for a moment: "If you haven't found someone to promote from within, I'd have to assume that you are looking for something you don't yet have in this company. What benefits are you looking for?" If you can get a straightforward answer to this, you should be able to shape your pitch even more sharply, precisely tailoring it to what the employer says he needs.

10. *How do you handle rejection?*

Rejection is part of just about any business. People don't always buy what you have to sell. The trick here is to separate rejection of your product from rejection of yourself: "I see rejection as an opportunity. I learn from it. When a customer takes a pass, I ask him what we could do to the product or price or service to make it possible for him to say yes. Don't get me wrong: You've got to make sales. But rejection is valuable, too. It's a good teacher."

11. *Tell me about a time when you said something really embarrassing.*

Don't dodge this one, but don't make yourself look like an oaf, either. Offer as innocuous a faux pas as you can dredge up: "A colleague of mine came to a party with his wife. She had put on a good deal of weight. Well, my colleague had been talking quite a bit about starting a family—and I just naturally put two and two together. "So when is the big day?' My colleague's wife just looked at me, 'What big day?' 'The baby!' I said. 'I'm not expecting.' Well, you can bet that's the last time I put two and two together like that! Fortunately, she took it all graciously—and seemed concerned that *I* was embarrassed. But I learned a lot about never assuming something without getting the facts. I mean, she could have been a client or a client's spouse. The stakes are often higher than you think. It was a painful but valuable lesson."

Clincher

Whenever possible, punctuate the interview with positive feedback. Don't praise the interviewer for being a nice guy or a brilliant person, but comment on his performance: "You certainly know how to get to the heart of the matter!" Or: "That is a thoughtful question. Give me a moment."

Don't Call Us ...

Resist the temptation to "open up" to the interviewer. A skilled interviewer will put you at ease and may even come on more as a friend than as a potential employer. Don't kid yourself. The interviewer is not your friend. She's not your enemy, either. But keep the relationship businesslike and always present your best: the qualities that make you a great employee, minus the various failings and foibles you as a person share with the rest of humanity.

12. *Why do you want to leave your current job?*

This is a basic question, hardly peculiar to the stress interview, but it is all the more difficult to answer in the context of other stress questions. Fortunately, employment advisers have come up with a neat acronym to cover this one. It's easy to remember, even under pressure: CLAMPS. The acronym stands for Challenge, Location, Advancement, Money, Pride (or Prestige), and Security. Expressed singly or in combination, any of these motivating factors should persuade the interviewer that you have a sound, intelligent, thoughtful reason for wanting to leave your current position.

13. *What do you most dislike about your current job?*

Typical of the stress interview, this question is expressed in negatives. But even when you are *invited* to be negative, avoid negativity. The interviewer will discount that *he* asked you to be critical, and he will remember only that you were a complainer. Worse, his or her *overall* impression of the interview will be negative. Moreover, while dissatisfaction with your present position may seem to *you* a very good reason to change jobs, it fails to address the needs of the target employer. Your answers should always address the needs of the employer. Remember, a successful used car salesman doesn't pitch you with, "Buy this car so that *I* can pay *my* mortgage and put *my* kids through college." He sells the value and benefits of owning this particular car.

How should you answer, then? Consider something like this: "I like everything about my current position." Then, go on to list some vital skills, abilities, and qualifications that position has given you or allowed you to hone. Conclude with: "I'm now ready for a new set of challenges and an opportunity for greater advancement and greater responsibility, an opportunity to bring all that I have learned to a more challenging and rewarding position."

14. *How many hours a week do you need to get your job done?*

In the context of a stress interview, this is a trick question. The "trick" is that if you reply with something like 40 hours, you risk labeling yourself as a clock watcher, yet if you say 60, you might be implying that you're slow, inefficient, and easily overwhelmed.

How do you avoid the trap? Whenever you are invited to mount the horns of a dilemma, simply decline the invitation. Instead of pinning your answer down to a specific number ("I work 47.2 hours each week."), reply, "I make an effort to plan my time efficiently. Usually, this works well. However, as you know, this business has crunch periods, and when that happens, I put in as many hours as necessary to get the job done."

It's not likely that the interviewer will press beyond this answer, unless she is "layering" questions as part of her high-stress tactic. If she persists, demanding that you furnish a number, turn her question around with a question of your own: "That really does depend on the project and the priorities. What's typical in your business/ department?"

15. *What do you consider an acceptable attendance record?*

This question demands little or no thought at all, depending on whether you are interviewing for a management/supervisory position or an entry-level job. If you're in management, be careful that your answer does not seem to evade responsibility. "I demand perfect attendance from my people" is not only an unrealistic response, it places the responsibility for good attendance entirely on the staff. Answer in a way that puts you front and center in the picture: "I believe that attendance is a function of motivation and management. If I do my job right, my staff people will be motivated, and attendance won't be a problem."

Clincher

The objective of the stress question is to lock you into a difficult, negative, or impossible set of answers. Reject this by redefining the question. "What *don't* you like?" can be answered by simply turning the *don't* into a *do.* "I like everything."

If you are up for an entry-level position rather than a management post, simply answer that you are strongly motivated, are excited about the job, enjoy working, and are rarely sick.

16. *What's the most difficult situation you ever faced on the job?*

Do *not* search your soul to find an answer for this one. The last thing you want to do is to dredge up a situation so difficult that it resulted in personal failure or general disaster. Expect a question like this—even if you're not in a stress interview situation—and come to the interview prepared with a story that has a *happy* ending—not just happy for you, but for your company as well.

Some tips: Do not discuss personal or family difficulties. Do not discuss problems you've had with supervisors or peers. You may discuss a difficult situation with a subordinate, provided that the issues were resolved inventively and to everyone's satisfaction. You could also answer this question by relating a situation that was particularly challenging for you; for example, the time you had to learn a new computer program before you could write a how-to article about it. It was difficult, but one of the most rewarding assignments you had.

17. *What kinds of people do you find difficult to work with?*

Now that you are thoroughly indoctrinated in the avoid-negativity-at-any-cost school of thought, you might answer this one quite simply: "I don't find it difficult to work with anybody." Or: "I get along with everyone." Neither of these is a bad answer, but

they are not very convincing. Use the question as a chance to show that you are a team player: "The only people I have trouble with are those who aren't team players, who just don't perform, who complain constantly, and who fail to respond to any efforts to motivate them." The interview is expecting a response centered on personality and personal dislikes. Surprise her by delivering an answer that reflects company values.

18. *Evaluate me as an interviewer.*

Here's one out of left field, and it can throw you for a loop. This person has been applying the pressure for a half hour or 45 minutes, and now he's asking you what you think of *him*? What is he after? A pat on the back?

Hardly.

This is your opportunity to signal to the interviewer that you understand and appreciate what he's trying to do. "Frankly, this has been the toughest interview I've ever had. But I understand and appreciate what you're after. You want someone who can think on her feet, who works well under pressure. What kind of interviewer do I think you are? Well, you've succeeded in seeing how well I perform under pressure."

19. *How would you respond if I told you that your performance in this interview has been poor?*

A body blow? The knockout punch? Only if you overlook the "if" in this question. The interviewer is not telling you that your performance was poor. He's asking you what you would say *if* he told you that. The key to responding to criticism is neither to defend nor accept it, but to learn from it. Here's an effective answer to the question: "I would ask you what it was that you didn't like. Where do you feel the problems were? If your response led me to conclude that I had miscommunicated with you, I would try to make myself clearer. If, however, you identified a deeper difficulty, I would ask your advice on how to correct it. Certainly, I don't relish being told that I have failed in some way. But even failure is valuable as a learning experience."

20. *I'm not convinced that you're right for this job.*

You have nothing to lose by taking the phrase "I'm not convinced" as an invitation to convince the interviewer once and for all that you *are* right for the job. Once again, the experience of veteran salespeople can serve to guide you. When a salesperson meets resistance, she probes for soft spots through that resistance by asking questions. You should do the same: "Why do you say that?" Or: "What will it take to convince you?"

Let the interviewer tell you what he needs, then give it to him:

> **Interviewer:** I'm not sure that you have enough supervisory experience.
>
> **You:** Of course, you can find people who have been supervising longer than I have, but if you look at what I've accomplished in my department—a 15 percent reduction in costs, a record for high customer satisfaction—wouldn't you agree that I am an effective supervisor?

Probe with your questions, invite the interviewer to review his needs, and respond to each of those needs. Each time you present your qualifications, invite agreement: "Wouldn't you agree?" In a stress interview, the interviewer's expressions of doubt are a challenge—or request—to you for more information, more reasons to say yes.

Clincher

Sucking up is an ugly synonym for dishing out empty flattery. *Empty* flattery has no place in an employment interview. Flattery, however, is another story. Take the opportunity to provide positive feedback to the interviewer—not empty flattery, but flattery based on the interviewer's actions, questions, and comments: "That's hardly your run-of-the-mill interview question. You've obviously given this issue a great deal of thoughtful consideration."

The Least You Need to Know

➤ Exploit the stress interview not to reveal "the real you," but to reveal the person the prospective employer wants "you" to be.

➤ The employer is less interested in the specific answers to his stress-producing questions than in how you behave—your tone and body language—under stress.

➤ Avoid making emotional responses to emotionally provocative questions.

➤ Try to translate the stress interviewer's negative questions into positive responses.

➤ Defuse difficult questions by turning them around as questions you ask the interviewer.

Chapter 24

What to Do at a Brick Wall

> **In This Chapter**
>
> ➤ Recognizing the "red flags"
>
> ➤ Preparing for objections
>
> ➤ What are the most frequent objections?
>
> ➤ Tactics for overcoming objections
>
> ➤ Dealing with illegal or offensive objections

Here's the good news: A prospective employer isn't going to summon you to an interview to tell you you're wrong for the job. If you're invited to fly into his air space, he's not likely to *try* to shoot you down.

But it does happen. And that's the bad news. In the course of the interview conversation, objections will arise. Sometimes the objections loom large enough to overshadow the areas of agreement. Your objective is to turn objections into opportunities that demonstrate why the employer was right to call on you in the first place. This chapter discusses the typical interview killers and not only how to beat them, but how to use them to help make your case.

Call to Action

The range of employer objections is as great as the range of reasons an employer may find to hire you, and a determined interviewer can turn any positive into a negative.

For example, a common red flag is a resumé that reveals a history of frequent job changes. If that's the case with you, you'd better prepare some answers to overcome the inevitable objection. However, if you've been with the same company for many years, you may well run across a potential employer who will object to that: "Why have you stayed with Acme Widget so long? Is security more important to you than challenge?" Other common objections you should prepare yourself to deal with include:

➤ Gaps in your resumé

➤ Insufficient experience

➤ Inadequate or inappropriate educational background

➤ Apparently poor career progress

➤ Over-qualification

➤ Fired from a job

➤ Concerns that you won't "fit in"

Objections in these areas can come at any time during the interview, but they typically come toward the end and may be triggered by the very effort you make to bring the interview to a positive close. As you may recall from Chapter 13, "Questions You Should Always Ask," the most effective way to bring an interview to a conclusion is to move the interviewer to some positive action: "Based on my background and all I have to offer, wouldn't you agree that I bring to the position everything you need?" While such a question invites a positive reply, it may also provoke objections.

And that's okay.

The objections, after all, are in the employer's mind and will figure in her decision whether or not to make an offer. Isn't it better that you know—*now*, before you leave the interview—what objections remain active? At least this will give you an opportunity to confront and perhaps overcome them.

Five Steps to Overcome Any Objection

If you're lucky, the employer will raise an objection that is readily overcome: a simple misunderstanding, perhaps, or something somehow left out of the interview discussion. Such objections can be addressed straightforwardly by restating the misunderstood item or by supplying a piece of data. If possible, work into the restatement some *fact* that contains the seeds of an argument to refute the objection. "Your concern, then, is that my three years in sales with Acme Widgets are not enough background for a sales manager." The "three years in sales" is a statement of fact.

Other, more complex objections involve the employer's feelings and his perception of you and your background. Overcoming these requires a more systematic, exploratory approach.

1. The Rephrase Step

The first step in overcoming a complex or difficult objection is to make that objection your own by restating it in your own words. This not only helps to ensure that you understand the problem, it shows the employer that you are eager to take on responsibility for problems, and that you are willing to make the employer's concerns your concerns: "So you are worried that, having managed the department at Acme for two years, I have insufficient supervisory experience?"

2. The Confirmation Step

Don't leave your rephrasing of the objection out there all by its lonesome. After you've rephrased it, confirm your understanding of the objection: "Do I understand you correctly?"

Two responses to this question are possible:

1. "No, that's not quite what I said."
2. "Yes. You understand me correctly."

Either response serves to keep the doors open, to prevent the interview from grinding to a negative halt. If the employer tells you that you have misunderstood his objection, *he* will restate it, thereby investing more time in you—which, in and of itself, is valuable to an interview. Second, in the course of restating the objection, both of you may come to a clearer understanding of just what it is the employer wants and needs. Finally, it's also possible that restating the objection may take some of the wind out of it, or put it into a context that makes it look less absolute.

> **Clincher**
>
> "What's in a name?" Shakespeare asked. While most may call an employer objection an *obstacle*, you should think of it as an *opportunity*. An objection is an opportunity to demonstrate your problem-solving skills—right on the spot.

If, on the other hand, the employer replies that you have understood his objection, you've accomplished two things. First, you've established that the two of you communicate successfully—in itself a positive achievement. Second, you've gotten the interviewer to speak again, which now means that it's your turn to talk. This will push the imperiled interview forward.

3. The Concession Step

Tread carefully here. Your next move should be to acknowledge the validity of the employer's concern even as you disclaim actual liability. You do this by conceding the feelings, not the facts: "I can see how you feel that way. It's certainly important to have an experienced leader in this position." All that has been conceded is the validity of feelings. There is no agreement as to the validity of the facts that have been asserted.

4. The Neutralizing Step

Having acknowledged the employer's negative feelings, it is now up to you to neutralize them by providing new information or by reintroducing vital information that the employer may be overlooking or discounting. If you managed to wedge in a fact when you rephrased the objection, you already have a leg up: "In my three years in sales at Acme, I've taken on increasing levels of responsibility. As I mentioned, the sales force at Acme always had a great deal of autonomy. We were free to sink or swim. I swam, and I made it my business to mentor others. I understood that my success depended on the success of the team. Team building—that's the single greatest leadership lesson I've learned over the past three years."

5. The Storytelling Step

Having set up a fresh approach to your information—an approach you hope will overcome the employer's objections by making him see your skills and qualifications from a different angle—state some *specific* accomplishment to support what you've just asserted. As always, your message will come through most clearly if you deliver it in the language of business—dollars: "In the last quarter, my own sales were up 26 percent. But what I'm most proud of is having played a role in bringing up sales for our entire unit—up 14 percent. This is what I mean by building a team. That improvement was due in no small part to my mentoring efforts."

Clincher

Don't think of an objection as criticism or doubt, but as a cry for help. The employer is having trouble making the decision to offer you the job. Help him make that decision.

The Charge Is Job Hopping

Objections about your employment history are the most common concerns interviewers raise; frequent job changes, especially, are likely to raise an eyebrow. This is easy enough to understand. Hiring is an expensive process, and, depending on the nature of the job, it may take a significant amount of time and, perhaps, training to get the new hire up to speed. No employer wants to make this investment if he feels the employee may soon leave.

An objection to job hopping should never take you by surprise. *You* know whether or not you've held several jobs over a relatively brief span of time, and, if this is the case, you should know that you must have an explanation ready.

Preparing the Defense

Too many job hunters devote a good deal of time to preparing a neat and orderly resumé. They plan it, compose it, type it up on the word processor, then print it out. And, evidently, never look at it again.

You need to study your finished resumé, not just with an eye toward tweaking and improving it, but in order to see it as a prospective employer might. If it becomes apparent to you that the duration of each of your positions has been relatively brief, you can be sure that this impression will be made even more vividly on the prospective employer. Don't cringe in the hope that the interviewer won't drop the bombshell. Take a proactive approach. Think about how you will meet—and make the most of—the objection that will almost certainly be raised.

The Best Light

Don't concentrate on making excuses for job hopping. Don't defend it. Don't justify it. Above all, don't talk about the personal problems or restlessness or feelings of dissatisfaction that may have motivated you to move from position to position. Instead, find an explanation that puts it all in the best possible light. For example:

> *You're right. I have held a number of jobs during the past five years. You know, most people stumble on their careers by default. They start a job, and they just stay in it long enough so that it becomes "what they do"—their career. I don't like things to happen just because they happen. I try to operate from firsthand knowledge and experience. Because of that, I've been willing to explore a number of job possibilities over the years. Now, at last, that experience has paid off. I've discovered, through firsthand experience, what I want to commit myself to: a position as widget control analyst with Smith Widgets. That's why I'm here.*

Gaps, Gulfs, and Gaffes

Anything that doesn't look 100 percent positive is likely to trigger an objection. Again, there is little excuse for letting yourself get ambushed by one of these situations. You can see the red flags dotting your resumé just as clearly as any potential employer can. Recognize them, and prepare to explain them—before walking into the interview.

There's a Hole in Your Resumé

Any lack of continuity in your employment history is certain to provoke questions. For most

Clincher

"An ounce of prevention," goes the cliché, "is worth a pound of cure." Try to structure your resumé so that there are no gaps. See Chapter 3, "Target: Interview," for gap-filling strategies.

employers, the ideal candidate is one whose career shows continuous employment and an uninterrupted upward trajectory. If there's a hole in your resumé, you'd better be ready to account for it.

Unless the gaps in your employment history correspond with coma or prison time, you *did* do something with that time. Talk about volunteer work, study, travel, freelance employment, consultant work. Express in the most productive terms possible whatever you did during those gap periods. If you *were* in prison, you may have done something useful with that time as well. What training did you receive? What did you study?

Perhaps you left "regular" employment to strike out on your own as a freelancer, an independent contractor, or a consultant. If you enjoyed any tangible degree of success in this endeavor, use it as your reason for having left a past employer and feature the "gap" prominently on your resumé and in interviews. Just be aware that unemployed job hunters habitually tell prospective employers that they are currently "consultants" or "contractors" or "freelancers" or "independents" or something equivalent. Unless you have some clients to show for it, there is a danger that the target employer may interpret all these terms as synonyms for *unemployment*. List your most prominent clients on your resumé.

Not Enough Experience

This is probably the most common objection of all, and the one that's hardest to overcome. After all, your experience is your experience: a matter of record.

Don't Call Us ...

Confronted with an objection that you lack experience, it's perfectly proper to respond by putting the experience you *do* have in the best possible light—showing, for example, how your experience in customer service applies to sales. However, resist the temptation to fabricate experience you don't have. If you're ever found out, fraud is a cause for summary dismissal.

But what is "experience?"

Few employers insist on your making a lateral move from Job A at Company A to Job A at Company B. Most appreciate your wanting to step up from Job A to Job B—maybe even to Job C. A leap to Job D will probably take a more earnest effort at persuasion, and, beyond this, most employers will, with justification, protest that you lack sufficient experience.

To make a step or two or three upward, you need to persuade the employer that you have a solid background, but even more important, that you have the confidence, will, skills, and ability to take on more responsibility.

When you meet with an objection that you don't have Job C experience, you might concede that, yes, you haven't done Job C before, but your experience with Job A and certain other elements of your personal background, education, and personality give you a strong foundation on which you can quickly build the skills necessary for the job. "Besides, it's a challenge. I'm motivated. I wouldn't want a job that didn't challenge me."

In Chapter 2, "On Your Mark," we talked about *transferable skills*—the skills you carry with you from job to job, in contrast to skills that are demanded by a particular job. When you meet an objection relating to experience, it's your cue to trot out your transferable skills. Show how the skills you have developed on your own, as well as those you use and have honed in your current or most recent position, are transferable to the target position: "Customer service is about people and about selling the company and the company's reputation with each and every service call I handle. So, while I've not had 'sales' in my job title, the skills I've honed these last two years have been sales skills. I really see no difficulty making the transition from selling the values of the company to selling particular products."

Wrong Degree, No Degree

Face it: If you want a job as chief of surgery in a large metropolitan hospital, you're going to need that M.D. degree, and no amount of talk about "transferable skills" or "related experience" is going to be accepted as a substitute. There *are* certain positions that require specific educational credentials. In business, however, educational requirements are not always carved in stone. Confronted with an objection concerning your education, you have three options before you throw in the towel and walk out the door:

Clincher

One last alternative: Get more education. If you find that doors are repeatedly slammed in your face, it's a pretty certain signal that you should consider going back to school.

1. Say "Yes, but ..." and present the strengths you do have, including practical experience, qualifications, and transferable skills. If you can make a convincing case, you may be able to circumvent the degree issue.

2. Agree that you would be happy and eager to pursue the required degree—with the target employer's assistance. Perhaps this firm is willing to assist you with a professional development program.

3. Using a polite, non-confrontational tone, ask the interviewer just what he expects the degree would do for you and the company: "I have a bachelor's, majoring in the field. What benefit would I—and the company—derive from my holding a master's?" Depending on the response, you may be able to make a strong case for the greater value of your practical experience in the field.

Climbing Down the Ladder of Success

Prospective employers like candidates with simple lives and simple careers, careers that might be represented graphically as a straight line rising at a 45 degree angle. Always up. Never down.

Life is not always like that.

Explaining a Salary Reduction

One way to avoid having to explain a salary reduction is to avoid volunteering salary information and certainly not listing it gratuitously on your resumé. If you somehow find yourself in the position of having to explain a reduction, however, show how you traded opportunity—or something of real value—for money. For example:

➤ "The opportunity to work independently on special projects was more than worth the 14 percent reduction in salary. I learned a great deal."

➤ "The opportunity to live in Chicago was worth a modest pay cut to me."

➤ "This is the industry I want to be in. Breaking in came at a price—a fairly substantial reduction in salary—but it's been worth it."

Explaining an Apparent Demotion

More difficult to explain in terms of an exchange of value for value is an apparent reduction in responsibility. If you were, in fact, demoted, you should either do your best to hide that fact or be prepared with a very good explanation. Try to ascribe the reason for the change to "staffing needs"; don't suggest that you failed to deliver satisfaction.

If the "demotion" is only apparent, go ahead and explain it:

➤ "I was excited about working at the Smith Company. When an opening occurred there, I grabbed it, even though it meant a title change from manager to supervisor."

➤ "For family reasons, I wanted to move to Chicago. I was willing to take a somewhat lower-level position to make the move possible."

I'm Overqualified!?

What objection can be more stupefyingly frustrating than the opinion that you are *"over-qualified* for the position?" In responding, take your cue from your own sense of frustration. You need to understand the objection. You need more information. Respond to the objection with a request for clarification. If possible, couple that request with a mini-review of the highlights of your practical qualifications:

I'm frankly bewildered by that statement. My understanding was that you needed someone to manage customer service. I've been running customer service departments for 15 years. I can meet the challenge—and it's a challenge I don't think anyone could be 'over-qualified' for. During my tenure at the Smith Company, I reorganized the customer service departments, so that costs were reduced by 13 percent, while reported customer satisfaction rose by 21 percent ...

> **Talk the Talk**
>
> To be **overqualified** means that you have too much experience or too much education to "fit into" a given position. The employer's assumption is that you'll become bored with the job and soon quit.

This should coax the interviewer into rethinking his position. If it doesn't, he's going to have to work that much harder to justify to himself—and to his supervisors—why you should *not* be offered the job.

If the employer cannot clarify the over-qualification objection, try something more probing: "Well, can you tell me, is there something specific you are concerned about?" This question may begin a fruitful discussion or it may yield a simple answer: "I think you'd find the position rather boring. I'm afraid you'd just use it as a stepping stone—and quit at the first opportunity." Now you have a real issue to address. Assure the interviewer that the position excites you and that you intend to commit effort and time to it.

You Were Fired

First of all, be certain to distinguish between being laid off—termination due to circumstances entirely beyond your control, such as corporate downsizing or a work-force reduction—and being dismissed due to what your employer perceives as your failure to perform or to some transgression your employer determines that you have committed. If you have been laid off, ensure that the target employer understands this and does not believe that you were fired.

> **Don't Call Us ...**
>
> When asked about the circumstances of termination, don't lie. Deceptive answers in an interview or on a job application are always grounds for summary dismissal a day later or ten years down the road. If you are caught in your lie, you will be fired—again.

But what if you were fired?

Be honest, but don't strip naked. Don't volunteer the information that you were fired. If you're asked, though, give a full and forthright reply that puts the event in its best possible light:

Clincher

If you were fired, try to put that event in perspective. If you can, find out how many others were fired, laid off, or even left voluntarily during the period in which you were dismissed. After responding forthrightly to the interviewer's question, add: "I am one of 38 people who have left so far this year."

The Skinny

It's important to establish or reestablish good relations with your former employer. That said, only about 10 percent of successful job candidates are actually subjected to a check of their references.

I have to say that my termination was my fault. I had personal problems at the time, which are now completely resolved. But, at the time, I was frequently late. My supervisor—with whom I am still very much on speaking terms—was under orders to reduce the workforce, and, quite honestly, my attendance record at the time gave him the reason he needed to let
me go.

Unless you can make an ironclad case that you were fired unjustly, don't blame other people for what happened to you. You will not be believed. However, you must also avoid wallowing in guilt. Just take responsibility, and, along with responsibility, take the opportunity to demonstrate that you understand how you failed and, more importantly, how to avoid repeating the failure. Create the impression that getting fired taught you about commitment and responsibility, taught you the "hard way," a way you'll never forget, a way that will benefit any company that employs you. You will not repeat your mistakes.

Of course, going into the interview, *you* know if you've got an unpleasant termination in your employment history. You must prepare a solid response to any objection this fact may elicit. One aspect of this preparation may be to contact your former employer. Ask her what she intends to say about you now:

I'm in the process of looking for a new job, and I'd like to see just how I stand with you. If you are asked as part of a pre- or post-employment reference check, how would you describe the circumstances of my leaving the company? Would you say that I was fired? Would you say that I was laid off? Would you say that I resigned? My problem is that, every time I tell a prospective employer about my termination, I blow another shot at a paycheck.

Perhaps you can persuade your former employer to use non-pejorative language in describing your termination.

"I'm Not Sure You Fit In ... "

Depending on who you are and the health of your ego, this objection can be truly devastating or merely offensive. It may also be illegal.

Making the Most of Diversity

If the interviewer tells you that he has doubts about how you would "fit in," respond with a probing question expressed in as neutral a tone as you can manage: "I don't understand that. Can you explain what you mean?"

If the employer's response touches on issues of gender, race, or age, you are well within your rights to remind him of the law. But do you want to initiate a lawsuit, or do you want to get a job? The more immediately effective alternative is to sell the employer on the value of diversity: "It's true that I bring a unique perspective with me—the perspective of the streets, of the working class, of the (African-American, Hispanic, Polish, Italian, Asian, whatever) community. You do business with these people and this community. I offer firsthand experience. Don't worry. I'll fit in here. More important, I can help to ensure that the Smith Company will 'fit in' with all the people it serves."

You should also think about whether you want to work for someone to whom race, gender, or age is such a source of contention. Hopefully, no one at your workplace will have to be sold on the values of diversity.

Hiring and the Law

Strong federal legislation bars employers from discriminating against any person on the basis of sex, race, age, national origin, or religion (Civil Rights Act of 1964, Title VII); nor can an employer discriminate against workers age 40 or older (Age Discrimination in Employment Act of 1967); nor can persons be barred from employment because of disabilities that do not prevent them from doing their assigned tasks (Americans with Disabilities Act of 1991, Title I). These are wonderful laws. The problem is that proving the occurrence of discrimination is often extremely difficult, time-consuming, and costly. When you are looking for employment, you probably don't want to take on additional difficulties, don't have much time, and can't afford a protracted legal battle. Know what your rights are, but realize that, confronted by objections that reflect prejudices and even illegal discrimination, you have to choose whether to enforce your legal rights or overcome the objection in order to press the interview to a successful conclusion. Remember, you can always decide to turn down an offer. But first you must get the offer.

The Least You Need to Know

➤ Examine your resumé carefully in order to identify the "red flags" that will wave before the eyes of a potential employer.

➤ Based on your employment history, make a list of potential employer objections; before you go into an interview, prepare strategies to overcome each of these.

➤ Learn to view objections not as rejections, but as the employer's request that you help him make it possible to hire you.

➤ Know your rights to protection from discriminatory hiring practices, but be aware that discrimination is difficult to prove and that you may choose to make certain compromises in order to secure a job offer.

Part 6

To Follow Through, Follow Up

Think you can kick back and relax, now that the interview is over? Better think again. What you do after the interview can be very important to "closing the sale."

Of course, you may find that your interviewing chores aren't quite finished. Employers are being increasingly careful these days—hiring the wrong person can be a very costly mistake—so you may be subjected to one or even more follow-up interviews. Read on for a chapter on making the most of this special interview situation.

Finally, there is what you need to do once all the interviews are over. The most important step is writing a thank-you letter—one that is not merely courteous (although that's important), but that actually helps close the sale. The final chapter tells you how to write such a letter.

Chapter 25

Nailing the Follow-Up Interview

In This Chapter

➤ Why a follow-up interview is a good thing

➤ Preparing for the follow-up

➤ Convincing the interviewer that you "belong"

➤ Closing the follow-up on a positive note

Let's begin by making sure we all know what we're talking about here. We've already discussed the common interview scenario—a screening interview (see Chapter 17, "Getting Through the Gatekeeper Interview,") followed by an in-depth or selection interview. It has been on the selection interview that most of these chapters have focused.

There is yet another possible interview scenario. Sometimes the selection interview is not the final interview. It may be standard practice for a particular employer to follow up an in-depth interview with yet another, or it may be that the earlier interview has left some questions unanswered, and the employer feels that a follow-up is necessary.

This chapter gives you some suggestions for handling such close encounters of the third kind.

You've Made the Cut—Now What?

First, convince yourself of this: If getting called to a selection interview following a screening interview is a good thing, being asked to a final *follow-up interview* after the

Talk the Talk

A **follow-up interview** may take place after an in-depth, or selection, interview. It is often the venue in which unresolved issues are discussed. Sometimes its main purpose is to deliver the offer and negotiate salary and other matters.

selection interview is even better. Sure, the *best* scenario would have been an offer at the end of the selection interview. After all, who wants to go through yet another high-stakes, high-stress meeting? Yet an employer would not ask you back just to tell you you're not right for the job or because he wants to confirm his suspicion that you're not right for it. Go into the follow-up interview confident that the employer is highly interested in you, and that his purpose in asking you to the follow-up is mainly to confirm his decision.

Does this mean you should assume the follow-up is a mere formality?

No.

Can you still (not to put too fine a point on the matter) blow it?

You bet.

Preparing for the Follow-Up Interview

If you are told, following the selection interview, to expect a follow-up, begin preparing for it immediately. While the interview just concluded is fresh in your mind, jot down a list of:

➤ Major issues raised

➤ Topics the interviewer mentioned more than once

➤ Issues the interviewer told you were key

➤ Issues you feel remain unresolved

➤ Questions you expected to be asked, but weren't

➤ Questions you were asked, but wish you had answered more effectively

➤ Mistakes you made: errors in information, inadequate information, and so on

➤ Questions you still have

Indeed, it's a good idea to make such a post-interview list, even if you *haven't* been advised of a follow-up. There are two reasons for this: First, a follow-up interview may be sprung on you unexpectedly, giving you little time for preparation; second, all interviews have valuable lessons to teach, and analyzing your performance will be helpful in subsequent interviews with other employers.

Study your list. Try to find or formulate answers to unresolved issues. Prepare discussion points for the topics that are clearly of greatest interest to the employer.

Anticipating the Issues

Compile and review your list. Expect that the follow-up interview will focus on some or all of the
issues either emphasized in the previous interview, left unresolved in that interview, or conspic-
uously absent from it.

Can you be certain that your list covers all of the
issues that may be addressed in the follow-up
interview? Of course not. But you can reasonably
anticipate significant overlap. You also want to
ensure that your own agenda is clear—that you
resolve any questions you still have.

Your Entrance

Even if you are very excited by the prospect of
employment at the target firm, you may find it
difficult to work up enthusiasm for yet another interview. *How much more can they put
me through?* Feelings of resistance or even resentment at being run through the mill
yet again are normal and to be expected. Acknowledge these feelings, then set them
aside. Exert whatever effort it takes to put yourself into a high-energy, positive frame
of mind *before* you walk through the door.

Like an Old Friend

Make your entrance like an old friend. Smile. Greet the interviewer or interviewers
warmly and with firm handshakes all around. Your objective is to deliver the impression that this follow-up visit is a great pleasure for you—a step along the road to
becoming a full member of the team.

The Name Game

The single most impressive demonstration of your enthusiasm sounds simple. For
some people, it *is* simple. For others, it requires a singularly demanding feat of
memory.

When you make your entrance and exchange greetings, call everyone by their name.
Okay, this isn't all that exciting if you interviewed one-on-one with the boss. But if
you met three, six, eight, or more people and can now shake hands with each and say
"Mr. Thomas, great to see you again … Ms. Perkins, how are you? … Mr. Edwards,
good seeing you again …" and so on, rest assured you will create an impression the
interviewers will discuss among themselves and admire. If these folks do become your
colleagues, coworkers, and supervisors, they will talk about your "amazing memory"
for months afterward.

> **Clincher**
>
> If the salary issue was left
> untouched in the screening or
> selection interview, it's certain to
> be a principal subject of the fol-
> low-up. The main purpose of
> some follow-up interviews is
> salary negotiation. Review
> Chapter 12, "Money Talk."

The name game takes effort, especially when you have so much on your mind. In a high-stress situation, you're lucky if you can manage to remember your own name. Yet the effort is very much worth it. Of course, no one's memory is perfect. If you can greet four out of six interviewers by name, you're doing very well. As you greet an interviewer whose name you cannot recall, keep the handshake warm, look the person in the eye, and say, "Nice to see you again. I'm sorry, I can't recall your name … " The other person will respond—"Bill Reynolds"—and you should then repeat the name: "Of course! Mr. Reynolds."

Don't Call Us …

Unless you were specifically invited during the previous interview to use an interviewer's first name, don't do so now. Use surnames, and don't ask for permission to use first names.

Connect a Face with a Concern

Connecting a face with a name challenges your memory; you may really have to stretch to associate an issue with the person who raised it. But, again, the effort is worth it. At the selection interview, try to take mental note of who raised what issue. Immediately after the interview, jot this down. Review your list of who said what before going into the follow-up meeting. People enjoy being given ownership credit for their ideas: "Ms. Kelly, I remember from our first meeting that cash flow is a particular concern of yours. As I said before, I agree that it's a key issue, which I would address with a special incentive program. May I share my ideas with you?"

You're Already There

Inertia is the tendency of a body in motion to keep moving at a constant velocity and of a body at rest to remain motionless. Inertia, in short, is resistance to change, and it is as operative in the realm of human behavior as it is in physics. A key to overcoming inertia is to *imagine* change. If you can get interviewers to see you as a member of the team, it will be that much easier for them to say yes. Your mission during the follow-up interview is to pull off a kind of balancing act. Without creating the impression that you believe the job is "in the bag," you should behave as if you are already part of the team.

➤ Using the interviewers' names will help achieve this impression.

➤ Speak about the long-term future whenever possible, as if you believe that you will have a stake in the company.

➤ While you should use *would* instead of *will*, avoid *if*.

Let's linger over that last point for just a moment. It would be presumptuous to say "I *will* start a new incentive program in this position," but it is effective to offer: "I *would* start a new incentive program." Do *not*, however, feel obliged to add, with modesty, the qualifying conditional phrase: " … *if* I am hired." The interviewers are well aware that your employment is still an "if" proposition. You need not remind them.

Choose Your Pronoun

One of the most effective means of stimulating the employer's collective imagination so that you are perceived as one of the team is simply, whenever possible, to use the pronouns *we* and *us* (and the possessive *our*) in place of *I*, *you*, and *your*: "*Our* concern has to be cash flow" is a far more effective statement than "*Your* concern has to be cash flow." It demonstrates common cause and your wholehearted engagement with the prospective employer's enterprise.

Engage Problems

Speaking of engagement, you should address as aggressively and as enthusiastically as possible any problems or difficult issues raised in the course of the follow-up. Adopt and broadcast the attitude that this company's concerns are now—*already*—your own. Demonstrate an ownership interest in all issues raised: "We need to tackle that. I've given it considerable thought since we last met, and I have a few suggestions. Would you like to hear them?"

Be Positive

Don't shy away from any problems or doubts the interviewers may express. Review the tactics for overcoming objections, discussed in Chapter 22 and take to heart the advice given there to learn to regard interviewer's objections not as potential reasons for rejection, but as the employer's request that you help him to make the decision to hire you. If it was important to create a positive impression and maintain a positive tone during the selection interview, it is even more crucial to establish a positive atmosphere in any follow-up meeting. Do not brush aside or downplay any doubts or concerns that may be expressed, but accept them as challenges—that is, as opportunities to excel, to show that you are precisely the kind of problem solver the firm needs.

Don't Call Us ...

Don't ask obvious or basic questions during the follow-up interview. Also avoid questions to which you should already have the answer: "What does Acme Widgets make, anyway?"

By the same token, you should not introduce any markedly negative questions or concerns at this point: "Since the first interview, I've heard some terrible things about your company." By all means, ask questions, but postpone discussion of any potentially negative issues until *after* you have received an offer.

Wait Until They "Gotta Have You"

If salary is one of the issues raised at the follow-up interview, don't lose your grip on the negotiating principles discussed in Chapter 12, the most important of which is to try to delay the discussion until you are confident that the interviewer or interviewers have reached the *"gotta-have-you"* point. The employer will be willing to shell out more money to someone in whom he has confidence and in whom he has invested time and attention.

Talk the Talk

The **"gotta-have-you"** point is that stage in the interview when the candidate senses that the interviewer or interviewers have decided to make an offer.

Making Your Exit

Ideally, the follow-up interview will conclude with a job offer, a salary discussion, joyous concord, and hearty congratulations all round.

But it may not end this way.

If it doesn't, don't be alarmed. But do try to push the meeting to a positive conclusion.

Do's and Don'ts for Bringing It to a Close

It is the responsibility of the interviewer or interviewers to bring the follow-up meeting to a close. If the closing signal comes—"Well, I have no further questions"—without an offer having been made, that's your cue to help out:

➤ "I've enjoyed our meeting. Is there anything else—any additional information I can provide that will help you make your decision?"

➤ "These have been exciting meetings. What more do you need to know in order to make your decision?"

If you feel highly confident about the interview, you might close with a question that pushes the interviewers to act: "Based on all that you've learned about me, wouldn't you agree that I am fully qualified for this position?" However, avoid asking such questions as:

➤ "Did I get the job?"

➤ "Am I hired?"

➤ "Well, how about it?"

➤ "What are my chances?"

➤ "How does it look?"

Do I Shut Up Now?

If the follow-up interview does not conclude with an offer, do, at the least, push for closure: "When do you expect to reach your decision?" Once you have an answer to this, the meeting is over. You've either made the sale, and that means—as all sales veterans know—that it's time to shut up, or you haven't. And if you haven't made the sale at this point, you need to leave the decision at long last in the hands of the employer. But although it is time now to be silent, your work is not done, as we shall see in the final chapter.

The Least You Need to Know

➤ Make a special effort to remember the names of multiple interviewers when you first meet them, so that you can greet these people by name at the follow-up interview.

➤ Prepare for a follow-up by jotting down notes—important concerns, unresolved issues—*immediately* after the first selection interview.

➤ Speak and act as if you already have a long-term stake in the company; make its concerns your own.

➤ Whenever possible, use the pronouns *we* and *us* (and the possessive form *our*) instead of *I*, *you*, and *your*.

➤ If the interview closes without an offer, ask the interviewers if they need any additional information to facilitate a decision.

The Morning After

A sigh of relief. The interview's over. Nothing to do now but wait for the employer's decision. It's out of your hands now. Waiting is hard, but at least you don't have to *do* anything else.

Well, you *should* feel relieved. And maybe you could even get by putting your feet up and taking it easy until the phone call comes. But this is not the best way to use the post-interview period. The interview may be over, but your interview work is not finished.

More to Do

Your most important post-interview task is to write a thank-you letter. Mail your letter within one day of the interview. In part, this is a courtesy that no employer demands, but most expect. Failure to send a letter will almost certainly be noticed. Courtesy alone is an important enough reason to write and send a thank-you letter, but there is an even more important reason. The letter is an opportunity to keep your candidacy in the forefront of the employer's mind, to address one or two issues left unaddressed or unresolved in the interview, and, most important, to push the "sale" to a successful conclusion.

Never send a thank-you note on a postcard or—ugh! on a greeting card. This is a business situation and warrants a friendly, but respectful business letter, either on your personal stationery or on standard 8½"×11" typing paper, mailed in an appropriate envelope. Type the letter. Do not write it by hand.

Don't Call Us ...

Do not directly quote any earlier cover letters or your resume in the thank-you letter. This should be a fresh communication.

Clincher

Some interview experts suggest that you send a thank-you letter to *everybody* you spoke with during your interview. This is not always practical. What if you accidentally leave one person out? If you are confident that you can send letters to all the interviewers, do so. Otherwise, target the lead interviewer only.

Four Steps to Thank–You Letters That Mean Business

I have used the phrase "thank-you letter" rather than "thank-you note" purposely. A single-sentence "note" fails to take advantage of this opportunity for follow-up communication. Write a four-paragraph letter, with each paragraph devoted to a separate "selling" step:

1. Begin by thanking the interviewer and saying how much you enjoyed meeting with him or her.
2. Tell the interviewer how excited you are by the prospect of working in the target position at this particular company.
3. Review interview highlights and selling points.
4. Establish closure: Reiterate your understanding of when you expect to hear from the employer again.

Address the letter to the lead interviewer—if there was more than one interviewer—and be certain to ask the addressee to convey your regards and thanks to the others with whom you spoke. If it's impossible to identify a single lead interviewer, write to more than one of the people with whom you met. Don't send copies of the same letter to multiple addresses. Each should receive a different letter.

The following is an example of an effective thank-you letter.

Jane Smith
1234 East 56th Street
Eden, New Jersey 01234
Telephone: 201-555-5555
Fax: 201-555-4444
E-mail: jsmith@compunerd.com

(Tip: Include full communications information in your letterhead. Make it easy for the employer to communicate with you.)

Mr. Kent Bromide
Executive Vice President
Acme Widget Company, Inc.
5678 Regal Street
Pine Barren, New Jersey 02345

(Tip: Address the letter to the lead interviewer, if you met with more than one person. Be certain to include his or her full and correct title.)

Dear Mr. Bromide:

(Tip: Unless you were invited to use the addressee's first name during the interview, don't use it now. Surname only, please.)

Thank you for the opportunity to interview for the position of assistant sales manager. I was greatly impressed by the intelligence and energy of everyone with whom I spoke at your offices, and I was very grateful for the warm reception and the sincere interest shown in me.

(Tip: Begin with thanks. Be sure to remind the reader of what position you interviewed for. A liberal dollop of praise and flattery doesn't hurt, either.)

The prospect of working at Acme is very exciting. You have forged a great team, and I would be thrilled to become part of it.

(Tip: Convey enthusiasm for the job.)

I was delighted by our conversation, particularly by the prospect of creating a special incentive program. As I mentioned, I was instrumental in designing just such a program for Smith Widget, which resulted in a 26 percent increase in order volume within two quarters after its introduction. That experience taught me a great deal, which I hope I will have the opportunity to apply at Acme.

(Tip: Gracefully hit a highlight or two of your qualifications, emphasizing what you can do to benefit the employer's company, not what you want from the company.)

Thanks again for the interview. I look forward to hearing from you, as you mentioned, before the end of the month.

(Tip: Reiterate whatever closure you have been promised. This serves not only as a reminder to the employer, but lets him know that you are expecting action.)

Sincerely,

Jane Smith

(Tip: End with a conventional polite "complimentary close." Don't repeat thanks or "hoping to hear from you," or anything of the kind. This is a friendly but businesslike communication.)

Pursue the Issues

At the beginning of this chapter, I painted a picture of relief and relaxation following the interview. Actually, if you're like most job candidates, you'll spend at least part of the post-interview period fretting over the important information you *forgot* to convey to the interviewer. Read on to find out what to do.

Those Unanswered Questions

The thank-you letter is not the place to include questions *you* forgot to ask. A request for additional information should not be disguised as thanks. However, if you are aware of having left unanswered one or two of the interviewer's more significant questions, you could include the answer here: "I have given additional thought to your question concerning XYZ, and I'd have to conclude that, while there is no single right way to carry out this type of operation, the ABC method is probably the most efficient and cost-effective. I'd be quite pleased to discuss this further with you."

"I Forgot to Mention ..."

The thank-you letter can also be used as a vehicle to convey one or two significant items of information that failed to find their way into the interview. Again, keep these comments brief. If an item merits detailed discussion, invite an additional meeting. It's best to restrict mention of these interview omissions to a paragraph in the thank-you letter; you can insert this paragraph before the final paragraph of the letter. Sending a separate letter devoted to such omissions will not create an impression of conscientiousness, but, rather, of disorganization and absent-mindedness. Noting one or two omissions is fine, but going on at length about business you should have resolved in the interview venue is neither appropriate nor impressive in a positive way. Also, make certain that what you mention contributes actively and positively to closing the sale. If it doesn't, don't bother inserting the information.

Don't Call Us ...

Don't launch into long discussions. The thank-you letter should not be a chore to read. Keep your comments brief, suggesting further discussion wherever appropriate.

Zapping Doubt

You've dutifully written and mailed your thank-you letter, but this still isn't reason enough to call a halt to your post-interview thought processes. As objectively as possible, review the interview in your mind. Did you say anything that might have created—or reinforced—doubt in the employer's mind? If you believe that you have, ask yourself what you could say to counteract this unwanted impression.

This is no exercise in idle self-criticism. While you don't have the entire interview to do over again, no law bars you from making a telephone call. Let's say that you were asked to furnish the interviewer with a start date. You were a bit surprised by the question—you *shouldn't* have been, but you were—and you quickly calculated that you wanted to give your current employer a month's notice and you wanted another month's worth of vacation time for yourself. "I could start in two months," you replied.

The corners of the interviewer's mouth turned down. His eyes narrowed. But then the interview went on, and you thought nothing of this verbal and nonverbal exchange—until now.

Of course! The interviewer's body language was telling you something. Two months is too long. Rather than risk losing the offer, you recalculate. Your current employer can do with two weeks' notice, and you can do with a week off. Pick up

Don't Call Us ...

Although you should not hesitate to correct an important omission or error with a phone call, don't make more than one phone call of this kind. You can't afford to give the impression that you make a lot of mistakes, which you then correct by dribs and drabs in a series of afterthought calls.

the phone and make a call: "Hello, Mr. Thomas. This is Jane Smith. I just realized that I made a mistake during our meeting. You asked me when I would be available to begin work. I'm afraid I miscalculated when I told you that I couldn't start for two months. I'm very excited about the position and wouldn't want to wait that long. I could start as soon as three weeks from the date of offer."

The Silent Treatment

"No news," the old saw goes, "is good news."

In truth, no news is no news, and the silence following an interview can be deafening. That's why it's important to obtain a promise by the end of the interview that you will be contacted by a certain date. If that date comes and goes without word, you have a good reason to phone the employer and remind him that you had expected to hear from him by now. Ask about the status of the decision, and always ask if you can supply any additional information that might help bring about a decision. Conclude the call by asking for a new decision date. If this date is at all tentative, secure the employer's permission for a check-in call at the end of the week.

Clincher

Don't devote the rest of your professional life to calling the silent employer. Press on with your job search. Bid for more interviews with other companies.

Silence in and of itself is neither a positive nor a negative sign. Don't be afraid that you are being too pushy or overanxious by checking in with the employer. You can be certain that passivity will not influence the employer's decision positively and may even make a negative impression. Checking in and asking if the employer needs further information may be perceived as being a pest, but it's more likely that it will be interpreted as enthusiasm and a desire to make the sale and get the offer. In the face of silence, the more aggressive approach has a greater chance of eliciting an offer than the passive attitude.

Briefing Your References

Another way to use the interval time between interview and offer is to contact your *reference network,* especially anyone you mentioned as a reference. Brief them. Bring them up to date on your interview: "It went really well with Acme Widget. You remember that I interviewed for a slot as assistant sales manager? I'm waiting for word from them. You might get a call from them. Do you have a few moments now to go over some points I'd like you to reinforce concerning my background and qualifications?"

Talk the Talk

Your **reference network** is the set of colleagues, clients, supervisors, and others whose names you have furnished as references.

It's important that you take nothing for granted. Fully prep your references. Make sure they know:

➤ Who may be calling them

➤ What position you interviewed for

➤ What points about yourself you would like emphasized

You should be as specific as possible about these points. Spell them all out for your reference. Remind her of details. Recommendations and references are most effective if they are specific rather than general, built on concrete nouns and verbs (he did this, he accomplished that, he achieved such and such) rather than on vague adjectives (he's a nice guy). It's up to you to review the specifics with your reference. It may even be up to you to supply those specifics.

Depending on the nature of your relationship with your reference, you may want to ask him to call the employer rather than advising him to wait for the employer to call. Review the points you'd like him to make.

What to Do with Success

Don't decide whether to take a job until you get an offer. Your goal should always be to get an offer. The more offers you get, the better you'll feel about yourself, your qualifications, and your ability to communicate effectively in an interview. Moreover, it's never wise to burn bridges. Treat each interview and offer seriously and graciously. You can never tell with whom you may be doing business at a later time.

CPR

What if the employer calls to tell you that one of your references gave a negative report about you? This is not likely to happen (if for no other reason than the reference's fear of slander litigation), but it's not impossible.

Respond by expressing surprise: "I'm very surprised to hear that, and I really don't understand. There must be some misunderstanding." Next, express your thanks to the target employer: "I'm very grateful that you are taking the time and effort to inform me of this." Finally, tell the target employer that you will speak to the reference immediately, and that you will report back: "Let me discuss this with _____ and see what's going on. I'm sure this can be resolved to your satisfaction. I'll call back with a report of what I discovered."

You must not jump to conclusions or take rash action. Do speak with your reference to determine just what went wrong. Assuming some misunderstanding occurred and the reference had intended to give a positive report concerning you, you should ask him or her to call the target employer immediately. If, however, the reference tells you that he or she cannot be positive about you, don't argue. Try to get the whole story, and report it yourself to the target employer. Put the situation in the best light possible and offer at least two alternative references: "This is, of course, very awkward. I was unaware that Mr. Smith had these feelings about this particular issue. May I ask you to call Mr. Josh Johnson and Ms. Clara Rappaport, who will give you a more accurate and objective appraisal of my qualifications?" Be certain to call these alternative references, informing them completely of the situation, before you mention their names to the target employer. It's usually not a good idea to have the alternative references call the target employer. Such a move smacks too strongly of frantic "damage control"; just furnish the names to the employer and invite *him* to make the call.

Obviously, the best way out of this disagreeable situation is to prevent it. Don't use references about whom you have even the slightest shadow of a doubt.

Accepting the Offer

Unless you are 100 percent certain that you want the job, you need not leap to accept the offer. If you need 24 hours to reflect and ponder, ask for it. If you do accept the offer, do so graciously and with enthusiasm: "Great! I'm really eager to begin."

Confirming the Offer

If you are not given the terms of the offer in writing, you have three choices:

1. You can request the terms, including a job description, in writing.

2. You can accept a handshake and a verbal offer and hope for the best.

3. You can accept the handshake and the verbal offer, but follow up with a memo of your own summarizing your understanding of the terms.

In most larger organizations, the terms of the offer and a job description are usually recorded, in writing, clearly and carefully. In smaller companies, the owner-manager may be accustomed to less formality. If you are uncomfortable requesting written terms in such a situation, your best alternative is to accept the offer as you understand it, then follow up with a memo:

Date: *Today, 2000*
To: *I.M. Boss*
From: *A. Workman*
Re: *Terms of employment*

Mr. Boss:

I just wanted to ensure that we are in full agreement as to the terms of my employment here at Acme.

1. *My job title is _____.*

2. *My duties and responsibilities include _____.*

3. *My salary is _____.*

4. *I am entitled to _____ paid vacation days, _____ sick days, and _____ personal days.*

5. *Regular working hours are from _____ to _____.*

This is my understanding of the terms. If this reflects your understanding as well, please sign this memo and return it to me.

Thank you.

Workman

Such a memo should offend no one and will serve to clarify and correct any misunderstandings or potential misunderstandings. There's a lot to be said for the informal, person-to-person, handshake approach, but it's also good to remember the words of movie mogul Samuel Goldwyn: "A verbal agreement ain't worth the paper it's written on."

Your First Few Weeks on the Job

In some ways, your first weeks on the new job are an extension of your employment interview. You and your employer are still getting to know one another, your expectations, your needs, wants, and methods of working. Make no mistake, too, you *are* being judged and evaluated. Most employers have a stated "probation period" of three to six months, during which you may be "terminated" with little or no notice.

Now is the time to make good on your promises, even as you evaluate what your new job has to offer you. Request honest feedback: "Don't hold back. I want to do the best job possible, and your comments will help me."

While it's true that no supervisor wants an employee who delivers a barrage of questions before executing the simplest of tasks, be certain to establish clear and frequently used lines of communication now. It's better to risk asking a few too many questions than to start off uncertain of your work. And you'll find that your questions will be best received if you ask them in the same context of enthusiasm that impressed the people who interviewed and hired you.

The Least You Need to Know

➤ Never fail to write a thank-you letter to the interviewer. It should be in the mail within one day following the interview.

➤ If the employer fails to contact you after the interview within the length of time promised, don't hesitate to call. It's better to risk being perceived as pushy than passively allowing an opportunity to slip away.

➤ Keep your reference network informed of your status following the interview. Brief them on what you would like them to say to the prospective employer.

➤ Remember: Your goal in the interview process is *not* to get a job. It is to get an offer. Only after you have secured the offer can you choose whether or not to take the job.

Talk the Talk Glossary

ASCII text Also called "DOS text" or "text only." A computer-generated text without the special formatting and font options word-processing software introduces. ASCII text is not very attractive, but you can be certain that any e-mail recipient can read it.

baby boomer Anyone born during the sharp increase in birth rate following World War II, that is, between 1947 and 1961.

behavior-related questions Questions aimed at assessing a candidate's character, attitude, and personality traits by asking for an account of how the candidate handled certain challenging situations.

benefit (of a product) Something good a product or its **features** (*see* next page) do, or are perceived to do, for the buyer; for example, the high-speed processor on that new PC makes you feel more productive. The *benefit* of the processor—a perceived increase in productivity—may justify the buyer spending more money for it.

bona fide occupational qualification (BFOQ) An employment criterion that permits discrimination based on personal attributes in certain cases; for example, a women's bathing suit manufacturer needs to hire models for its catalog. No men need apply. A delivery company needs drivers capable of lifting 80 pounds. The applicant who is disabled by a chronic bad back and is therefore incapable of repeated heavy lifting may legally be rejected.

buy signal A term, borrowed from the sales profession, meaning a verbal or non-verbal cue that suggests the prospective employer is responding positively to what the candidate is saying.

cold call An unsolicited employment query/application made via the telephone. The target employer doesn't know the caller and hasn't asked for the call.

dynamic listening   Listening with the mind and imagination, not just the ears. It is based on the listener identifying the interests he or she had in common with the speaker and responding to the speaker's themes in such a way that the conversation is energized by active give and take.

executive briefing   A condensed summary, no more than a half-page long, in narrative paragraph form, of the candidate's resumé.

feature (of a product)   An attribute of the product; for example, a high-speed microprocessor that makes one PC faster than another. (*See also* **benefit.**)

flex time   An arrangement that allows employees to adjust their morning start and evening quitting times to suit their preferences, family schedules, and even evade rush-hour traffic congestion.

follow-up interview   An interview that may take place after an in-depth, or selection, interview. It is often the venue in which unresolved issues are discussed. Sometimes its main purpose is to deliver the offer and negotiate salary and other matters.

freelancer   A person who offers services for hire, independently of a regular or permanent employer. (*See also* **independent contractor.**)

golden parachute   A liberal severance compensation package that is agreed to, by contract, at the time of the job offer. A golden parachute usually includes several months or more of severance pay and other goodies, such as stock or stock options and outplacement assistance.

Gopher   A series of electronic menus from which the Internet user can access just about any type of textual information.

gotta-have point   The stage in the interview when the candidate senses that the interviewer or interviewers have decided to make an offer.

group dynamics   The systematic study of how groups operate, how members persuade one another and fail to persuade one another, how conflicts develop, and how consensus is reached.

home page   An Internet site created by an individual or organization; it contains hypertext links to data relevant to the individual or organization. The home page is roughly equivalent to an electronic table of contents.

independent contractor   A person or company hired by another firm to perform certain services. The independent contractor is not a regular, permanent employee of the hiring firm. Whereas a freelancer works independently of an employer, an independent contractor may be a company or an employee of a company (other than the hiring firm). (*See also* **freelancer.**)

informational interview   An interview the *job hunter* requests in order to gather information about a particular company or an entire industry. The purpose of such an interview is to enlarge your business network, to meet potential employers, to learn from them, and to allow them to make your acquaintance. Immediate employment is not an objective of the informational interview.

jet lag   A temporary disruption of bodily rhythms caused by high-speed travel over multiple time zones. Symptoms include drowsiness, headache, and even flu-like symptoms.

job board   A site on the World Wide Web on which employers post job openings and job searchers reply and/or post resumés.

lay-off   Termination of an employee for reasons unrelated to his or her performance or behavior. Lay-offs are usually the result of economic reversals or mergers (in which certain departments or individuals become "superfluous").

layering   An interrogation technique that rapidly builds, piles, or "layers" one question on top of another.

line extension   A new product or service that is a continuous, logical development of the products or services a firm currently offers. For example, a maker of breakfast cereal may introduce a line of snack foods (such as chewy bars) based on the cereal.

mission   The more or less concise formulation of the purpose, goals, and objectives of an entire organization or department.

network   An informal set of business and personal contacts the job hunter develops in order to acquire information and employment leads.

overqualified   Having too much experience or too much education to "fit into" a given position. The employer's assumption is that the overqualified employee will become bored with the job and soon quit.

panel interview   An interview in which (typically) five to twelve interviewers, assembled at one time and in one room, ask the employment candidate questions. The purpose of this mass interview is to expose the candidate to as many decision-makers as possible in a short time. Also called a *group interview*.

pocket square   A decorative handkerchief intended to be tucked into the breast pocket of a suit.

positive visualization   A mental exercise in which one imagines what success in a given context will look and feel like. A runner might prepare for a race by *seeing* herself leaping the hurdles. A job candidate might visualize herself successfully answering the most difficult questions or accepting a congratulatory handshake at the end of a great interview.

problem-solving question   Poses a hypothetical scenario or sets a hypothetical task and asks the candidate to formulate solutions and procedures.

reference network   The colleagues, clients, supervisors, and others whose names you have furnished as references.

screening interview A preliminary interview, typically conducted by a junior-level Human Resources staffer, for the purpose of screening out unqualified job candidates, so that (theoretically) only qualified candidates are interviewed by the supervisors who are actually authorized to hire.

selection interview The in-depth interview conducted by the person (or persons) who has the authority to hire. In larger organizations, this interview is often preceded by a **screening interview** (*see* above).

sequential interview An interview in which the candidate is passed from interviewer to interviewer, to be met with privately in the office of each. Also called a *serial interview*.

skills The intellectual and creative tools the candidate can offer an employer. Skills that can be applied to a number of different jobs and work environments are called **transferable skills** (*see* below).

stress interview An employment interview that uses harsh, high-pressure techniques—such as long silences, deliberately offensive questions, impossibly difficult questions, very brusque questioning style—to test the candidate's mettle. The stress interview is most often used to evaluate candidates for high-pressure jobs in which difficult or hostile customer contact is anticipated.

transferable skills Skills specific to the individual rather than to a particular job. Transferable skills describe a function—that is, how the individual works with people, data, or things. For example, knowing how to write computer programs in the C++ programming language is a job-specific skill, whereas the ability to analyze and synthesize information is a skill that can be transferred from job to job.

upsell To use the customer service function as an opportunity to offer customers accessories and other products related to their original purchase.

Information Sources for Job Searches and Interview Preparation

Sources of Sources

Burwell Directory of Information Brokers (Houston: Burwell Enterprises, updated frequently); if not available in your local library, dial 713/537-8344.

Directories in Print, 10th Ed. Detroit: Gale Research, Inc.

Encyclopedia of Business Information Sources, 10th Ed. Detroit: Gale Research, Inc., 1994.

Glossbrenner, Alfred and Emily. *Finding a Job on the Internet* New York: McGraw-Hill, 1995.

Reader's Guide to Periodical Literature. Updated continuously. Available in most libraries.

Career Forecasts and Outlook

Krantz, Les. *Jobs Rated Almanac, 3rd Ed.* (New York: Wiley, 1995).

Occupational Outlook Handbook (U.S. Department of Labor, updated frequently). Available from NTC Publishing Group, 225 W. Touhy Ave., Lincolnwood, IL 60646.

Occupational Outlook Handbook for College Graduates (Washington, DC: U.S. Government Printing Office, updated frequently).

Smith, Carter, ed., *America's Fastest Growing Employers: The Complete Guide to Finding Jobs with Over 300 of America's Hottest Companies* (Holbrook, MA: Adams Publishing, 1994).

Industries and Fields (General)

Dictionary of Holland Occupational Codes, Dictionary of Occupational Titles, and *Standard Industrial Classification Manual.* These three reference works, available in public libraries, list virtually every occupation imaginable.

Encyclopedia of Associations (Detroit: Gale Research, Inc., frequently updated). Lists 25,000 organizations, associations, clubs, and other nonprofit membership groups, many of which are rich sources of industry and employment information.

Godin, Seth, ed. *The Information Please Business Almanac and Desk Reference* (New York: Houghton Mifflin Company, updated annually).

National Trade and Professional Associations of the United States (Washington, DC: Columbia Books, Inc., updated annually).

Newsletters in Print (Detroit: Gale Research, Inc., updated frequently).

Communications Industry

Telecommunications Directory (Detroit: Gale Research, Inc., updated frequently).

Computer Industry

Computers and Computing Information Resources Directory (Detroit: Gale Research, Inc., updated frequently).

Information Industry Directory (Detroit: Gale Research, Inc., updated frequently).

Government Employment

United States Government Manual (Washington, DC: U.S. Government Printing Office, updated annually).

Sources of Information on Specific Companies

The Adams Jobs Almanac (Holbrook, MA: Adams, updated annually). Also consult this publisher's *JobBank* series, which lists jobs in specific cities, metropolitan areas, and regions.

Corporate and Industry Research Reports (New Providence, NJ: R.R. Bowker/Martindale-Hubbell, frequent editions).

Corporate Technology Directory (Woburn, MA: Corporate Technology Information Services, Inc., 1993).

Hoover, Gary, et al., eds. *Hoover's Handbook of American Business* (Austin, TX: The Reference Press, issued annually).

Job Seeker's Guide to Private and Public Companies (Detroit: Gale Research, Inc., updated frequently).

People with Clout (Contacts)

Contacts Influential: Commerce and Industry Directory (San Francisco: Contacts Influential, Market Research and Development Services, updated frequently).

Richardson, Douglas B. *Networking* (New York: Wiley, 1994).

Standard and Poor's Register of Corporations, Directors and Executives (New York: Standard and Poor's, updated frequently).

Starer, Daniel, *Who Knows What: The Essential Business Resource Book* (New York: Henry Holt, 1992).

The *Who's Who* series. Consult these volumes in the reference section of the public library.

Online Resources (General)

Richard Nelson Bolles's *Job-Hunting on the Internet, 2d Ed.* (Ten Speed, 1999) and Mary B. Nemnich's and Fred E. Jandt's *Cyberspace Job Search Kit, 3d ed.* (Jist Publishing, 2000) are excellent places to start your search for online information sources.

Once you're online, check out:

➤ The *RiceInfo Gopher*, which presents Internet resources by subject area. You can get to the RiceInfo Gopher through the Web (**www.riceinfo.rice.edu**) or by Gophering to **riceinfo.rice.edu**.

➤ *Clearinghouse for Subject-Oriented Internet Resource Guides* (from the University of Michigan's University Library and School of Information and Library Sciences). You can reach this through anonymous ftp (**una.hh.lib.umich.edu**), Gopher (**gopher.lib.umich.edu**), Telnet (**una.hh.lib.umich.edu.70**), or the Web (**www.lib.umich.edu/chhome.html** or **www.http2.sils.umich.edu/~lou/chhome.html**).

➤ The *Gopher Jewels*, which extracts menus from the Internet's major Gopher sites and classifies them by subject. Get to the Gopher Jewels via the Web (**www.galaxy.einet.net/gopher/gopher.html** or **www.galaxy.einet.net/GJ/index.html**) or Gopher to **cwis.usc.edu**.

➤ The *United States Library of Congress*. The Library maintains a service called LC MARVEL, a subject-oriented view of the Internet. You can reach MARVEL via

303

Gopher (www.**marvel.loc.gov**), Telnet (www.**locis.loc.gov**), or the World Wide Web (**www.lcweb.loc.gov/homepage/lchp.html**).

The five most-visited employment-related Internet sites are the following:

➤ America's Job Bank (**www.ajb.dni.us**). A government site run jointly by the U.S. Department of Labor and some 1,800 state employment offices. Neither employers nor job seekers are charged a fee.

➤ **CareerPath.com**. A site combining the resources of six major city newspapers from Boston, Chicago, Los Angeles, New York, San Jose, and Washington, D.C., which draws its job postings from newspaper help wanted ads and from corporate Web sites. No fee to job seekers.

➤ **HotJobs.com**. Allows job seekers to use a "Personal Search Agent" to find the jobs that fit customized criteria.

➤ **Monster.com** (formerly Monster Board). The biggest and most popular of the job boards.

➤ JobOptions (**www.joboptions.com**). Formerly called E-Span. Job seekers find it user friendly.

Online Resources (Education)

Those interested in academic positions should consult:

➤ *The Chronicle of Higher Education* (Gopher to **chronicle.merit.edu** or crawl the Web to **www.chronicle.merit.edu/.ads/.links.html**) and the *Academic Position Network (APN)*, a growing clearinghouse of employment opportunities (Gopher to **wcni.cis.umn.edu:11111** or use a Web browser to reach **gopher:// wcni.cis.umn. edu:11111/**).

➤ More specialized is *Academic Physician and Scientist* (Gopher to **aps.acad-phy-sci. com**).

➤ *Texas A&M University* offers a clearinghouse site on the Web at **www.agenifo. tamu.edu/jobs.html#otherorgs**); *Rice University* offers one at **gopher:// riceinfo. rice.edu:70/11/Subject/Jobs** or directly by Gopher at **riceinfo.rice.edu**; and the *University of Minnesota College of Education* offers another at **rodent.cis.umn. edu:11119** (via Gopher) or **gopher:// rodent.cis.umn.edu:11119/** (via Web). The Minnesota site is specifically for elementary, middle school, and junior and senior high school positions.

Online Resources (Government)

Jobs with the federal government are accessible using:

➤ The *Dartmouth College Gopher* (at **dartcms1.dartmouth.edu** or via the Web at **gopher://DARTCMS1.DARTMOUTH.EDU:70/11/fedjobs**—be sure to type this one with the capital and lowercase letters indicated here).

➤ *FedWorld*, a database prepared by the National Technical Information Service of the U.S. Department of Commerce. You can Telnet to **fedworld.gov**, FTP to **ftp.fedworld.gov**, or take the Web to **www.fedworld.gov**. If you prefer, you can dial up FedWorld's BBS directly at 703/321-8020 (set your communications software to 9600 bps, 8/N/1).

Online Resources (Science and Technology)

For positions in science and technology, try:

➤ *CareerMosaic* on the World Wide Web at **www.careermosaic.com**. Not only will you find job postings here, you can also download a variety of profiles of high-tech corporations.

➤ *Monster Board* at **www.monster.com**. Of course, be certain also to search for specific companies and fields.

Online Resources (Healthcare)

Health care professionals will want to explore:

➤ *MedSearch America* (via the Web at **www.medsearch.com** or via Gopher at **gopher.medsearch.com**) in addition to using keywords for finding specific firms and institutions.

Online Services (Commercial)

A few of the large commercial on-line services provide employment- and career-related sites and services:

➤ *AOL (America Online)* provides a "Career Center," which includes a host of resources, the most popular of which is JobOptions, formerly known as E-Span. This site can be accessed via the World Wide Web as well as through AOL.

➤ *Compuserve* offers less in the way of employment features than AOL, but still serves up a vast array of vocational and professional forums. As with AOL, JobOptions is just a click.

➤ *Prodigy*'s offerings are slimmer than AOL's or CSi's. Here you'll find the Prodigy Classifieds and the Career Bulletin Board.

People:

Data:

Things:

Skills Inventories

A People Skills Inventory

Rate your skill levels from 1 to 4, with 4 being the strongest. Notice that the skills are arranged in approximate order of complexity, from lowest to highest. For example, "following instructions" (the first item listed) is a simpler skill than "coaching and mentoring" (the last item).

I am good at ...

WITH PEOPLE AS INDIVIDUALS:

Following instructions	1	2	3	4
Serving	1	2	3	4
Listening	1	2	3	4
Communicating verbally	1	2	3	4
Communicating in writing (letters, memos)	1	2	3	4
Diagnosing, evaluating, and analyzing	1	2	3	4
Persuading	1	2	3	4
Recruiting and motivating	1	2	3	4
Selling	1	2	3	4
Instructing and training	1	2	3	4
Coaching and mentoring	1	2	3	4

WITH PEOPLE IN GROUPS:

Communicating	1	2	3	4
Representing	1	2	3	4
Guiding group discussion	1	2	3	4
Persuading and motivating	1	2	3	4
Formal public speaking	1	2	3	4
Performing and entertaining	1	2	3	4
Managing and supervising	1	2	3	4
Consulting and advising	1	2	3	4
Negotiating and resolving conflict	1	2	3	4
Pioneering (leading innovation)	1	2	3	4

A Data Skills Inventory

Here's a checklist for data skills. As in the people-skills inventory, the transferable skills are listed from least complex (lowest level) to most complex (highest level). In addition, they are gathered into more-encompassing groups.

I am good at …

SORTING:

Copying	1	2	3	4
Data entry	1	2	3	4
Record keeping and filing	1	2	3	4
Retrieving information efficiently	1	2	3	4
Helping others retrieve information	1	2	3	4
Memorizing and paying attention to detail	1	2	3	4

GATHERING:

Compiling	1	2	3	4
Searching and researching	1	2	3	4
Observing (in order to gather data)	1	2	3	4

MANAGING:

Comparing (similarities? differences?)	1	2	3	4
Computing	1	2	3	4

	1	2	3	4
Analyzing	1	2	3	4
Organizing, systematizing, prioritizing	1	2	3	4
Step-by-step, goal-oriented planning	1	2	3	4
Visualizing (drawing, creating graphics, etc.)	1	2	3	4
Synthesizing, developing, improving	1	2	3	4
Problem solving	1	2	3	4
Developing the "big picture"	1	2	3	4

CREATING:

	1	2	3	4
Daydreaming	1	2	3	4
Imagining	1	2	3	4
Improving	1	2	3	4
Designing	1	2	3	4
Inventing and innovating	1	2	3	4

A Things Skills Inventory

Ditto for "things" skills, except that, here, the larger groupings (WORKING WITH MACHINERY AND VEHICLES, WORKING WITH MATERIALS, etc.) are not necessarily hierarchical; that is, each grouping is its own ladder, so that the skills involved in working with machinery and vehicles are not necessarily less complex than those you use in working with materials or working in construction.

I am good at ...

WORKING WITH MACHINERY AND VEHICLES:

	1	2	3	4
Operating	1	2	3	4
Controlling (including driving)	1	2	3	4
Maintaining	1	2	3	4
Repairing	1	2	3	4
Assembling	1	2	3	4

WORKING WITH MATERIALS:

	1	2	3	4
Sewing, weaving, basic woodworking, etc.	1	2	3	4
Finishing	1	2	3	4
Carving	1	2	3	4

Sculpting	1	2	3	4
Precision hand work	1	2	3	4

CONSTRUCTION WORK:

Rough carpentry, framing, etc.	1	2	3	4
Finish carpentry	1	2	3	4
Remodeling	1	2	3	4

WORKING WITH LIVING THINGS:

Gardening	1	2	3	4
Farming	1	2	3	4
Caring for animals	1	2	3	4
Training and handling animals	1	2	3	4

BODY SKILLS:

Strength	1	2	3	4
Endurance	1	2	3	4
Dexterity	1	2	3	4
Athletics	1	2	3	4

Index